ROUTLEDGE LIBRARY EDITIONS:
THE HISTORY OF
ECONOMIC THOUGHT

Volume

THE STOCKHOLM SCHOOL
AND THE DEVELOPMENT OF
DYNAMIC METHOD

THE STOCKHOLM SCHOOL AND THE DEVELOPMENT OF DYNAMIC METHOD

BJÖRN A. HANSSON

Routledge
Taylor & Francis Group

LONDON AND NEW YORK

First published in 1982 by Croom Helm Ltd

This edition first published in 2017
by Routledge
2 Park Square, Milton Park, Abingdon, Oxon OX14 4RN

and by Routledge
711 Third Avenue, New York, NY 10017

*Routledge is an imprint of the Taylor & Francis Group, an informa
business*

© 1982 Björn A. Hansson

British Library Cataloguing in Publication Data
A catalogue record for this book is available from the British Library

ISBN: 978-1-138-29250-5 (Set)
ISBN: 978-1-315-23288-1 (Set) (ebk)
ISBN: 978-1-138-23020-0 (Volume 5) (hbk)
ISBN: 978-1-138-23022-4 (Volume 5) (pbk)
ISBN: 978-1-315-38662-1 (Volume 5) (ebk)

Publisher's Note
The publisher has gone to great lengths to ensure the quality of this
reprint but points out that some imperfections in the original copies
may be apparent.

Disclaimer
The publisher has made every effort to trace copyright holders and
would welcome correspondence from those they have been unable to
trace.

The Stockholm School and the Development of Dynamic Method

BJÖRN A. HANSSON

CROOM HELM LONDON

©1982 Björn A. Hansson
Croom Helm Ltd, 2-10 St John's Road, London SW11

British Library Cataloguing in Publication Data

Hansson, Björn A.
  The Stockholm School and the development of
  dynamic method.
  1. Economic development
  2. Economics—Sweden—Stockholm
  I. Title
  339.5   HB199

ISBN 0-7099-1225-0

Printed in Great Britain by
Biddles Ltd, Guildford, Surrey

Table of Contents

Preface

All Scandinavian sources cited in this work have been translated by the author, while all the cited correspondence between the Swedes and the non-Scandinavians remains in the original English. I would in particular like to thank Dr. M. Milgate, Dr. R.M. Goodwin, Dr. K. Velupillai and Miss Victoria Chick who have been very helpful during different stages of my work. Furthermore, the work could not have its present shape without the help through correspondence, private talks and access to unpublished material of Professor Sir John Hicks, Lady Ursula Hicks, Mrs. Getrud Lindahl, Professors Erik Lundberg, Gunnar Myrdal, the late Bertil Ohlin, Otto Steiger, Björn Thalberg, and William P. Yohe. Mr. C. Szalwinski provided the secretarial assistance and was responsible for typesetting the manuscript to printer's specification. Finally, there would not have been any book at all without financial assistance from Lunds Universitet (Lund), Kungliga Vetenskapsakademien (Stockholm), Stiftelsen Siamon (Stockholm) and the British Council.

It goes without saying, that all errors and interpretations are entirely my own responsibility.

Björn Hansson

Chapter 1

Introduction

Interest in the development of economic theory in Sweden in the period after Wicksell was heightened by Ohlin's article in Economic Journal (1937A-B) where the existence of a "Stockholm School" was mentioned for the first time. Of course, this interest had been partially awakened already by the Wicksellian flavour of Keynes' Treatise on Money[1] which was followed up by the translation into English of Wicksell's Interest and Prices and Lectures.[2] After most of the major Swedish works had been translated in the late 1930's a consensus arose on the nature of the contribution of the Stockholm School, which has been aptly summed up by Winch:

----

[1] This is of course only true for the Anglo-Saxon world since Wicksell's works were certainly known in the Germanspeaking countries, which was the basis for Myrdal's somewhat caustic remark on Keynes' Treatise:

"J.M.Keynes' new, brilliant, though not always clear, work, A Treatise on Money, is completely permeated by Wicksellian influence. Nevertheless Keynes' work, too, suffers somewhat from the attractive Anglo-Saxon kind of unnecessary originality, which has its roots in certain systematic gaps in the knowledge of the German language on the part of the majority of English economists" (Myrdal 1939, pp.8-9).

[2] Cassel's Theoretische Sozialökonomie from 1917 had already been translated in 1923 as The Theory of Social Economy and his writings had a certain influence on Dennis Robertson (cp. Robertson 1926, p.5). Furthermore, it is not unlikely that it was through Cassel's work that Keynes got to know Wicksell's ideas on the normal rate of interest.

"Swedish economists, building on a Wicksellian foundation, developed a body of analysis which is separate from, but paralell to, that associated with the name of Keynes" (Winch 1966, p.170).

However, this consensus was only based on a few articles in economic journals and no monograph existed which analysed the contribution of the Stockholm School in any detail. It is therefore not surprising that the debate started anew in the 1960's when Landgren's dissertation (Landgren 1960) - a complete work devoted to the Stockholm School - appeared and challenged this commonly held view. Landgren's standpoint was in its turn attacked later by Steiger in his dissertation of 1971 (Steiger 1971), which consequently has as its subtitle: "Eine Anti-Kritik". The renewed interest in the Stockholm School is perhaps best illustrated by the fact that almost a complete issue of History of Political Economy was devoted to the question. This issue contained a translation of an article by Ohlin (Ohlin 1933C-D) and papers by Brems, Patinkin, Steiger and Yohe. However, these earlier works concentrated on the macroeconomic theory and the economic policy of the Stockholm School and its relation to the Keynesian revolution. In fact, the connection between Keynes and the Swedes has been obscured by the concentration on these issues. The substantial contribution of this disseration, although it will partly cover the same ground as the earlier works, is therefore to analyse these issues from a different angle; namely, the development of dynamic method within the Stockholm School. Furthermore, this new approach has certain points of contact with the very recent development in dynamic theory, since some of the methods discussed in this work have actually surfaced again in the modern debate.

1 - The main purpose of the work.

The core of the work is a reconstruction of the development of dynamic method by some Swedish economists between 1927 and 1937.[3] The reconstruction is considered to be a necessary basis for tackling the following three questions within the history of economic thought.

The first question relates to <u>the existence of a School</u>. Our reconstruction will show that there was an interrelated development of dynamic method, and this development, once it was under way, was almost completely isolated from outside influences. Furthermore, the construction of the different methods was probably a unique accomplishment, except for intertemporal equilibrium. Indeed, it is held that their ideas on macroeconomic theory and economic policy cannot prove the existence of a particular school, since these ideas were influenced by outside sources and they were therefore not unique. Hence, it will be argued that the development of dynamic method is the essential element of the Stockholm School. To support this proposition it is necessary to show that the outside influence on the development of the dynamic method was insignificant. But on the other hand it does not matter whether they took most of their macroeconomic ideas from foreign sources.

The second question refers to <u>the nature of the Swedish origin of the Stockholm School</u>, which in this case refers mainly to the the possible influence of Wicksell and Cassel. It will be shown that they could only have had a direct effect on the macrotheoretical propositions. Hence, in the macroeconomic sphere the Swedes chiefly analysed changes in the general price level with a savings-

---

3 'Dynamic methods' refer to notions such as temporary equilibrium, disequilibrium sequence analysis etc. (cp. Ch.II). The term has been used in a similar way by Hicks for classifying models according to the manner in which they deal with the dynamic character of reality (cp. Hicks 1965, pp.28-29). The discussion of dynamic method is not a methodological discussion in any philosophical sense, like for example the advantages of a deductive or an inductive method.

investment mechanism, and they explicitly referred to Wicksell's theory as their starting-point. However, even if they leaned heavily on Wicksell's theory for analysing changes in the price level, they did not take up his strictly sequential analysis in Interest and Prices (cp. Wicksell 1936, p.136f.) It is in Lundberg's Studies in the Theory of Economic Expansion that we first find an explicit comment on Wicksell's procedure in Interest and Prices. Of course, that does not exclude the idea that Wicksell's and Cassel's analyses of the cumulative process created a climate of opinion which might have been generally conducive to the development of dynamic methods, but this common background is only proof of an indirect and very loose influence; indeed, it is of an almost trivial character. Furthermore, the proposition that the development of economic method constitutes the Stockholm School implies that their constructions of notions such as the 'method of expectations' (Myrdal 1927) and intertemporal equilibrium (Lindahl 1930) are theoretical breaks with an earlier tradition. The explanation of this issue is worthwhile given the possibility that the Swedish or other predecessors may have had a tangible influence on the character of these notions.

The third question takes up the relation between the Stockholm School and the Keynesian revolution. This relation is located within the macroeconomic sphere. The analysis in this work does not entail a step by step comparison between Keynes' development prior to and inclusive of the General Theory and the concomitant development in Sweden. It is instead a comparison between certain macrotheoretical propositions of the Stockholm School, independently of whether these propositions are original or not, and Keynes' finished construction in the General Theory. It is therefore necessary to analyse the macroeconomic theories of the Stockholm School, which we are particularly well-placed to do once we have sorted out the dynamic method involved, since it is not possible to state the exact character of their macroeconomic ideas without understanding the nature of the applied equilibrium notions. Although the Stockholm School in its mature stage analysed the effects on output during a dynamic process as well as output changes as a part of the equilibrating mechanism between savings and investment, nevertheless their analysis of the equilibrating mechanism is a dissection of the composition of the factors constituting the ex post equalities, and is never the matter of determining the equilibrium level of output and employment. We cannot therefore find the principle of effective demand in the work of the Swedes. Furthermore, there is no evidence that they considered their analysis as a complete substitute for the propositions of orthodox theory, since the latter were still supposed to play some role.

The analysis of the development of dynamic method is in itself of interest in relation to the current evolution within economic dynamics, as is shown by the development in the late 1960's and the 1970's when mathematical economists moved away from the use of intertemporal equilibrium, in part due to the problems of including money in this method, and made attempts to develop different notions of temporary equilibrium (cp. sect. II:3). These developments bear a remarkable resemblance to what was going on in Sweden in the first half of the 1930's. In fact, there is an indirect link over time between the modern practitioners and their Swedish counterparts, since the former drew on Hicks' development of temporary equilibrium (cp. Weintraub 1979, p.68) and Hicks in his turn was clearly influenced by the development of the same notion within the Stockholm School.[4,5] Strictly speaking, however, it is beyond the scope of this work to pursue any further comparison between the Swedes and the modern development of disequilibrium methods. This work does therefore not contain any assessment of the intrinsic value of the Swedish contribution to the development of dynamic method as such, and the main argument is not affected even if the Swedish contribution is considered to be of no value for this development, because the reconstruction is still considered to be a necessary basis for tackling the above mentioned questions within the history of economic thought.

Our original contribution is to have studied the Stockholm School from the viewpoint of the development of dynamic methods which makes it possible to analyse the above mentioned questions

----

4 This has been conceded by Hicks himself:

> "For the moment, however, I got more from
> Sweden than I did from Cambridge. It was
> Myrdal's Monetary Equilibrium, which showed
> me the power of a short-period analysis in
> which expectations (certain or uncertain)
> are treated as data: and Lindahl ["Lindahl's
> influence was chiefly personal, as his
> writings were (then) mainly in Swedish. But
> he was himself in London rather often at
> that time" (ibid., p.309 n.2)] who showed me
> the usefulness of translating 'dynamic
> equilibrium' into 'macro' terms. Where I
> got with their aid is indicated by the paper
> "Wages and Interest: the Dynamic Problem" "
> (Hicks 1963, pp.308-309; cp. Hicks 1973,
> p.143).

5. This link is even more explicit in the case of J-P.Benassy, who was supervised by Debreu and Bent Hansen for his dissertation Disequilibrium Theory (cp. Benassy 1975, p.503,n.2). His ideas on disequilibrium seem to have emanated from Hansen (1951), and this work in its turn profited from Hansen's direct contact with Lindahl (cp. Hansen 1951, p.viii).

from a different and more appropriate angle. This work is therefore different from the other major works concerning the Stockholm School since they have dealt with the School from different viewpoints. Hence, Landgren and Steiger have concentrated on the Swedish contribution to macroeconomic theory and economic policy for the purpose of making a comparison with Keynes' General Theory, but do not analyse the dynamic method involved. Yohe, on the other hand, is closer to our own viewpoint since he draws the proper conclusion that "the extension of Wicksell's work by the Stockholm School has been more in the area of method than in theory" (Yohe 1959A, p.294). However, although his main purpose is to show "that a substantial share of the Wicksellian doctrine has survived and has permeated the works of the Stockholm School" (ibid., p.161), he has not traced explicitly the interrelated development of the dynamic method among the Swedes, and he has therefore missed the particular stage in the development of the Stockholm School where Wicksell's contribution was of a direct importance.[6]

2 - The idea of a reconstruction as an expository device.

In this work, the central arguments are erected using a procedure which is referred to as a 'reconstruction'. This procedure is a teleological exercise in the sense that the period under consideration is, with the advantage of hindsight, characterized by the stages it exhibits in the evolution of dynamic methods. It is important to stress that a later method is not just a fusion of earlier methods. On the contrary, the process is

----

6 Yohe also has a tendency to interpret their models within a framework which gives them a flavour of mechanical dynamics instead of expectational dynamics (for an explanation of these terms cp. Ch. X Note 5 and 6). The most evident example of this type of interpretation is given by Yohe in his mathematical formulation of Lindahl's note of 1953 on the theory of the multiplier (cp. Yohe 1959B, pp.165-166).

such, that a subsequent method is partly constructed by elements which have been transposed in a critical way from earlier methods. <u>The momentum of the development lies therefore in the attempt of each method to overcome some of the inherent limitations in earlier methods.</u>

The method of a reconstruction has been adopted for three separate reasons. The first is the simple fact that the members of the Stockholm School very seldom referred in any detail to each other's works, and it is therefore necessary to find substantive evidence which can help to show the connection which existed between its individual members. Secondly, quite often a particular work contains an explicit analysis of the method to be used for solving certain problems, but our analysis shows in fact that the actual application of the method cannot give the results aimed at. For example, Lindahl used temporary equilibrium to explain forced savings, but from his explicit definition of this method it must follow that if temporary equilibrium rules, then such a phenomenon cannot even exist (cp. sect. IV:3:3:1). Another example is Myrdal's attempt to use his method of analysing tendencies at a point in time to explain a cumulative process, but his method is a single-period analysis and cannot therefore be used for developing a multi-period sequence like the cumulative process (cp. sect. VI:2:1). However, this type of contradiction between explicit method and its use provides a momentum for the development of the dynamic method itself, since it may serve as a catalyst for later attempts to develop the method in such a way that these shortcomings are superceded. The last reason stems from the fact that it is possible to utilize more recent developments in dynamic method to help to characterize the formal propositions and assumptions that will define a particular method. The more exact mathematical formulations of intertemporal equilibrium in the 1950's will thus help us to analyse the inconsistencies in Lindahl's formulations of 1929 (cp. sect. IV:2:3a:2).

The most important conclusion proved in this reconstruction is the existence of a unified theme - namely the search for a proper dynamic method - and its development by mutual influence among the participants. The existence of a unified theme refutes the division of the Stockholm School into the 'neo-Wicksellians' (Ohlin, Myrdal, Lindahl) and those interested in sequence analysis (Hammarskjöld, Johansson, Lundberg, Svennilson) (cp. Palander 1941, pp.5-6; Steiger 1971, pp.41-42). It is obvious that Lindahl's and Myrdal's works of 1927-1932 are different from those which come later on. But our main point is to show that their works actually functioned as stepping-stones to the subsequent development. Furthermore, Lindahl's contribution of 1934 onwards is not only a stepping-stone to the development of sequence analysis but part and parcel of that very development. It seems likely that this mistaken dichotomy has arisen from a one-sided concentration on the macroeconomic propositions of the so-called 'neo-Wicksellians', so that their contributions to dynamic method have been overlooked.

Once we have been able to reconstruct the unified theme, then we can also give the rationale behind our decision to start our analysis in 1927 and end in 1937. With Myrdal's dissertation things started to move slowly, since it awakened interest in anticipations and dynamic methods; and after Lundberg's contribution to sequence analysis in 1937 there seem to be no fundamental changes in the dynamic method then existing. For example, Svennilson's dissertation may indeed show that he must be considered as a member of the Stockholm School, since he gives a more sophisticated analysis of certain elements within sequence analysis, in particular the role of anticipations and plans. However, his work does not form part of our reconstruction since it does not entail a revision of the inherited method or the production of a new one. On the other hand, when we reach Bent Hansen's dissertation of 1951, we find a level of sophistication which is more a matter of revision of the older methods than mere refinements. But Hansen's construction is not influenced only by the earlier contribution of the Stockholm School, since the works of Hicks, Lange and Samuelson also played a role in his development.[7] Thus we are no longer able to speak of a fairly isolated development of dynamic method within the Stockholm School, which was one of the characteristics of our notion of a School, but we must now see the matter as an up-to-date attempt to fuse the Stockholm School with the subsequent development of dynamic method.[8]

---

7 Bent Hansen gives the following account of the different methods which had influenced him:

> "The analytical equipment used is not new, but neither is it outmoded. It employs the terminology and technique of the Stockholm School, as presented by Erik Lindahl, and some of the lines of reasoning of that school of thought whose pioneer is J.R.Hicks [Samuelson and Lange can probably be included in this "school of thought"]. Naturally there are traces of influence from J.M.Keynes, but the analysis of this book can hardly be described as 'Keynesian'" (Hansen 1951, p.viii).

8 We can describe this problem by referring our aim to the picture given by Joan Robinson in her review of Myrdal's <u>Monetary Equilibrium</u>:

> "After the confluence of the 'Cambridge' and the 'Swedish' traditions of monetary theory, it is interesting to look back and see how the two streams were flowing while they were still divided by contours of language" (Robinson 1939, p.78).

Hence, our aim is to analyse how the Swedes came to form one School and how it was evolving before it started to mix with the Keynesian ideas in 1936-1937. Bent Hansen's contribution consequently came long after the two streams had started to flow together.

3 - An outline of the work.

This section is intended to provide a schematic outline of the work to provide the reader with an overview of the whole, before he has to plunge into the detailed analysis of the contribution of the different members of the Stockholm School.

The chapter on the analytical framework gives a classification of the different dynamic methods developed by the Swedes, and the analysis of these methods has been pursued from the perspective of sequence analysis. The aim is to give the meaning of the central categories used in the subsequent chapters.

It is possible to divide the period under consideration into four separate stages, where each stage is characterized by a specific dynamic method. The first stage is represented by Myrdal's dissertation, which shows how anticipations of an uncertain future are an independent part of the data which determines a 'long run' equilibrium position. The crucial factor for the further development of the Stockholm School was the treatment of anticipations and uncertainty as part and parcel of the theoretical core, and their placement on the same level as preferences, technical conditions and given resources.

Lindahl's construction of intertemporal equilibrium in 1929 constitutes the second stage. This concept grew out of a critique of comparative statics as a tool for handling dynamic problems, and its aim was to describe the traverse between two equilibrium positions. It seems that one of the reasons why Lindahl gave up this method was that he realized that it could not tackle imperfect foresight in a meaningful way. This weakness provided the rationale for the next stage, namely, temporary equilibrium, whose object was to analyse cumulative processes. The development of dynamic methods then became intertwined with Wicksell's savings-investment mechanism, i.e. the indirect relation between savings and investment via changes in the general price level. However, we will show that since it is an equilibrium approach, temporary equilibrium cannot really give a proper analysis of this mechanism. In fact intertemporal equilibrium as well as temporary equilibrium are examples of an equilibrium approach, which means that they refer to situations where the plans are consistent over several periods or one period respectively, and they are formally represented by a system of simultaneous equations. Both Lundberg and Myrdal criticized this equilibrium approach, since the simultaneity could not explain the link between consecutive periods, i.e. the way in which the events in one period determine the outcome in the coming periods. Thus Lindahl was not really portraying a process over time.

The last stage culminates in 1937 with Lundberg's disequilibrium sequence analysis, but this notion is preceded by a long and protracted development, which in fact makes up the bulk of the work. Myrdal was once again the one who pushed the development in the right direction with the publication of Monetary Equilibrium (Swedish ed. 1932, German ed. 1933). This laid the foundation for the disequilibrium approach with the notions of ex ante and ex post, which made it possible to analyse a situation where the ex ante plans were incongruent while the ex post analysis showed which factors made up the ex post equality.

Hammarskjöld constructed some important elements for the coming sequence analysis. His idea of windfall profit as a link between periods gave the first, though incomplete, formal sketch of a sequence analysis. The discussion of the unit period where the length was coupled with the realization of unchanged plans later became a standard assumption within the Stockholm School.

It will be shown that Ohlin's work in 1932-1934 made no direct contribution to the development of dynamic method. But he furthered the macroeconomic analysis with his insistence that a disturbance could emanate from an autonomus change in consumption, and it did not have to come from the capital market as was generally assumed by Myrdal and Lindahl. Ohlin also stressed that changes in output and real income could be a part of the equilibrating mechanism between savings and investment.

Lindahl finally came back on the scene with two works in late 1934 and early 1935 respectively. Building on Myrdal and Hammarskjöld, Lindahl formulated the first proper algebraic expression of a single-period analysis, which exhibits how incongruent ex ante plans lead to determinate ex post results. Lindahl also discussed the problems in building a sequence analysis, but his own construction is an equilibrium sequence analysis which assumes that there is equilibrium in each period. In this respect Lundberg went beyond Lindahl, since his sequence analysis builds on disequilibrium within the separate periods. However, there is still an equilibrium notion in Lundberg's analysis, namely, the assumption of constant response functions over the process.

The penultimate chapter examines the immediate Swedish reaction to the General Theory. The critique was mostly directed against Keynes' equilibrium constructions (i.e. his method) and as such it shows the complementary character of the Swedish contribution. However, if Keynes' method is taken for granted then the Swedish critique of Keynes' theoretical propositions is ill-founded. Furthermore, since the Swedes did not separate Keynes' method from his theory, they did not perceive the General Theory as an outright challenge to orthodox theory, and at the same time they did not see the possibility of fusing their own insights in dynamic methods with Keynes' theoretical propositions (cp. sect. 5 App. I).

The last chapter summarizes the result of the work.

The work finishes with an appendix which gives our definition of Keynes' principle of effective demand together with a sketch of how the Swedish method can be grafted on to Keynes' theory.

Chapter 2

The Analytical Framework

The analytical framework is to a great extent dictated by the ideas belonging to the Stockholm School. This is most obvious from the fact that our examination of different dynamic methods uses 'sequence analysis' as the point of reference. The overriding aim has been to construct a classification which is fine enough to distinguish between the different dynamic 'methods' developed by the Swedes. Therefore it is no surprise if this classification is too coarse to catch the differences between the methods belonging to the current development of disequilibrium analysis.

1 - Sequence analysis as the point of reference.

The different dynamic methods are considered here as separate <u>analytical</u> attempts to tackle what is considered to be the economic reality. It is obvious that quite often there is a close relation between the idea of what the economic reality 'really is like', or what is supposed to be the pertinent feature of reality [1], and the method applied to analyse this reality, in the sense that the former gives the rationale for choosing a particular method. In what follows we will denote the notion of what the economic reality 'really is like' as the <u>object</u> for the economic analysis and each dynamic method will if possible be connected with its implicit object.

Our classification is based on the concepts developed by the Stockholm School for the purpose of

---

1 This notion is akin to Schumpeters's <u>vision</u>, which is the preanalytical cognitive act preceding the economic analysis proper (cp. Schumpeter 1954, p.41). It can certainly include Hicks' idea of the existence and non-existence of different types of markets (cp. Hicks 1946, pp.135-140; Hicks 1956, pp.56-57; pp.73-75; pp.77-78).

sequence analysis.[2] Sequence analysis, which is just one type of dynamic method, is related to that particular economic object where the timing of economic events is of paramount importance.[3] A sequence signifies here a recursive model where the outcome at the end of period t, i.e. at the point of time t+1, is completely determined by the actions undertaken during the period, and the actions in their turn are derived from the plans formed at the beginning of the period, i.e. at the point of time t. Furthermore, the results of period t are linked in a derterminate way, fixed at the point of time t, with the plans for period t+1. Hence, following this procedure it is possible to determine the outcome for some periods ahead in time. The irreversibility of the sequence analysis refers to the fact that a unilateral dependence over time is used in this analysis in contrast to a mutual interdependence (cp.

----

2 There is no common term for this process amongst the Stockholm School, Lundberg used 'sequence analysis' (cp. Lundberg 1937, p.51), Lindahl 'the general theory of development' (cp. Lindahl 1939B, p.51), Ohlin 'process analysis' (cp. Ohlin 1937A, p.58).

3 The importance of timing coupled with unilateral dependence are both characteristics of processes in real calendar time:

"The modern sequence theory is not like the equilibrium theory directed towards a study of conditions of an economic system isolated from time but towards a study of how in a time sequence one condition is developed from a subsequent one" (Svennilson 1938, p.3).

It is for example interesting to see that the Swedes took great interest in working out each step involved in the adjustment process implied by the multiplier. Keynes, on the other hand, was mainly interested in determining the equilibrium level of output and employment and just mentioned that an adjustment process existed (cp. sect. 2 App. I).

Svennilson 1938, p.4).[4] However, even sequence analysis contains an equilibrium notion in the shape of constant expectation functions, which is a variant of our general notion of equilibrium:

"It is the invariance of behaviour [routine behaviour] over a certain period which gives significance to the concept of equilibrium" (Hahn 1952, p.803).

The central idea in Swedish sequence analysis is the notion that a plan epitomizes economic behaviour, which means that all economic actions are directed towards fulfilment of plans based on expectations of the future and that the plans will be revised in the light of the actual results. This provides for the discontinuous character of sequence analysis, in the sense that the continous flow of actions, in realizations of plans made at an earlier stage, will sooner or later be interrupted because of incongruent plans, which will lead to the formation of new plans. Hence the crucial role of expectations, since they represent the connection between preceding events and the new plans.

----

4 This is in conscious contrast to Hayek's construction of a watertight difference between equilibrium analysis and causal analysis:

"an explanation in terms of causation which must necessarily be treated as a chain of historical sequences. What we find here is not mutual interdependence between all phenomena but a unilateral dependence of the succeeding event on the preceding one" (Hayek 1941, p.17).

Because we hold that sequence analysis contains a notion of equilibrium, i.e. constant expectation functions (cp. below sect. 5), and this notion could certainly be related to Hayek's own idea of 'equilibrium analysis', namely, "[a] logical analysis of the different plans existing at one moment" (Hayek 1941, p.18 n.1).

Chapter 2   17

Sequence analysis may be said to be made up of two separate parts, namely, the single-period analysis and the continuation analysis. The first part is concerned with an analysis of what is going to happen during a single period, showing how certain ex ante plans at the beginning of the period lead to determinate ex post results at the end of the period. The second part analyses the effects of the ex post results in the current period on the plans for the subsequent period. It is obvious that both parts are necessary components in a sequence analysis, since the latter is supposed to determine a process spanning several consecutive periods. However, it is interesting to notice that Myrdal laid the foundation for the single-period analysis in <u>Monetary Equilibrium</u> without mentioning continuation analysis.

It is valuable to look through the Swedish eyes at other methods related to other objects, because this gives a useful indication of the way the members of the Stockholm School, at least in its mature form, might have characterized different dynamic methods. It is thus in line with Lindahl's idea that general dynamic structures, i.e. sequence analysis, should precede the construction of more particular methods (e.g. the static method cp. sect. IX:2). Our viewpoint is therefore basically the foundations laid by the Swedes during the period under consideration.

2 - The static method.
The static method, which refers to a stationary society,[5] deals in particular with the conditions of static equilibrium:

----

5 This type of society is roughly represented by an unchanged supply of factors of production:

"a society which retains unchanged from year to year the same population, the same area of territory and the same amount of capital, and remains on the same level of technical achievement" (Wicksell 1934, p.7; cp. p.207).

"the _static_ aspect of the problem of equilibrium, i.e. the conditions necessary for the maintenance, or the periodic renewal, of a _stationary state of economic relations_" (Wicksell 1934, p.105).[6]

Examples of this method are stationary state and proportional growth models, which means that the process has a reiterated character. Stationary state could be interpreted in sequential terms, as saying that the ex post results of the previous period lead to such ex ante plans for the current period that the same ex post result will be determined for this latter period, and so on (cp. Lindahl 1954, p.27). In the proportional growth model several quantities are changing from period to period, but the change

----

6 Robbins noticed that there exist two separate conceptions of stationary equilibrium:

"It is perfectly true that in both the Clarkian [and the Wicksellian] and the Classical construction [and the Marshallian] the quantities of of the factors of production are constant. But - and this is the fundamental difference which it is desired here to exhibit - _in the one, this constancy is the condition of equilibrium; in the other, it is simply one of the resultants of the equilibrating process._ In the Clarkian state, population and capital are to be constant - they are _not allowed_ to vary. In the classical constructions, population and capital are constant, but this is because, together with wages and interest, etc., they have reached a position of rest" (Robbins 1930, p.204).

We are thus not referring to the Marshallian notion of a long period equilibrium which implies a position of rest towards which the system is tending at any moment of time. However, it is important to bear in mind that Keynes used a particular version of this notion in the _General Theory_ (cp. sect. 3 App. I).

between two consecutive periods is uniform and equal to the common growth rate. Hence, the ex post values for the former period will iniate such plans for the current period that the plans are uniformly expanded by the given growth rate, and the ex post results of the current period will then stand in the same relation to the ex ante plans of the subsequent period, and so on.

Those who used the static method did not really assume that its object, viz. the stationary state, existed in the real world, and this conception functioned mainly as a theoretical fiction:

> "Our assumption of a stationary economy represents only the simplest case which is theoretically conceivable, but which never quite comes to pass in reality" (Wicksell 1954, p.164; cp. Cassel 1923A, p.29).

But they would still assert that the economic laws valid for the stationary state would also be relevant for the existing reality (cp. Wicksell 1934, p.5).[7] The proper use of the static method has generally been for comparisons between stationary states or proportional growth paths, where the actual transition between two equilibrium situations is not taken into account (cp. ibid., p.152), i.e. comparative statics (cp. Robbins 1935, p.101).[8]

----

7 It is interesting to notice that 'the static point of view' was related to the theoretical part of economics while 'the more dynamic point of view', such as the accumulation of capital belonged to the practical part of economics (cp. Wicksell 1934, p.5; p.7).

8 This is in line with Lindahl's view of the static method:

> "the two purposes of the static theory are to explain the condition for a stationary equilibrium situation, i.e. for a reiterated process, and to make comparisons between alternative processes of this type" (Lindahl 1942, p.46).

One may say that plans and the realization of plans play no significant role within the static method, in the sense that the determination of the equilibrium conditions for the stationary state is achieved without any reference to plans. That is to say, it is implicitly assumed that plans and expectations are fulfilled, which is the same as saying that anticipations are not part of the data determining the equilibrium. In this method plans and expectations have instead been reserved for the analysis of disturbances around the equilibrium level, like the difference between the normal rate and the money rate in the cumulative process. But this analysis is completely separate from the determination of the equilibrium level itself. 'Dynamics', even as recently as the 1920s, referred basically to a qualitative account of how disturbances might arise and work themselves out through credit cycles or trade cycles. This is very aptly shown by Cassel in his distinction between the dynamic/concrete economy and the uniformly progressive economy [9], where the former are "the deviations which actual life shows from the uniform development" (Cassel 1929, p.19; cp. p.21, p.31). Dynamics therefore came to belong to the part of economics related to the so-called 'Theory of Money and Credit', intended as Vol.II of 'Economic Principles', while Vol.I was 'Value Theory' which analysed the determination of conditions of

----

9 The uniformly progressive economy is "characterized primarily by the uniformity of the growth of capital" (Cassel, 1929, p.33), and in the analysis of this case Cassel just assumed a given and constant growth rate (cp. ibid., p.89). This case, as has been noticed by Hicks, can be treated in the same way as the static case:

"It was, I believe, first shown by Cassel that a model of steady growth can be constructed which can be handled in much the same way as the static model" (Hicks 1965, p.13).

equilibrium.[10] From this period, Keynes' A Treatise on Money is here considered to be one of the most accomplished works in this genre, and it may be helpful to think of Keynes' work as Vol.II to Marshall's Principles of Economics. Hence, even if practitioners of dynamics were wont to analyse the observed reality in terms of trade-cycles or the like, that analysis would not challenge the propositions derived from the static method.[11] This idea of what dynamic theory was about formed the background for the Stockholm School when they started their attempts to develop dynamic methods. Thus it is important to realize, that the construction of new notions, like intertemporal equilibrium, constitutes a theoretical break with the older tradition.

3 - Intertemporal equilibrium.

The next method is intertemporal equilibrium, involving a sequence of periods which are different from one another. The outcomes of all periods are now determined at the beginning of the process by the existence of complete futures markets or perfect foresight. This method does not really portray a sequential process, since it makes no sense to say that the plans and outcome of the current period determine what is going to happen in the subsequent period, as the relative price exchangeratios and quantities are determined simultaneously for all

----

10 Thus Wicksell published his Lectures on Political Economy in two volumes, namely, 'Theoretical Economics' and 'On Money and Credit' respectively. Despite the fact that Wicksell actually attempted to show that there was a connection between value theory and monetary theory via the relation between the normal rate of interest and the money rate (cp. Wicksell 1936, pp.xxv-xxvi).
11 This is also true for Marshall's followers, even if they used his idea of a long period equilibrium (cp. above Note 6), since their analysis of the deviations from the long period norm did not affect the norm itself, unless the disturbance was unleashed by a change in one of the fundamental forces (cp. Keynes 1930A, p.137).

periods before the process starts (cp. Lindahl 1954, p.27).[12]

This method was first developed by Hayek in 1928 followed by Lindahl in 1929 (cp. Milgate 1979, p.1; sect. IV:2:3a:1), and it played an important role in Hayek's subsequent work in the 1930s while it was almost immediately given up by Lindahl. However, the notion only became widespread within the economic profession in the 1960s, but it had already been given a strict mathematical formulation by economists like Arrow and Debreu in the mid 1950s.[13] The demise of this notion probably started in the late 1960s when a younger generation of mathematical economists began to question its validity for analysing problems involving uncertainty and money (cp. Hahn 1973, pp.15-16), and different versions of temporary equilibrium were constructed to cope with these problems (cp. Weintraub 1979, p.102). From our point of view, it is particularly interesting to notice that Lindahl gave up the use of intertemporal equilibrium as early as 1930 for very much the same reason, and he formulated instead a notion of temporary equilibrium.

What is the object of this dynamic method? In the words of its inventor, the notion of intertemporal equilibrium has a "purely fictitious character"(Hayek 1941, p.21), and seems mainly to be normative, since "the functioning of the existing economic system will depend on the degree to which it approaches such a condition"(ibid., p.28). The same idea has also been put forward by one of the foremost figures in the resurgence of this method:

---

12 Hahn seems for similar reasons to consider this equilibrium notion to reflect an _inessential_ sequence (cp. Hahn 1973, p.16).

13 It would seem that the profession at large could not really have grasped what was going on until they had digested the less terse exposition of intertemporal equilibrium developed by Koopmans in his first essay in Three Essays on the State of Economic Science from 1957.

"the conceptual framework on which it
[intertemporal equilibrium] is based is
much better adapted to the examination of
the normative problems raised by the
organisation of economic activity over
time" (Malinvaud 1972, p.242).

Nevertheless, Hayek holds that the notion can also
"help to explain real events"(Hayek 1941, p.21),
since it tells whether the plans of the different
individuals are mutually consistent and may therefore
be realized, or "whether the present situation
carries the seed of inevitable disappointment to
some, which will make it necessary for them to change
their plans"(ibid., p.22; p.28).[14]
    It is important to notice that the analysis
pursued within this method must be in real terms; i.e.
it is a barter economy, and no commodity may
therefore serve solely as a medium of exchange,
because in the case of perfect foresight, where the
different plans are compatible but new contracts will
actually be signed over the whole sequence, there is
no reason to hold a commodity in the terminal period
which has no direct utility as a medium of exchange,
and since no further exchange takes place it has no
indirect utility either. In the case of complete
future markets, where the plans are reconciled before
the process starts, no new contracts are signed
during the sequence. The process of reconciliation

----

14 Hahn gives a similar account of the empirical
validity of intertemporal equilibrium:

    "it is motivated by a very weak causal
    proposition. This is that no plausible
    sequence of economic states will terminate
    if it does so at all, in a state which is not
    an equilibrium. The argument is
    straightforward; agents will not continue in
    actions in states in which preferred or more
    profitable ones are available. to them nor
    will mutually inconsistent actions allow
    given prices to persist" (Hahn 1973, p.7).

by which the equilibrium is established is therefore, if it is discussed at all, supposed to have a notional character, which means that no deals are concluded before all the plans are consistent, and in such a process a medium of exchange is superfluous. Hence, in both cases any good may serve as numeraire, which is just a convenience for expressing all the different exchange ratios in a common unit. However, several practitioners have proceeded as if fiat money was included in intertemporal equilibrium or they have made analogies to a money economy.[15]

4 - Temporary Equilibrium.

Temporary equilibrium only determines the complete outcome for a single period, and it is implied that equilibrium only rules for the current period. However, anticipations for the first period as well as for the forthcoming periods are included in the current plans due to the existence of capital goods. But there is no necessity that equilibrium will exist for the forthcoming periods, in the sense that the plans for these periods, made up at the beginning of the current period, will be consistent. Hence the temporary character of this equilibrium.

A continuation theory can be constructed from this method by assuming a string of periods all in temporary equilibrium. However, such an analysis

----

15 Both Hayek and Lindahl use this procedure, even if Hayek stresses that the analysis is in real terms (cp. Hayek 1941, pp.29-31; sect. IV:2:3a:2). Even a canonical text like Debreu's Theory of Value seems to contain such analogies. On the one hand, it is explicitly stated that "no theory of money is offered here, and it is assumed that the economy works without the help of a good serving as a medium of exchange" (Debreu 1959, p.28). On the other hand, a few pages later we are asked to "imagine that a certain good circulates as money at location s, at date t" (ibid., p.33). If such wordings are used by one of the leading mathematical economists, then it is no surprise that mainstream economists thought that money was perhaps after all included in this method.

looks identical to intertemporal equilibrium, since it must be assumed that the plans are from the outset consistent over all periods. That amounts to the existence of perfect foresight, since no prereconciliatory procedure, except for the first period, is supposed to take place. Due to the lack of a proper continuation theory, this method has instead fallen back on a procedure which is akin to comparative statics, which in this case means a comparison of alternative temporary equilibria (cp. Hicks 1965, p.65). This method is therefore most suitable for analysing an economy which has few, if any, futures markets, i.e. a spot economy (cp. Hicks 1946, p.136; Hicks 1956, pp.144-145). Temporary equilibrium has been used to analyse Marshall's fish-market which is Hicks' flex-price example (cp. Hicks 1965, pp.52-54), while Lindahl's case is more akin to Marshall's short period equilibrium since both production and sales are in equilibrium (cp. sect. IV:2:2; cp. sect. IX:5).

Money, both as a medium of exchange and a store of value, certainly plays a role in temporary equilibrium, since there are good reasons to hold money balances so as to hedge, or to take advantage of, expected and unexpected oppurtunities in subsequent periods. Hence, even Hayek, one of the staunchest proponents of the 'real' characteristic of intertemporal equilibrium, has extended his concept of intertemporal equilibrium so as to be able to take into consideration "the desire of people to hold money" (Hayek 1941, p.357). This extension, which looks similar to temporary equilibrium, goes as follows:

"The plans of the various individuals may be compatible with the extent to which they are definite, and yet the individuals may at the same time be uncertain about what will happen after a certain date and may wish to keep some general reserve against whatever may happen in that more uncertain future" (ibid.; cp. Hicks 1965, pp.58-59).

5 - Disequilibrium methods: Equilibrium and disequilibrium sequence analysis.

Finally we have the disequilibrium method which analyses single periods out of equilibrium and which signifies that the ex ante plans are not consistent but the ex post values are equal. This method implies two different versions of continuation theory, namely, equilibrium and disequilibrium sequence analysis. However, the equilibrium sequence analysis, although it starts out from a single-period analysis which allows for disequilibrium, as a continuation theory it assumes that each period is in equilibrium. Hence, this version is basically the same as intertemporal equilibrium (cp. sect. IX:4:5).[16] In the disequilibrium sequence analysis the process is represented by an array of single periods which are not in equilibrium, but there are constant rules of conduct which determine how the ex post results from one period influence the ex ante plans for the subsequent period (cp. sect. X:2). These rules represent the equilibrium notion within disequilibrium sequence analysis. But it is only a question of the maintenance of equilibrium for a short period of time, since the rules can not be assumed to stay constant for more than a few periods.

This method is the first with a meaningful sequential character to it in the sense that both cause and effect are involved. Hence, it is no longer the case of "mutual interdependence between all phenomena but a unilateral dependence of the succeeding event on the preceding one" (Hayek 1941, p.17). According to Hayek, the latter is the hallmark of real processes in historical time, i.e. what he calls "a chain of historical sequences" (ibid.).

---

16 Thus Hicks speaks of 'Equilibrium over Time' as depending on "the condition that the prices realized on the second Monday are the same as those which were previously *expected* to rule at that date" (Hicks 1946, p.132). Furthermore, if there are no unexpected (exogenous) changes in the preferences and the resources, then nothing has happened to disturb the plans made up at the preceding Monday and since "no one has made any mistakes, ... plan can continue to be executed without any revision" (ibid.).

We have thereby come as 'close' to the 'real world' as it is possible within a theoretical analysis, and as a result we have diminished "the width of the gulf which separates tnis exercise in economic logic [equilibrium analysis, cp. above Note 4] from any attempt directly to explain the processes of the real world" (ibid., p.39). This result is obviously of great importance if the ultimate goal of economic analysis is to explain these types of causal processes (cp. sect. IX:2). Consequently this method takes as its object a 'real world' where the sequential relations between formation of plans, actions and revisions of plans are of ultimate importance, which of course is a characteristic of plans and actions in real time.

The mathematical formulation of a model in disequilibrium sequence analysis, e.g. Lundberg's model sequences, looks very similar to models within mathematical dynamics.[17] But, from our point of view, the latter belongs to the static method because of its mechanical character, which here implies that the expectations are formed endogenously, i.e. there is a strict and stable relation between expectation and earlier events, and there is no place for revising the expectations due to the accumulated information (cp. Ch.X Note 5 and 6).

----

17 By this term we mean a type of model where the object under consideration is described by a system of differential or difference equations, and where the analysis considers the determinateness and stability of the system.

Chapter 3

The Method of Expectations
Myrdal's Dissertation (1927)

"the 'method of expectations' ... the
introduction of expectations as explicit
variables in a formal 'equilibrium' theory"
(Hicks 1973, p.143 n.11).

Prisbildningsproblemet och föränderligheten
(The problem of Price Formation and Change) is
Myrdal's doctoral dissertation of 1927. In the
preface he mentioned Cassel, Bagge and Lindahl. Both
Bagge and Lindahl had read the original manuscript
and given their comments to Myrdal. Lindahl was also
one of the examiners.[1] Cassel was Myrdal's supervisor
for the dissertation, but he was probably mostly
influential "in regard to general approach than to
details" (Myrdal 1958, p.242). In fact, Cassel's
ideas on price and value theory completely permeate
the work, while there is no evidence that Wicksell
had had any substantial influence on Myrdal's work
(cp. Note 5). This is examplified by Myrdal's
critique of Wicksell's theory of capital from a
Cassellian viewpoint (cp. Myrdal, 1927, p.54ff.).
With respect to the development of dynamic
method within the Stockholm School the most important
contribution of Myrdal's thesis resides in his
working out of the 'method of expectations', which
means that anticipations are part of the data. Thus
they play the same role as other immediate or primary

----

1 Lindahl reviewed the dissertation for the Economic
Journal (cp. Lindahl 1929C).

determinants of price.[2] The stress on anticipations
is particularly obvious in the later development of
the Stockholm School with the introduction of the ex
ante notion in Myrdal's <u>Monetary Equilibrium</u> and
Lindahl's emphasis on the plan as a central concept
in economic theory.

1 - Myrdal's purpose.
It will be useful in understanding the
background to Myrdal's method if we first look at
Cassel's handling of the dynamic problem:

> "Up to the present in our treatment of the
> pricing problem we have regarded these [the
> immediate price determinants (cp. Note 1)]
> as given factors. But these factors depend
> themselves upon a number of different
> factors of the economic and general human
> life. If we want to study the influence of
> these on prices, we have first to study
> their influence on the immediate
> determinants. It is only through these that
> more remote factors can affect prices.
> Hence all such inquiries bring us back to
> our solution of the pricing problem ... .
> Factors which thus influence prices from
> without are for instance, changes in the
> size of the population ... in a word, all
> the factors which give the economic life its
> mobility and vitality. In so far as these
> movements affect prices, and are in turn
> influenced by them, we have to deal with

----

2 Cassel mentioned the following three determinants:

> "the character of the dependence of the
> demand for finished products upon prices ...
> the technical conditions of production and
> the quantities of the available means of
> production ... . We call these three groups
> of determining factors of prices their
> immediate determinants" (Cassel 1923A,
> p.152).

dynamic problems of pricing. These dynamic
problems have, of course, a considerably
larger content than the static problem of
prices ... . It would, however, be a
mistake to imagine that solving the static
problem has nothing to do with the dynamic
problems. On the contrary, all questions of
dynamical pricing are converted first into
questions as to the effect of certain
movements and changes upon the immediate
determining factors of prices, and
consequently as to the determination of
prices by these factors in accord with the
causal already descibed" (Cassel 1923A,
pp.152-153).

Hence, for Cassel the dynamic problem was to gauge
the influence of the outside factors on the immediate
determinants, and after that the˜ pricing problem is
solved in the traditional way, namely, as a system of
simultaneous equations. It is crucial to notice that
Myrdal related his own purpose to this particular
passage by arguing that it is necessary to include
"the anticipated consequences [of "the effect of
certain movements and changes", from the quotation
above] as more or less probable possibilities"
(Myrdal 1927, p.7 n.4). Hence, the direct spur to the
dissertation seemed to have come from what Myrdal
considered to be Cassel's incomplete handling of the
dynamic problem, since the latter had left out the
problem of including the 'continual changeability'
which for Cassel was the main complication in the
dynamic case (cp. Cassel 1929, pp.18-19). The origin
of Myrdal's construction may therefore be
characterized as a theoretical attack on a problem
which was mentioned by Cassel but to which he did not

provide any solution.[3] The influence on Myrdal's
particular way of attacking the dynamic problem has
probably emanated from Knight, since in his Risk,
Uncertainty and Profit a future change could be
anticipated in advance and thereby it could be
included in the economic calculations (cp. Myrdal
1927, p.9; Knight 1921, p.35ff.). Myrdal's difference
with the latter is that Knight did not try to
establish a long run equilibrium which included
anticipations as a datum (cp. ibid., p.108).
However, this was done by Marshall and in his
Priciples risk was a part of the supplementary costs
(cp. ibid., p.25 n.4; Marshall 1961, p.377; p.400),
but Marshall assumed that the anticipations were
fulfilled in the long run and the factor of change
thus disappeared (cp. ibid., p.26; Marshall 1961,
p.360; p.424 n.1).

---

3 This characterization is similar to Cassel's view:

> "You say that you are tired of your
> theoretical studies and you look upon the
> English translation [of the dissertation]
> as a task which is too trying. ... . But do
> not think that you can leave the great
> problem of changeability, which you now have
> made a first attempt to put in its proper
> perspective within the economic theory.
> Such a bold venture is obliging. I have
> tried to widen the static viewpoint and to
> extract from it as much as possible. I also
> believe that the foundation I have given to
> this field must last and form the
> startingpoint in elementary teaching. ... .
> The foundation of the dynamic economy is
> your task and some day you have to reach
> such a clarity in this matter, that you can
> give the world an elementary and fully
> understandable guidance to the dynamics of
> the economy. This is after all the
> categorical imperative, which life has put
> in front of you" (Cassel to Myrdal, 9
> December 1929).

The point is that Myrdal put these 'anticipated concequences', or as he usually calls them the 'factor[s] of change', alongside the other immediate determinants.[4] The factor of change implies that "the changes whether they are completely foreseen or not exert their effects on the economic process long before they actually take place" (ibid., p.9; cp. p.7). Such effects are possible because "price formation takes place in human minds" (ibid., p.8; cp. p.33). The main reason for bothering about such effects is the fact that "means of production are permanently bound, so they could not be moved or adapted at all, or only with costs, to new circumstances of price formation" (ibid., p.17).

In his own eyes this construction amounted to a dynamic theory:

"the purpose is to complete the mental picture, to add a further deductive step towards the immense field of empirical facts, and to construct the third approximation, in addition to the stationary and the uniformly progressive economy [i.e. Cassel's first and second approximation respectively]: the equilibrium price formation of a society with non-uniform changes, and thereafter to put it into direct relation with the actual prices" (ibid., p.11).

The step has a 'deductive' and 'theoretical' character, since it is possible to use a deductive method when "the change [föränderligheten] is looked at prospectively, possible changes are discounted to one point of time, the existing moment"(Myrdal 1925, p.10; cp. sect. II:2). It is a 'further step' in the sense that it liberates the theory of price formation from the static assumption; that is, to Cassel's two

----

4 This idea is similar to Keynes' notion of a 'theory of shifting equilibrium' which is different from the 'theory of stationary equilibrium', where the former refers to "the theory of a system in which changing views about the future are capable of influencing the present situation" (Keynes 1936, p.293).

'approximations' (cp. Myrdal 1927, p.4), since Myrdal took into consideration non-uniform changes in the primary factors which for him are a characteristic of the reality. Moreover, to apply the dynamic theory directly to an explanation of the actual prices shows that it is not possible to come closer to reality in a 'theoretical' discourse.

The new determinant specific to the dynamic theory, i.e. the anticipation of changes, implies that <u>the dynamic normal will be different from the static normal</u>:

> "a normal price formation within a dynamic situation is not the price formation, which under similar circumstances would exist, if it could be anticipated with certainty that no new primary changes will from now on take place ... . Or expressed in a different way: the equilibrium price of the dynamic economy is by no means the price, which sooner or later would be realized if the reality became static" (ibid., p.7).

This is a critique of J.B.Clark's dictum "that the static forces set the standards, and the dynamic forces produce the variations" (as quoted and italicized by Myrdal from J.B.Clark, <u>The Distribution of Wealth</u> (1914, p.32), ibid. p.9). According to Myrdal, who in his turn referred to Knight, Clark did not realize that "the disturbances that progress causes" (as quoted by Myrdal from J.B.Clark 1914, p.29, ibid.) could be incorporated as anticipations into a theory which would still satisfy the conception of a long run normal. Hence, Myrdal's opinion on dynamic theory came out clearly in his reformulation of Clark's saying:

> "static <u>and dynamic</u> forces set the standard, and the dynamic forces produce the variations" (ibid., p.10).

This idea, that the equilibrium price of the dynamic theory has an existence in its own right and that it is different from the static equilibrium price, must be considered the most important proposition in Myrdal's dissertation.[5] Cassel deemed this result to be "extraordinarily important" (Cassel 1927). Furthermore, it is crucial to remember that the difference depends upon the inclusion of anticipations as a datum into the theoretical corpus, and thereby anticipations play the same role as the other price determinants. When Landgren much later refuted Ohlin's claims that static equilibrium price theory had neglected the role of anticipations, he gave several instances where neo-classical economists had mentioned anticipations and uncertainty (cp. Landgren 1960, pp.227-228; Ohlin 1937A, p.54; cp. below Note 11). Incidentally, D.H.Robertson voiced the same type of critique against Hicks' 'method of expectations' (cp. Hicks 1973, p.143 n.11). However, neither Landgren nor Robertson had seen that the inclusion of anticipations as a datum means that a different equilibrium position is determined compared to the static theory. But it should be kept in mind that Myrdal's equilibrium position was a long run normal while Hicks' position was a temporary equilibrium.

---

5 Static theory may not be a good approximation to reality, since the static prices are in general not the normal in relation to the actual prices; but, nevertheless, it can not be thrown overboard, because it still forms "a theoretical frame for a more sophisticated and deeper analysis" (Myrdal 1927, p.27; cp. p.6), in the sense that it functions as starting point for dynamic theory (cp. sect. 3 below about "completing the static equations"). In this context Myrdal naturally opted for Cassel's version:

"Professor Cassel's static theory of price formation has been the genetical and logical starting point, from which I have tried to study the dynamic problem" (ibid., p.vii).

2 - The construction of a concept of dynamic equilibrium.

Both static and dynamic theory use the idea of an equilibrium (cp. Myrdal 1927, p.8 n.1; p.11), which signifies "that there exists an equilibrium position for the economy towards which the actual price formation tends" (ibid., p.5; cp. pp.8-9; p.18). This notion is so central to Myrdal that he held that "theoretical analysis _is_ nothing else than a study of such equilibrium situations and their assumptions, as well as the causes which hinder their continuous realization" (ibid.). The main hindrance to 'the continuous realization' of an equilibrium position is the factor of inertia or frictions, which means that the means of production cannot be adapted to changes without involving cost and time (cp. ibid., pp.12-13). However, Myrdal could not exclude this factor in the construction of dynamic equilibrium since it is the raison d'etre for the factor of change. On the contrary it has to have the same place as every other primary factor in the price formation (cp. ibid., p.14).[6] But it is still necessary to eliminate that element of inertia which is due to the fact that "the movement is not instantaneous but takes time" (ibid., p.15). This is possible by imagining "that the movement has come to an end" (ibid.). It is precisely this time factor which "alone represents the connection between the actual price formation and its normal equilibrium situation" (ibid., p.16; cp. p.15), and it could therefore be excluded in the construction of a dynamic theory.

Thus Myrdal gives the following definition of the dynamic normal:

----

6 The opposite idea is of course the so-called 'atomistic' situation where means of production are completely mobile and divisible. In such a case no difference will ever exist between market and natural prices, since any exogenous change will be immediately followed by a restoration of equilibrium, i.e. the economy is always in equilibrium (cp. Myrdal 1927, p.12; Lindahl 1939D, pp.274-275).

"it gives a determined and precise meaning
to the concept of equilibrium price
formation, if we thereby understand the
economic situation, which would exist at
each moment of time, if the movements of the
factors of production, caused by the changes
which have already taken place, were
instantaneous, though with the same cost as
in reality, inclusive of the interest losses
during the time of the movement" (ibid.,
p.15; italics omitted).

However, it is not enough to look at the effects of
'the changes which have already taken place', it is
also necessary to include the effects of those
changes that are due to the fact that "the conditions
of a period of transition considerably affect the
conditions [i.e. the primary determinants of prices]
of the subsequent normal settlement of prices"
(Cassel 1923A, p.154; cp. Myrdal 1927, p.15 n.2).
These so-called 'secondary effects' may arise because
of the fact that the actual prices deviate from the
equilibrium price during the process towards the
equilibrium position (cp. Myrdal 1927, p.15).
Though, Lindahl added that it seemed difficult to
understand this construction, since "one can see no
end to the effects, which should be included in the
timeless act" (Lindahl 1941, p.239 n.1).[7]
    The dynamic equilibrium, like its static
counterpart, must imply that at each moment of time
there exists an equilibrium level towards which
actual prices are tending. But this tendency will be
more or less continuously disturbed by changes in the
primary determinants which are not completely

----

7 Garegnani has answered this type of critique by his
assumption that the changes in 'the persistent
forces' are "once-for-all changes, and that, after a
period of transition, gravitation to the new long-
period values would again assert itself" (Garegnani
1976, p.28). Hence, after a period of transition the
deviations of actual prices from the normal price
will not any longer influence the equilibrium
position.

anticipated (cp. Myrdal 1927, p.18), i.e. 'the dynamic forces produce the variations' (cp. above).[8]

Among the Swedish commentators it was Lundberg who gave the most explicit critique of Myrdal's equilibrium notion when he stated that the difference between two consecutive <u>actual</u> prices could influence the supposedly 'governing' equilibrium position.[9] According to Lundberg, it was therefore necessary "to base the determination of the governing situation on a dynamic analysis" (Lundberg 1930, p.154), but he did not know of "any method to determine these ... equilibrium situations and even to show that they exist" (ibid.).[10] In fact, this is a direct challenge to the whole idea of the existence of a tendency towards a long run normal, which is possible since expectations are now a part of the data. Later

---

8 Hicks described this latter notion as "[a] picture, of actual values chasing a 'moving equilibrium'(the equilibrium values of which are determined statically)" (Hicks 1965, p.23).

9 Lindahl was not "convinced of the value of the author's construction" (Lindahl 1927, p.7), since the meaning of Myrdal's dynamic equilibrium was not unambiguous and Lindahl could think of at least six possible interpretations. Later on he reacted against Myrdal's attempt to exclude time, and he thought of it as a "neck-breaking attempt" (Lindahl 1941, p.239) which was very close to the 'atomistic' assumption.
Ohlin was certainly more positive:

> "While this [Myrdal's dynamic equilibrium] may appear to be a peculiar construction, it is no doubt more realistic than the earlier static equilibrium" (Ohlin 1937A, pp.54-55).

10 Thus Hicks says that "the tendency to (static) equilibrium is itself a dynamic matter" (Hicks 1965, p.18). The method used by Samuelson to solve this problem was to show that a particular static system is a stationary solution to a dynamic system and the latter is characterized by a system of differential equations.

we will examine Lundberg's influence on the dynamic
method used by Myrdal in <u>Monetary Equilibrium</u> (cp.
sect. VI:2:1).

3 - Two dynamic methods.

It is interesting to look at Myrdal's slightly
obscure distinction between two dynamic methods,
since they relate to the methods later developed by
the Swedes.

For Myrdal the dynamic price formation gave rise
to two different problems:

> "One problem is how a price situation
> [Myrdal must here refer to a normal
> situation] is transformed into another one.
> The question bears here upon the causal
> effects <u>forward in time</u> from the changes
> actually taking place. However, the changes
> have also effects <u>backwards in time</u>, since
> they have been anticipated. The latter
> problem is the primary one from a
> theoretical point of view. Because it is
> the price situation, in which the
> anticipations have been a codeterminant,
> which is hit by the changes and which
> thereby develops into a new one. An
> analysis of the former problem therefore
> necessitates that the latter problem is

solved" (Myrdal 1927, p.21).[11]

The primary method is formulated as "a mutual functional relation at a point of time" (ibid.). This system of interdependent equations must have the same formal character as a static system, where certain factors due to anticipations of changes have been included. Thus Myrdal spoke of "completing the equations of static price formation" (ibid. p.48; cp. Lindahl 1929B, p.80). For the existence of an equilibrium, i.e. in cases where there is a solution to the system of interdependent equations, Myrdal must assume that the anticipations are mutually consistent, which is guaranteed by the assumption of 'objective risk' (cp. sect. 4 below). This solution will give the dynamic equilibrium price, which will now function as the centre of gravitation for the actual prices.

The secondary method deals with "one-way causal effects proceeding in time" (ibid.). This must imply that if the anticipated changes in the primary factors are partially or completely wrong, then the secondary method would handle the time consuming process where the determinants of a new equilibrium are formed (cp. ibid., pp.19-20; Palander 1941, p.10). If the anticipations are correct then the normal prices will of course stay unchanged.

----

11 Lundberg refuted the idea that the anticipations could have an independent existence:

> "anticipations have no _direct_ causal effect backwards in time from the expected future situation, on the contrary anticipations during a given earlier period must be completely founded on the constellation of prices under this period and the previous ones". (Lundberg 1930, p.156; cp. Landgren 1960, p.227)

But even if the pre-existing prices are the arguments of the expectation function that does not determine the _form_ of the function, and this form could therefore be said to be determined independently by the anticipations.

Furthermore these changes have to have an 'exogenous' character, in the sense defined by Hayek:

> "the equilibrium, as defined in the first sense [the plans are mutually compatible, i.e. more or less Myrdal's first problem], may be disturbed by an unforeseen development of the (objective) data and to describe this as an exogenous disturbance. In fact, it seems hardly possible to attach any definite meaning to the much used concept of a change in the (objective) data unless we distinguish between external developments in conformity with, and those different from, what has been expected, and define as a 'change' any divergence of the actual from the expected development ... all this means that we can speak of a change in data only if equilibrium in the first sense exists, that is, if expectations coincide" (Hayek 1937, pp.40-41).

This interpretation also makes sense in Cassel's formal construction of the determination of prices, which is a system of simultaneous equations where changes in the immediate determinants are of necessity exogenous to the system and have to be explained by inductive methods, since they are parts of the dynamic/concrete economy (cp. Cassel 1929, pp.18-19). Needless to say, Myrdal gave no explicit the indications that he had understood that his first method presumes that anticipations are consistent and that his second method deals with exogenous changes.

We might, with hindsight, interpret the first method as an ex ante analysis, in the sense that anticipations, which Lindahl later developed into the notion of plans, determine the development for the forthcoming period whilst at the same time there is no guarantee that the anticipations are fulfilled. This method, in conjunction with Lundberg's criticism, could then be seen as a forerunner to the formulation in Monetary Equilbrium, but it will only give the tendencies at a point of time and there is no presumption that the anticipations are correct.

It is also possible to guess how the notion of temporary equilibrium could have grown out of Myrdal's first method, because Myrdal presumed that the long run equilibrium is continuously disrupted by unfulfilled anticipations amongst other things (cp. Myrdal 1927, p.18), which means that in real time the same equilibrium situation only rules for a short period. Then it is easy, at least retrospectively, to arrive at the conclusion that the equilibrium is only determined for <u>one</u> short period, since for later periods the anticipations are either not congruent, or do not conform to the exogenous changes, which is what justifies the introduction of the notion of 'temporary equilibrium' (cp. sect. IV:2:3b). Furthermore, this 'conjecture' is justified by the fact that once the assumption of objective risk is dropped, then there seems to be no possibility of keeping the idea of a long run norm (cp. sect. 4).

In the same way, the second method is related to what happens at a transition point in a sequence analysis; namely the process in which the ex post results from the outgoing period influence the ex ante plans for the forthcoming period. However, in a sequence analysis the two methods are fused in determining the sequence from a given starting-point. Thus the first method is used in the ordinary ex ante way, while the second method shows how ex post result will be transformed into ex ante plans determining the development of the next period. The Swedes later concentrated their attention on the first problem, i.e. "the primary one from a theoretical point of view" (Myrdal 1927, p.21), while they always considered the second problem to be a more complicated question (cp. sect. IX:4:5).

4 - Objective and subjective risk.
Myrdal's handling of risk sheds further light on the difficulties inherent in his dynamic method.

The notion of objective risk has the following meaning:

"we take ... the individual entrepreneur's complex of experiences and faculty of judgement as given and we furthermore assume this entrepreneur to be in a given situation, then a certain conception of the future is fixed as being for him the objectively correct one" (Myrdal 1927, p.98; cp. p.98 n.1; p.101; p.103).[12]

It is 'objective' in the sense that all irrational factors of the entrepreneur's mind have no effects on his estimation of risk (cp. ibid.). However, the important point is that the risk is objective, or logical (Keynes' term), in relation to the individual entrepreneur's given experience.[13]

---

12 A.G.Hart made the following comment on the meaning of Myrdal's objective risk:

> "they [Myrdal and some other Swedish economists] mean ... not the 'risk' as it would be estimated with full knowledge of all elements of the situation - when, of course, a given outcome would be regarded as either certain or impossible, not merely as likely - but as it would be estimated from the data available to the actual estimator by an ideal estimator" (Hart 1942, p.547 n.2).

13 Here Myrdal was obviously influenced by Keynes' Treatise on Probability. He actually builds on the following passage from Keynes:

> "To this extent, therefore, the probability may be called subjective. But in the sense important to logic, probability is not subjective ... . A proposition is not probable because we think it so. When once the facts are given which determine our knowledge, what is probable or improbable in
> (Note continued on following page)

The anticipations are now 'correct', thus
ensuring that a dynamic equilibrium exists in the
following sense:

----

these circumstances has been fixed
objectively, and is independent of our
opinion. The theory of probability is
logical, therefore, because it is concerned
with the degree of belief which it is
rational to entertain in given conditions,
and not merely with the actual beliefs of
particular individuals, which may or may not
be rational" (Keynes 1921, p.4; cp. Myrdal
1927 p.98 n.2).

Thus, Keynes spoke about a relation between two types
of propositions, one type which represents "the given
conditions" or "corpus of knowledge" (ibid.),
Myrdal's given experience of the entrepreneur, and
another type in which we might have rational belief.
The theory of probability then tells us:

"what further rational beliefs, certain or
probable, can be derived by valid argument
from our direct knowledge. This involves
purely logical relations between the
propositions which embody our direct
knowledge [the corpus] and the propositions
about which we seek indirect knowledge.
What particular propositions we select as
the premisses of our argument [cp. Myrdal
1927, p.108] naturally depends on subjective
factors peculiar to ourselves; but the
relations, in which other propositions stand
to these, and which entitle us to probable
beliefs, are objective and logical" (ibid.).

Keynes' account makes all probabilities conditional.
We cannot simply speak of the probability of an
hypothesis, but only of its probability relative to
some evidence which partially entails it. When in
ordinary speech we speak of the probability of some
outcome, i.e. the probability seemingly
unconditional, in Keynes' opinion we then assume
implicitly a standard body of evidence.

"[that if entrepreneurs always acted
according to the objective risk, their
anticipations] would on the average be
realized according to the law of great
numbers, if the single entrepreneur had a
sufficient number of oppurtunities to test
them" (ibid., p.96; cp. 98; p.99).

This connection between anticipations and outcome is
"obviously regulated by the 'law of large numbers'"
(ibid., p.118; cp. p.99 n.2; pp.187-188). Thus the
connection does not hold for a single act of a single
entrepreneur, but only for the aggregate
anticipations and the aggregate results of several
entrepreneurs over a period of time (cp. ibid.,
p.118; p.121).

If we now abandon the assumption of objective
risk, which means that we take at face value the fact
that the estimation of risk is "completely subjective
and specific to the person and for the moment of
time" (ibid., p.103; cp. p.96), then an 'irrational'
moment or 'emotive' factors can "be expected to have
a directly disruptive inference on the intellectual,
i.e. a non-emotional process" (ibid., p.183; cp.
p.98; p.99; p.105; p.111). The inclusion of 'emotive'
factors has the effect that "we annihilate the
connection broadly speaking between the
anticipations and the results" (ibid.; cp. p.188).
However, this new factor is not part of the ex ante
investment calculation since it is "concealed during
the process and it first emerges in the
entrepreneurial results" (ibid., p.188).

Myrdal only devoted a couple of pages to this
issue and he gave no hints whatsoever as to its
consequences for his equilibrium construction. But
this new factor seems to overthrow the whole idea of
a long run equilibrium. It implies that the
anticipations are not congruent, which means, in
turn, that endogenous changes have to ensue, so that
a long run equilibrium cannot exist. Myrdal's
critique of Marshall for assuming that the
anticipations were fulfilled in the long run (cp.
sect. 1) appears therefore to be misplaced. In fact,
this is a proof of the inherent difficulty to include
anticipations among the data for determining a long

run equilibrium.

These complications due to the non-existence of objective risk might be one of the reasons why Myrdal never mentioned long period norms in <u>Monetary Equilibrium</u>.

Chapter 4

The Equilibrium Approach
Lindahl's Development of
Intertemporal and Temporal Equilibrium
(1929-1930)

"that in each of these short periods of time
individuals have full knowledge of the
prices ruling during the period, and that
they allow their actions concerning supply
and demand to be determined by these prices,
which are therefore consistent with their
actions. The price situations will then be
equilibrium states in the sense that there
will be equality between supply and demand
during the period" (Lindahl 1939C, p.159).

The main aim of this chapter is the analysis of the
notions of intertemporal and temporal equilibrium
developed by Lindahl in "The place of Capital in the
Theory of Price" of 1929 and The Rate of Interest and
the Price Level of 1930. It is crucial to understand
that intertemporal equilibrium mainly grew out of
Lindahl's critique of comparative statics, and it is
therefore not related to Wicksell's ideas on the
cumulative process, while temporary equilibrium
evolved in response to certain weaknesses in
intertemporal equilibrium. Temporary equilibrium was
applied to the analysis of the equilibrating
mechanism between savings and investment during a
cumulative process, an analysis, which, as we will
see, is evidence of the inadequacies of temporary
equilibrium for this purpose. Furthermore, during
the cumulative process this equilibrating mechanism
looks akin to Keynes' principle of effective demand,
but the explanation of an equilibrium situation shows
that they are different theories.

1 - The object of Lindahl's analysis.

Right from the beginning Lindahl focused on finding a theory for explaining changes in the price level, which goes hand in hand with an attempt to construct a method for dealing with dynamic processes. The fusion between the notion of temporary equilibrium, which does not emanate from Wicksell, and Wicksell's theory for changes in the price level in the book of 1930 is therefore a sequel to the theories and methods dealt with by Lindahl in his earlier works.

1.1 - A critique of the quantity theory of money.

In his article "Om förhållandet mellan penningmängd och prisnivå" (On the Relation Between the Money Supply and the Price Level) of 1929, Lindahl mainly discusses different versions of the exchange equations to assess "which formulation of the relation between money supply and price level has the most real content" (Lindahl 1929A, p.1). After weighing the pros and cons of the different versions, in the process of which he refers frequently to Hawtrey's Currency and Credit (3rd ed. 1928), Lindahl opts for that version where PT relates to "the consumers' outlays for consumption purposes during a certain period. The saved part of the money income has therefore been left out" (ibid., p.11). (Incidentally, PT has the same meaning as the PQ which Lindahl later used in his formulation for determining the price level; cp. sect. 1:3). Hence, the idea of relating the consumers' outlay on consumption goods has probably emanated from Hawtrey. However, Lindahl was at the same time critical of Hawtrey's inclusion of investment in capital goods in the consumers' outlay, because of the problem to find a price which represents capital formation (cp. ibid., pp.10-11; Hawtrey 1928, p.46).

However, from our point of view, it is more interesting that Lindahl states the following dynamic problem:

> "during real dynamic conditions, when the transactions of commodities undergo obvious changes, the price level broadly speaking varies in proportion to the relation between

the money supply and the transaction of commodities [M/T], whereas the velocity of money should broadly speaking be unchanged" (Lindahl 1929, p.3).

Such a proposition is based on the idea that there is a causal relation running from changes in money supply to changes in the price level, and as a corollary the quantity theory appears "as the natural starting-point for making intelligible the factors which determine the general price level" (ibid., p.13).

It is of no particular interest to describe Lindahl's analysis of this problem, except to say that his negative conclusion led him to put forward his own method. However, this method is only stated in vague terms and must be considered more as a statement of his intentions and a discarding of the quantity theory approach;

"When elucidating the present causal connection [between M and P] one has to go down to the deeper lying factors, which could be studied most appropriately by starting from the conducted monetary policy. The general theory for the changes in the price level must therefore be founded on other lines than those which the quantity theoreticians have followed. For this theory the simultaneous changes in the money supply and the velocity of money appear as being of a more subordinate importance, even if by themselves they could offer a lot of interest" (ibid., p.18).

But on the other hand, it does show that already in this article Lindahl is groping for a theory to explain 'changes in the price level' during 'real dynamic conditions', which for a long time became the main object within the Stockholm School.

1.2 - A critique of comparative statics and the explicit formulation of a dynamic scheme.

Lindahl's aim was to analyse the effects on the price formation "due to the existence of a _time factor_ in production" (Lindahl 1939D, p.271), and he showed how capital goods can be included in the determination of a static equilibrium (cp. ibid., pp.301-309). But at the same time he was critical of this solution, since the static method postulates an equilibrium situation with determinate relative prices as already existing, which implies the following for the relative prices:

> "that the values in question are a necessary condition for the continuation of the stationary state, but not that they are a necessary consequence of certain given functions concerning supply, demand, etc. For if other prices were conceived to be introduced into the system, a dynamic process would set in, concerning which nothing definite can be said without more precise assumptions as to anticipations and planning, etc. A stationary state may possibly arise in the course of time, but it may differ more or less from the original state on account of what has happened in the mean-time" (Lindahl 1939D, pp.310-311).

Thus the point is that the dynamic process _itself_ will influence the new stationary state (cp. Note 10 Ch. III). Lindahl's object is now to find a method to analyse this type of dynamic process. But he had first to show that comparative statics was not a suitable method for handling this problem.

Comparative statics 'solves' the problem by actually circumventing it in the following way:

> "a _comparison_ between independent stationary communities which are conceived to exist in isolation and which, in respect of the factors determining prices, show both resemblances to and differences from each other" (ibid., p.311).[1]

However, the comparative static method can only be fruitful if the differences between the two stationary states are "confined to one or a few of the factors determining prices, while the others are regarded as unchanged"(ibid.), but then it is implicitly assumed that the unchanged immediate price determinants "are quite as well adjusted to one stationary state as to another" (ibid., p.312). Lindahl considered such an assumption to be unrealistic, since it is very likely that the other factors determining prices have to change if a new stationary state is to be reached. This means that even if a comparative static analysis is possible, in the sense that a new equilibrium situation is determined, the 'factors determining prices' that differ between the two situations are so numerous that a comparison is not very interesting.[2]

It is this flaw in the comparative static method plus the necessity to look into the dynamic process itself, which explain why Lindahl developed intertemporal equilibrium as a formal attack on the dynamic problem. Hence, <u>intertemporal equilibrium emerged from the shortcomings of comparative statics in handling some of the problems related to the inclusion of the time factor in production</u> and it was not directly aimed at solving any particular macrotheoretical problem (cp. ibid., p.271).

---

1 Lindahl did not use the term 'comparative statics' but the method described above is the same as the 'comparative statics' of Robbins (cp. Robbins 1935, p.101). Later on Lindahl considered that one of the uses of static theory was comparative statics (cp. Note 7 Ch. II).

2 The problem of the measurement of the quantity of capital poses a quite particular problem for the comparative static method, because the quantity of capital could be the same in two stationary states, thus invalidating the above criticism. However, the <u>economic</u> meaning of this 'quantity' is still unclear since the method of measurement is based on "a purely conventional idea" (Lindahl 1939D, p.317).

1.3 - Wicksell's theory of changes in the general price level and the notion of temporary equilibrium.

Lindahl starts from the following Wicksellian idea:

> "changes not only of relative prices but of the price level as a whole, can be explained in terms of the relationship between the demand for and the supply of goods" (Lindahl 1930, p.245; cp. p.235; Wicksell 1935, pp.159-160).

Thus the starting-point is not 'the mechanism of payment' but 'the general theory of price formation'. But the latter was mainly developed to determine relative prices for a static equilibrium, i.e. a reiterated process, while Lindahl was interested in explaining a dynamic process of changes in the price level, i.e. where the immediate price determinants are changing. Therefore he had to find a method which could fulfill the following requirements:

> "it must include the treatment not only of relative prices in each period, but also of the price relations between the different periods included in the dynamic process. If an average for these 'intertemporal' price relations is worked out, an expression is found for the relative position of the price level in different periods. In this manner it should be possible to arrive at a theory of change in the value of money" (ibid., pp.141-142).[3]

We will show below that Lindahl developed the notion of temporary equilibrium to solve this problem (cp. sect. 2:3b).

Having decided not to base his ideas on the quantity theory, Lindahl constructs his own version of the exchange equation:

----

3 From Lindahl's discussion which follows on pages 147-150 it is obvious that he refers to the undiscounted prices.

"in each period the portion of the total nominal income that is not saved is equal to the total quantities of goods and services consumed during the period, multiplied by their prices" (ibid., p.142).[4]

This equation is written as: $E(1-s)=PQ$.[5] Hence, following Wicksell's idea from above, it is the relation between nominal demand $[E(1-s)]$ and the supply of consumption goods (PQ) which determine the price level for consumption goods (cp. ibid., p.146; p.235). (Incidentally, this formulation is almost identical to Keynes' fundamental equations (cp. Keynes 1930A, p.122).) However, Wicksell included goods, services, raw materials, etc. in the general price level. The fact that Lindahl only looked at the relation between demand and supply of consumption goods is therefore a development of Wicksell's formulation. In this context, Ohlin has suggested a possible influence from D.H.Robertson and Hawtrey on the Stockholm School:

"Erik Lindahl was, as far as I know - just as later Myrdal (1933) and myself (1934) - not conscious of being specifically

---

4 A similar formulation was already mentioned in "The Place of Capital" as $s_t = i_t K_{t-1} - \sum P_t^r X_t^r$ (cp. Lindahl 1939D, p.329), although the supplied quantities are here a function of the prices from all periods (cp. sect. 2:3a:1). According to Steiger the same idea is already to be found in Lindahl's lecture notes of 1925 (cp. Steiger 1971, p.175).
5 P: a price index for goods and services consumed (inclusive of the producer's own consumption), the different price having been weighed by the total consumption of each category of goods.
 Q: the total quantity of consumption goods and services supplied and consumed, weighted by their prices. So PQ must be equal to the money value of total consumption for the period in question, i.e. $P_t Q_t = \sum P_t^r Q_t^r$.
 E: total nominal income.
 s: the proportion of income which is saved.

influenced by R.G.Hawtrey, but in some
degree by D.H.Robertson. Later on I have
often wondered whether Hawtrey's simple
approach, presented already in the 1920's,
of opposing total outlay and total income
and of studying seperately the factors
behind 'consumers' outlay' and 'traders'
outlay' may not have unconsciously
influenced Lindahl and all of us in our
attempts to show the simple meaning of
Wicksell's   saving-investment
analysis"(Ohlin 1960, pp.2-3, as quoted in
Steiger 1976, p.358 n.24).

We have shown above that Ohlin's suggestion of an
influence from Hawtrey is in fact correct, since
there is a direct relation between the latter's idea
of opposing consumers' outlay and consumers' income
and Lindahl's formulation in "Om förhållandet mellan
penningmängd och prisnivån" (cp. sect. 1:1). Though
we can see no direct influence from Robertson even if
he is mentioned by Lindahl in The Rate of Interest
(cp. Lindahl 1939C, p.236 n.2. The reference to
Robertson on p.199 n.1 does not exist in the Swedish
version, cp. Lindahl 1930, p.69). We would therefore
describe the influence on Lindahl in the following
way: the idea of analysing changes in the general
price level via the relation between total demand and
total supply has almost certainly come from Wicksell;
although there is evidence that the separation of the
total demand, the total supply of consumers' outlay
and the production of consumption goods to determine
the changes in the price level for consumption goods
has been taken from Hawtrey. The latter approach was
then further developed by Keynes in the Treatise
where the determination of the price level of
consumption goods and the price level of new
investment goods are independent of each other (cp.
Keynes 1930A, p.122; p.129; Keynes 1939, pp.225-226).
It will be shown below that Keynes' formulations
influenced the subsequent works of the Stockholm
School.
        In Lindahl's The Rate of Interest we have
finally a formulation of what became one of the main
objects of analysis for the Stockholm School, namely,
an explicit dynamic analysis of price changes, which

necessitates an amalgamation of dynamic method and macroeconomic analysis. It is important to notice that although their macroeconomic theory drew heavily on Wicksell, their dynamic method was at least at the beginning not influenced by Wicksell's explicit sequence analysis from Interest and Prices. On the contrary, they used their own brand of methods to elucidate the cumulative process as portrayed in Wicksell's Lectures.

2 - The dynamic method.

This section contains an analysis of intertemporal and temporal equilibrium. The two methods have an important common feature in that they both follow an equilibrium approach, and it is crucial that it is this common trait which was singled out for criticism by Lundberg and Myrdal. It is also interesting to notice that temporary equilibrium seems to have grown out of Lindahl's own dissatisfaction with intertemporal equilibrium as a tool for dynamic analysis.

2.1 - The equilibrium approach.

The equilibrium approach has the following characteristic:

> "an explanation of a price situation as a state of equilibrium, in the sense that there exists a mutual connection between supply and demand on the one hand and actual prices on the other, and that, therefore, at existing prices exchange can continue until full satisfaction has been attained" (Lindahl 1939D, p.339 n*; cp. Lindal 1939C, p.159).

Hence, for each individual and commodity the anticipated price achieves a balance of demand and supply and all expectations are therefore fulfilled, though it has to be added that the assumption of perfect foresight for the period ahead is "a necessary condition for an explanation of a price situation as a state of equilibrium"(ibid.).

Suppose for example that the anticipated quantities were not fulfilled while the prices were (e.g. the prices could have been fixed in advance, as in Lindahl's "A Note on the Dynamic Pricing Problem" of 1934) so that realized quantities do not tally, it might then be said that there is "no mutual dependence between prices and the factors affecting prices at a given moment, but instead a <u>one-sided</u> causal connection in one direction or the other"(ibid.). The result is a change in plans and there will exist a connection between the prices prevailing in consecutive periods (cp. ibid., p.274). In fact, this is the first time that Lindahl mentioned a method which has a disequilibrium and a sequential character, but at this point of time in his development he considered that such a situation is only relevant for markets where the transactions are "unusually sensitive to price change, especially on the stock and produce exchanges" (ibid., p.340 n*).

Lindahl did not mention any tatonnement process or the like, but at the same time he held that "the determination of prices involves time" (ibid., p.273). However, the problem of 'false trading' is avoided by the assumption of perfect foresight, which guarantees that the plans are based with certainty on definite prices, which will also be the actual prices

when the plans are realized.[6] This is in fact the
exact meaning of a mutual connection between demand
and supply on the one hand and prices on the other.

2.2 - The period as an analytical device for attacking dynamic conditions.

According to Lindahl, the principal difference
between dynamic and stationary conditions is that in
the former case the factors determining the prices,
i.e. the immediate price determinants, are
constantly changing (cp. ibid., p.318; p.330).
Instead of having a reiteration of the same state as
in the stationary case, we have a system which is
moving, which implies that the price determinants as
well as the prices are changing. Hence, the actors
must in each period anticipate not only what is
happening in the immediately following period, but
also what is supposed to take place in later
forthcoming periods. It is no coincidence that
Lindahl's definition of the dynamic problem sounds
very similar to Myrdal's discussion of the same

---

6 Hicks analyses the problem with trading at 'false
prices' but that does not lead to any serious
misgivings in his analysis, since the markets are
only supposed to be open on 'Mondays', which is the
same as the transition points in the Stockholm
School, and it is implied that all markets proceed
"quickly and smoothly to a position of temporary
equilibrium" (Hicks 1946, p.123). This is the
rationale for using the equilibrium approach:

> "We are supposing that trading continues, on
> the Monday, until supplies and demands are
> brought into equilibrium; this is essential
> in order for us to use the equilibriun
> method in dynamic theory. Since we shall
> not pay much attention to the process of
> equilibration which must precede the
> formation of the equilibrium prices, our
> method seems to imply that we conceive of
> the economic system as being always in
> equilibrium" (ibid., p.131).

problem, since the former was very familiar with the content of Myrdal's dissertation (cp. sect. III:1), though we shall see below that Lindahl's two separate attempts to solve this problem, i.e. the notions of intertemporal and temporal equilibrium, are certainly very different from Myrdal's notion of equilibrium.

The dynamic conditions imply in reality continuous changes in data but for analytical reasons Lindahl assumed the following:

> "we imagine it [the dynamic process] to be subdivided into periods of time so short that the factors directly affecting prices, and therefore also the prices themselves, can be regarded as unchanged in each period. All such changes are therefore assumed to take place at the transition points between periods. The development of prices can then be expressed as a series of successive price situations" (Lindahl 1939C, p.158; cp. Lindahl 1939D, pp.318-319).

The only obvious change between the two works is that Lindahl in The Rate of Interest puts more stress on the fact that the period has to be short, for the factors determining the prices cannot otherwise be assumed to stay constant.

It is important to notice that the idea of dividing the dynamic process into periods was introduced into the Stockholm School as an heuristic device, and Lindahl gave no reason why it might be realistic as well as merely helpful to use this device. This latter argument was first taken up by Hammarskjöld (cp. sect. VII:2) and was then developed by Lindahl, when he put forward the concept of plan as the fundamental notion in the analysis of economic behaviour. In fact the 'period' used by Lindahl is actually the length of a production period or, what amounts more or less to the same thing, Marshall's short period, since there is a mutual connection between demand and supply and the actual prices (i.e. we are certainly not dealing with Marshall's market period; cp. Lindahl 1939B, pp.66-68). Furthermore, the 'period' used in intertemporal equilibrium emanates from the period of production as used in Austrian capital theory to depict a roundabout process of production (cp. Lindahl 1939D, pp.296-297).[7]

2.3 - Two versions of the equilibrium approach.

2.3(a) - The notion of intertemporal equilibrium.

2.3(a).1 - Intertemporal equilibrium.

Lindahl's aim is to analyse dynamic conditions as defined above. Hence, the primary factors are "assumed to undergo change from one period to another. In this way a movement arises in the system" (Lindahl 1939D, p.330). However, his mathematical formulation shows that there is no 'movement' in any meaningful sense (cp. ibid., pp.321-330), since it is a <u>simultaneous</u> determination of all prices, quantities and interest rates for all periods under the assumption of equilibrium within

---

7 Ohlin seems therefore to be slightly mistaken in the following remark:

"[Lindahl in 1930 follows] the Wicksellian line of approach by means of period of time, perhaps somewhat under the influence of Mr. D.H.Robertson in this ... respect" (Ohlin 1937A, p.55).

However, the period approach was already taken up in 1929 from Austrian capital theory in general and not from Wicksell in particular.

each period, i.e. an intertemporal equilibrium.[8]
Consequently Lindahl stated that "all prices in all
periods included in the dynamic process thus become
linked together [simultaneous determination] in a
uniform system" (ibid., p.330). However, Lindahl
never mentioned the existence of futures markets, so
there is no possibility of reinsuring the fulfilment
of future actions. Still, he assumed that all
individuals make binding plans for each future period
before the dynamic process starts (cp. ibid., p.324).
Lindahl had therefore to assume that the individuals
behave as if they knew that their anticipations were
correct, which, incidentally, is assumed in
connection with the first case of imperfect foresight
(cp. sect. 2:3a:3).

But despite the assumption of perfect foresight
and the necessity of simultaneous determination,
Lindahl would have considered his formulation as
exhibiting what we must call a fictional movement:

> "Although individuals must ... be supposed
> to be aware both of future prices and of the
> forms of functions that determine the
> dependence of supply, demand and the
> technical coefficients on these prices,
> economic developments must nevertheless be
> regarded not as determined beforehand, but
> as the result of the actions of individuals"
> (Lindahl 1939D, p.285).

This passage shows in a conspicuous way the
contradiction between Lindahl's attempt to analyse
dynamic processes, which must have a sequential

---

8 Lindahl does not acknowledge the influence of
Hayek's "Das Intertemporale Gleichgewichtssystem" of
1928 in "The Place of Capital", but in The Rate of
Interest of 1930 Hayek's article is mentioned (cp.
Lindahl 1939C, p.142 n*). In fact, the word
'intertemporal' is first used by Lindahl in the
latter work where he refers explicitly to Hayek. But
it still seems likely that Lindahl worked out the
concept of intertemporal equilibrium without having
previously seen Hayek's article (cp. Milgate 1979,
p.6).

character, and the shackles which the notion of intertemporal equilibrium placed upon such an analysis. For, on the one hand the economic development is formally 'determined beforehand', but on the other hand we 'must nevertheless' assume that there is a real process over time.

In the intertemporal formulation the immediate price determinants are given in advance for each period. The problem is then to find "what ... prices and rates of interest, and which goods will be produced and consumed in all these periods" (ibid., p.322). With this formulation of the problem, Lindahl probably thought that he had shown that the prices were "a necessary consequence of certain given functions concerning supply, demand etc.", which the static theory could not show (cp. sect. 1:2). But intertemporal equilibrium can only give the equilibrium prices within each period and these periods must be related in a particular way to the prices in the other periods. Hence, if we start with a price vector for the first period which is different from the one which represents intertemporal equilibrium, then a dynamic process will ensue which is different from the one determined by the intertemporal formulation. Thus, this formulation was unable to overcome the problem of the static formulation, namely, that it postulated an equilibrium situation as already existing (cp. ibid.). We could state our critique against Lindahl just by a slight rephrasing of his criticism of static theory; the prices in question are a necessary condition for the continuation of the intertemporal equilibrium, but they are not necessary consequences of certain given functions concerning supply, demand, etc. However, Lindahl tried to overcome this flaw by his assertion of a 'fictional' movement. Hence, once again we can see that Lindahl set out to do a certain thing, but his formal device hindered his accomplishment of it.

In fact, Lindahl spoke of applying intertemporal equilibrium in a way which we would denote as comparative dynamics:

"to investigate ... the manner in which a given process is altered by the introduction of primary changes of different kinds. Here

the *ceteris paribus* premiss must be used
with special care, for a foreseen change in
one factor affecting prices must be
connected with more or less widespread
changes in other factors" (Lindahl 1939D,
p.337; cp. p.340).

We have seen that comparative statics had to be
introduced as a means of circumventing the dynamic
process, which might be permissible if 'changes in
other factors' were not too widespread (cp. sect.
1:2). Hence, we could argue that in an analogous way,
Lindahl himself seems to have realized the limitation
of his intertemporal approach, since he began to
speak about comparative dynamics as a device for the
analysis of dynamic processes.

2.3(a).2 - A critique of Lindahl's notion of
intertemporal equilibrium.[9]
    On the one hand Lindahl stated the following:

"[If the numeraire is equal to one in each
period] the problem is determined except for
a multiplicative factor for each period. On
the basis of the given data, we can
therefore not determine the absolute height
of the price level including the rate of
interest during the initial period, nor the
movements of the price level during the
following periods ... . From this we can
draw the important conclusion that the
assumption of perfect foresight does not
necessarily contain any conditions with
regard to the movements of the general price
level. The price level may vary in an
arbitrary way, that is, all prices may be
proportionally increased or diminished from
one period to another, without any
consequences for the real import of economic
transactions" (Lindahl 1939D, pp.327-328).

On the other hand, Lindahl realized that the general

----
9 See also the appendix to this chapter.

Chapter 4

price level could change "during the dynamic process on account of a change in the value of the monetary unit" (ibid., p.336), which gives rise to the following problem:

"in the analysis of the development of interest rates and of the factors intimately connected therewith - for example income and saving measured in monetary units - is it necessary to take these circumstances into account. For our reasoning regarding the rate of interest to be applicable, it is evidently necessary that the general price level should remain fairly stable" (ibid.).

Thus the development of the general price level is arbitrary but at the same time it has to stay fairly constant.

This contradictory analysis of the development of the general price level arises from the fact that Lindahl failed to draw the proper distinction between discounted and undiscounted prices. His intertemporal formulation gives a solution which represents the discounted relative prices, and these prices are relative to the numeraire for period one. Thus there is a strict relation between the relative prices of different periods, and this is expressed by the various own rates of interest, i.e. there is one development of the relative prices. The rate used by Lindahl in his equations is in fact the own rate of interest for the numeraire during the period in question.

In an intertemporal system there is no problem in dealing with fluctuations from period to period in the value of the numeraire-commodity, i.e. the problem with capital gains, since it is possible to separate these value changes from the own rates of interest (cp. eq. (3) in the appendix to this chapter). There is naturally a problem of 'realism' if the relative value of the numeraire fluctuates, while it is still supposed to fulfil the 'functions of money'. At the same time, Lindahl's remarks that the general undiscounted price level within a period is arbitrary if correctly anticipated, are not correct. This is because the relative prices within the undiscounted system for a particular period have

to be the same as the _relative_ prices expressed in
the discounted prices for the same period, and his
equations represent a numeraire system which implies
that the absolute height of the price level is given
once a numeraire is chosen (cp. Wicksell 1919,
p.224). Lindahl's remarks show that he gave the
numeraire commodity the same qualities as if it were
fiat money. This mistake is repeated later in The
Rate of Interest (cp. Lindahl 1939C, pp.147-150).
Hence, unlike Hayek he had not realized that
intertemporal equilibrium can only pursue an analysis
in real terms (cp. sect. II:3).

Lindahl's basic mistake is therefore not to have
included the necessary normalization of his system
which must follow from his Fisherine approach to the
rate of interest, where "individuals can exchange
present for future income among themselves" (Lindahl
1939D, p.288; cp. p.272). One might however say that
he would have been on the verge of solving the
problem, if he had explicitly said that the reason
that he only dealt with the own rate of interest of
the money commodity implied that the other own rates
had to fall in line, since an arbitrage could always
be done via money [10], a fact that he was probably
aware of. If he had solved this problem, he might
have seen much more easily that his system is
actually a numeraire economy and not a monetary
economy.

2.3(a).3 - Intertemporal equilibrium applied to
successive approximations of dynamic conditions.

In "The Place of Capital" Lindahl attacked the
dynamic problem via three different approximations.
He started with a static case and then introduces
"successively more complicated assumptions" (Lindal
1939A, p.10; cp. Lindahl 1939D, p.284). However, the
analysis is still within a static framework, which
should be compared with his later approach in which
he turnd the problem around so that the dynamic
framework is the starting-point (cp. sect. IX:2).
It is useful to analyse these approximations, since
it gives a clue as to why Lindahl gave up the notion

----
10 This means that $P_{q,t+1}/P_{Q,t+1} = (1+i_t)(P_{q,t}/P_{Q,t})$.

of intertemporal equilibrium.

The starting-point is thus the case with perfect foresight as described in section 2:3a:1. Lindahl then introduced the following assumption:

> "that people have the same ideas regarding the future and everyone is certain that these ideas will be realized. We also assume that these views regarding the future have such a character that they would be completely fulfilled if it were not - and there lies the difference from the previous case - that ["completely", in the Swedish edition (cp. Lindahl 1929B, p.73)] unforeseen events ocurred from time to time" (Lindahl 1939D, p.338).

Furthermore, it is assumed that these unforeseen events "take place at the point of transition from one period of time to another" (ibid., p.339). This implies that at a point of transition, a system of equations has to be solved exactly in the same manner as in the case of perfect foresight. The prices and quantities given by the solution will actually be fulfilled at least for the first period. But for later periods unforeseen changes will lead to a revision of the plans at the point of transition, and a new system of equations will then determine what is going to happen in the following periods. Hence, only the anticipations of the first period in a dynamic sequence are certainly correct, because of completely unforeseen changes at the transition points.

Despite the fact that the individuals alter their plans at transition points, they are still supposed to behave as if their anticipations were certain, i.e. their behaviour include no consideration of risk. Therefore the behaviour is the same as in the case of perfect foresight. Consequently, in the English edition Lindahl denoted this first case of imperfect foresight as 'Imperfect foresight: Perfect foresight for short periods only' (cp. ibid., p.339; Lindahl 1929B, p.73), while it has no such subtitle in the Swedish version.[11]

Finally we have the case of __imperfect foresight__ where the agents no longer consider their anticipations as certain. Instead it is assumed "that people's ideas regarding the future have the character of probability judgements" (Lindahl 1939D, p.348). Hence, risk and the valuation of risk are part and parcel of the problem, and Lindahl basically reiterated the ideas on risk given by Myrdal in his dissertation. This is the first example of a case with truly __imperfect__ foresight, since in the previous case the behaviour was in fact identical to the behaviour under perfect foresight. This is also in line with Lindahl's view of combining perfect foresight with the nonexistence of risk (cp. ibid., p.287).

However, it is not so clear whether Lindahl considered the equilibrium method as being valid for this case, since he stated that his comments on this case were outside the scope of the paper. But at the same time he gave the following proposition:

"How a certain price situation is determined under these more complicated assumptions could be clarified by a system of simultaneous equations only in the special 'hybrid' case discussed by Myrdal, where dynamic elements [i.e. anticipated consequences of future changes discounted

----

11 Lindahl wrote later that he had used the notion of temporary equilibrium to analyse this case (cp. Lindahl 1939A, p.10). But this seems to be a misuse of this notion, since his analysis of this case involves a full intertemporal solution and the analysis is not only related to the plans for the immediate period. Nevertheless, it is true that this intertemporal equilibrium has a __temporary__ character, in the sense that it is very often disturbed, i.e. each situation of intertemporal equilibrium exists only for a short period in real time. Even later Lindahl denoted a similar case as 'jumping equilibria' while intertemporal equilibrium was called 'moving equilibrium' (cp. Lindahl 1954, p.28 n.11).

to the present moment (cp. sect. III:1)]
are included in a static system ... . But
the introduction of the risk factor would
mean that we could not as before work with
functions referring to total quantities. We
should be obliged to descend to individual
functions, since the special mark of the
fully dynamic problem is the difference
between different individuals" (ibid.,
p.349).[12]

Therefore it seems likely that Lindahl thought that
the case of imperfect foresight could also be solved
by his system of equations for intertemporal
equilibrium, but the system had now to be made up of
separate functions for each individual. However,
this would still only be true for Myrdal's case with
objective risk, since the anticipations would not
otherwise be correct and a solution would thus not
exist (cp. sect. III:4). It would seem that Lindahl
later became aware of the fact that his formulations
were only valid for objective risk, and that that was
one of his reasons for giving up the intertemporal
approach. Hence, temporary equilibrium grew out of
the shortcomings of intertemporal equilibrium as a
method for attacking dynamic problems.

2.3(b) - The notion of temporary equilibrium.
    Lindahl started from the following assumption:

    "that in each of these short periods of time
    individuals have full knowledge of the
    prices ruling during the period, and that
    they allow their actions concerning supply
    and demand to be determined by these prices,
    which are therefore consistent with their
    actions. The price situations will then be
    equilibrium states in the sense that there

----

12 Lindahl has added "only in the special case ...
system" to the English edition, while this passage is
unbroken in the Swedish version. The passage has
also been broken up into two different paragraphs in
the English edition (cp. Lindahl 1929B, p.81).

will be equality between supply and demand during the period. The formation of prices can in this way be expressed in a system of equations for each period" (Lindahl 1939C, p.159).

He later described this idea as analysing "the dynamic process as a series of temporary equilibrium situations, by which I tried to get a connection with the ordinary static theory" (Letter to Frisch, 23 October 1934) [13], which shows that he coined the label 'temporary equilibrium' before the publication of Hicks' Value and Capital. With hindsight he thought of temporary equilibrium as a 'logical' idea:

> "Since one can imagine, that at a certain point of time all individuals make all sorts of mutual contracts concerning what is going to happen during a coming short period, and at the transition point to the next period they will then make new contracts of the Walrasian type due to the fact that they have changed their plans during the period" (ibid.; cp. Lindahl 1939C, p.159; cp. Lindahl 1939B, p.66).

However, the idea of contracts was first introduced into the Stockholm School by Hammarskjöld (cp. sect. VII:3:1).

----

13 Hicks has also noticed this relation between static theory and the use of the notion of temporary equilibrium for analysing dynamic processes:

> "By using the week [i.e. Lindahl's initial period], we become able to treat a process of change as consisting of series of temporary equilibria; this enables us still to use equilibrium analysis in the dynamic field ... . Thus, without abandoning our model to stationariness, we have preserved the essentials of the static machinery" (Hicks 1946, p.127; cp. Lindahl 1939B, p.68).

It seems at first sight that Lindahl discussed exactly the same formal method as devised for 'Imperfect foresight: Perfect foresight for short periods only'. However, the manner in which Lindahl constructed the equation $E(1-s)=PQ$ shows that the equilibrium quantities of P and Q are only determined for one period. This is because the inclusion of imperfect foresight implies that "ideas regarding the future have the character of probability judgements based on different alternatives, and these judgements vary individually" (Lindahl 1939C, p.151). Therefore Lindahl considered it possible to apply the notion of intertemporal equilibrium only for the case of perfect foresight. Hence, by 1930 Lindahl had changed his mind concerning the possibility of using intertemporal equilibrium for imperfect foresight, which we proposed that he still considered possible in 1929. He probably altered his view on the implication of imperfect foresight, since he did not even mention the notion of objective risk in The Rate of Interest, which in Myrdal's framework was a crucial assumption for the consistency of the plans. It is also noticeable that in "The Place of Capital" Lindahl assumed perfect mobility (cp. Lindahl 1939D, p.274), while in The Rate of Interest frictions are taken into consideration, which makes the validity of objective risk even more tenuous.

However, it was perhaps not 'illogical', for the reasons cited above, to assume the existence of consistent plans for the first period: hence the notion of temporary equilibrium. So it would appear that Lindahl developed this notion because of the restrictive assumption necessary for using intertemporal equilibrium as an instrument for analysing dynamic processes. Therefore an obvious link exists between the two notions.

The application of the notion of temporary equilibrium implies a restriction in the range of the demand and supply function, since they are only directly related to the expected prices of the current period, i.e. the initial period under analysis. In intertemporal equilibrium on the other hand, these functions are explicitly dependent on expected prices both from current and future periods, since anticipations relating to the later periods "[affect] people's actions and thus constitutes a determining factor in the price situation of the initial period" (ibid., p.339). If we compare Lindahl's construction of temporary equilibrium with Hicks' formulation, then the only obvious difference seems to be that Hicks assumes that "the plans which are adopted in any given week depend not only upon current prices but also upon planner's expectations of future prices" (Hicks 1946, p.124). However, Lindahl must include anticipations for several periods, since the equation to determine the general price level is an aggregate of the individuals' equations where E is a subjective and forward-looking concept (cp. below Note 18). For the case of imperfect foresight this concept of income implies that the anticipations of events belonging to future periods will differ. But this will not affect the compatibility of the plans for the first period. However, in later periods, certain individuals must necessarily be dissatisfied with their plans for the first period since they have now <u>realized</u> that their income expectations for later periods, which influenced the subjective income for the first period, were wrong.

In "The Dynamic Approach" of 1939 Lindahl gave a somewhat similar explanation why the equilibrium concept used in <u>The Rate of Interest</u> has a temporary character:

> "The dynamic element is not overtly present in the equilibrium equation in each period, unless the equation is made so complicated that it also includes anaticipations referring to future periods [which we hold that $E(1-s)=PQ$ does at least implicitly]. The dynamic element itself lies in the incompatibility of these anticipations, and this becomes manifest at the beginning of each period when the parties undertake the commitments valid for the period [must be at least one period later than the initial one for which temporary equilibrium rules]. In other words, during each period there is present a latent disequilibrium [the anticipations for later periods are not compatible], and that is the reason why the equilibrium achieved during the period is

found to be only temporary" (Lindahl 1939B, p.69).

Thus Lindahl had once again shown the close connection between imperfect foresight and the 'temporariness' of temporary equilibrium.

2.4 - Lundberg's and Myrdal's critique of the equilibrium approach.

In this section we will mainly discuss Lundberg's critique [14], since some of Myrdal's critical points are to a great extent similar to Lundberg's, and the rest of Myrdal's arguments will be dealt with in Chapter VI.

Lundberg's criticism relates explicitly only to intertemporal equilibrium in "The Place of Capital". He attacked mainly the following idea related to 'Imperfect foresight: Perfect foresight for short periods only':

"the accommodations [to the disturbances] are outside the system, they are not explained, but are looked upon as data for the next equilibrium period. The successive sequence of equilibrium points is not explained" (Lundberg 1930, p.157; cp. Myrdal 1939, p.122).

What is lacking, in Lundberg's opinion, is therefore a method which could describe this accommodation process. Therefore Lundberg was critical of the intertemporal methods as a method which is supposed to be a development of the static method, since in the case of perfect foresight there is no "question of a successive determination of prices for the different equilibrium periods, instead all prices are

----

14 There is no reason to believe that Lindahl did not know about Lundberg's article, since Lindahl was supposed to have seen the article during its manuscript stage (cp. Lundberg 1930, p.135). Furthermore Lindahl "liked it so much ... that for several years it was on his bedside table" (Letter from Lundberg to the author, 14 February 1979).

determined simultaneously" (ibid., p.157). That is
to say, there is no 'link' between the periods, which
amounts to the accomodation process. This method is
therefore characterized "as a typical statical system
where the existence of different prices under
different periods only expresses an intertemporal
equilibrium" (ibid., cp. pp.142-143). In fact,
Lindahl himself later described his method as
introducing "dynamical problems within the static
framework" (Lindahl 1939A, p.10), since with this
method "the entire static apparatus may be employed
in the analysis of a dynamic sequence" (Lindahl
1939B, p.68; cp. his letter to Frisch quoted above in
sect. 2:3b). Even later Lindahl equates stationary
and 'correctly anticipated' processes, since both use
a system of simultaneous equations which omits
temporal causation (cp. Lindahl 1954, p.27).

It is very likely that Lundberg's and Myrdal's
critique of the equilibrium approach played an
important role in Lindahl's development, since he had
given up this approach in his "A Note on the Dynamic
Pricing Problem" of 1934.[15] Particularly important
was the fact that they showed that there was no real
causation between the periods, and that Myrdal in the

----

15 B.Caplan only mentioned Myrdal's influence on
Lindahl's transition (cp. Caplan 1941, p.561), but
that is probably due to the fact that Caplan, like
most other commentators, had not seen Lundberg's
article.
Myrdal's critique is, according to Landgren, proof
that a School has never existed (cp. Landgren 1960,
p.229). But it seems to show the contrary, since
Lindahl took the critique ad notam which proves that
there was mutual influence amongst the members, and
also Landgren considered this to be a characteristic
of a School (cp. ibid., p.225). Furthermore,
Lindahl's work from 1934 links together the older
members of the Stockholm School, the so-called 'neo-
Wicksellians', with the younger members, Hammarskjöld
et. al., who were doing sequence analysis right from
the beginning (cp. sect. I:2). However, Landgren
was correct in saying that Myrdal was critical of the
period analysis, but we will show that Myrdal himself
had to use this method (cp. sect. VI:2:1).

meantime developed a disequilibrium approach in _Monetary Equilibrium_.

3 - The savings-investment mechanism during a cumulative process.

3.1 - Introductory remarks.

In this section we will analyse the equilibrating mechanism for savings and investment used by Lindahl and at the same time compare it with Keynes' principle of effective demand. We will see that the assumptions underlying temporary equilibrium must be violated in order to encompass the equilibrating mechanism.

In his book _Penningpolitikens mål_ (The Goal of Monetary policy, 1924; revised edition in 1929) Lindahl set up norms for regulating the price level. These norms were related to the overriding aim of monetary policy, namely, "to lessen the risks, which not completely anticipated events imply for the economic activity, and thereby lead to a minimum of disturbances inside the economic life" (Lindahl 1930, p.7, italics omitted). _The Rate of Interest_ is related to the earlier book in the sense that he now "investigates those problems which are connected with the realization of the two norms for the value of money, discussed in the earlier work, namely, an unchanged level of price and the regulation of the price level in inverse proportion to productivity"(ibid., p.5;cp. p.9), i.e. the means of fulfilling the norm; and consequently the Swedish title of _The Rate of Interest_ is _The Means of Monetary Policy_.

It is important to notice that the entire exercise is related to policy norms which include only the price level and there is no mention of the level of employment as being part of the norm. However at the same time Lindahl considers that this programme "smooth[s] out the business cycles" (ibid., p.8), where these cycles of course involve unemployment and cuts in the level of activity. Hence, this could be taken as a first proof that Lindahl does not aim at determining the equilibrium level of output and employment, which is the explicit aim of the principle of effective demand. Instead he is interested in finding the determinants behind the changes in the price level, and thereby he might be able to find a policy norm which could dampen the business cycles.

3.2 - Assumptions.

The analysis is based on the following assumptions concerning the monetary system: a closed economy, a free currency, all granting of bank credit is centralized with the central bank, and there are no cash holdings (cp. Lindahl 1939C, pp.139-140). Lindahl has thus adopted the Wicksellian idea that the theory has to be tested under "the simplified assumptions ... which imply inter alia that there are no cash holdings in the community" (ibid., p.141; cp. Wicksell 1898, p.76; Wicksell 1936, pp.70-71), since both Wicksell and Lindahl hold that a theory worked out for such conditions would be more general than the quantity theory.[16]

In the example described below we have a case of "a stationary equilibrium suddenly disturbed by a lowering of interest rates, which is expected to endure" (ibid., p.162). The production of capital goods and stocks can increase but there are no unemployed factors of production. It is also assumed

----

16 According to Steiger The Rate of Interest "marked a decisive break with Knut Wicksell's famous theory of changes in the general price level" (Steiger 1978, p.422) for the following reason:

"By using Wicksell's suggestion of a 'perfect credit system' Lindahl showed that the Wicksellian approach did not lead to a theory of the value of money which is generally valid, because it could not explain changes in the general price level in a society with no cash holdings" (ibid.).

But this is certainly wrong, since that is exactly the way in which Wicksell himself used this assumption. Hence, Lindahl did not break with Wicksell on this point.

"that all individuals believe that the existing prices of consumption goods will be maintained" (ibid.), i.e. if the prices change at a transition point they are supposed to stay the same for all forthcoming periods.

3.3 - The equilibrating mechanism.

3.3.1 - The savings paradox.

We shall first analyse the equilibrating mechanism by looking at the so-called 'savings paradox':

"How can a lowering of the loan rate of interest which is generally supposed to have a tendency to decrease (voluntary) saving, thus cause an increase in total saving?" (ibid., p.174)

The mechanism is the following; the fall in the rate of interest increases the relative price of capital goods in relation to consumption goods, which leads to an increase in investment, since total saving must equal the total value of real investment [17], there must be such a change in the price level and in the income distribution that new savings will be

---

17 New real capital could be formed since it is assumed that forced savings have taken place (cp. Lindahl 1939C, p.183). Wicksell would have endorsed Lindahl's findings, while Hayek would deny them completely, since in his world the results of forced saving will <u>always</u> have a temporary character (cp. Wicksell 1935, p.199; Hayek 1935, pp.55-58).

Chapter 4   75

forthcoming to match the new investment.[18] Hence, in this process it is <u>the change in income distribution</u> due to the change in the price level which will play the role of an <u>equilibrating mechanism</u>:

> "In every case given, the shift in the price level will be sufficiently large to cause such a change in the distribution of incomes that total saving in the community will correspond to the value of real investment, the extent of which is primarily determined by the rate of interest" (ibid., p.175).

Lindahl shows also the converse case where savings are running ahead of investment due to an increase in the money rate of interest. This will lead to a fall in demand for consumer goods and the ensuing fall in the price level will cause such a variation in the distribution of income that the increased savings due to the increased rate of interest are balanced by dissavings from loss-making entrepreneurs, i.e. 'abortive' savings.

---

18 The income for a certain period is defined as the rate of interest on the capital value of all capital goods including human capital (cp. Lindahl 1939C, p.144). The capital value is the expected yields where, in the case of imperfect foresight, due regard has been given to subjective probabilities and risk evaluation (cp. ibid., p.145). Therefore it is obvious that Lindahl's concept is subjective and forward looking. Nominal income can now change because of alterations in the capital values:

> "a change in the <u>ideas</u> of individuals concerning future productivity and prices ... can in itself influence capital values and, thereby, nominal income also" (ibid., p.154; cp. Myrdal 1927, p.44).

Saving for a period is then defined as the difference between income and the value of the consumed services for the period, and it is equal to the net increase or decrease in the value of capital (cp. ibid., p.144).

Before further discussion of the equilibrating mechanism, we have to look at the role of temporary equilibrium in this process. In the savings paradox the increase in nominal income for entrepreneurs due to the rise in the price level must be unexpected, since they only anticipate the change in the relative price level but not the change in the price level itself (cp. ibid., p.181). This interpretation is backed by Lindahl's additional note to the English edition, where he says that "[the] 'unintentional' part of saving and investment that brings about equality in a retrospective calculation should thus not be included" (ibid., p.250 n.*) in the savings determined before the period in question. This is also vindicated by the description "that during each period the supply of saving adjusts through the change of the income distribution" (Lindahl 1930, p.126). Henceforth, it is not a planned change before the period but an unintentional one during the period. But at the same time Lindahl must rule out the possibility that the entrepreneurs, who realize during the period that their incomes have increased, change their investment demand during the period, which would otherwise shatter the whole equilibrium approach. It is therefore impossible to analyse the savings paradox etc. with the help of temporary equilibrium, since, strictly speaking, the equilibrium approach can not handle unforeseen events during a period. This drawback with the notion of temporary equilibrium might have been one of the reasons for Lindahl's abandonment of it.

At the beginning of the period planned and realized investment is greater than the planned saving, which depends on the money rate of interest and the expected income for the period. This will lead to such an increase in the price level that the nominal income and the distribution of income will change until savings ex post, which depend on the same money rate of interest but on the new level of income [19], will equal the increase in the total value of real investment. Therefore the mechanism is akin to effective demand since changes in income are the active factor in bringing about the equality between savings and investment, though Lindahl assumes that savings depend on the money rate of interest while Keynes introduces the marginal propensity to save. But this similarity only exists during the disequilibrium process represented by the cumulative process. Once the new stationary state is reached, which is characterized by "a larger amount of capital, a lower rate of interest and a higher price level" (Lindahl 1939C, p.181), the rate of interest will play its orthodox role by balancing savings and investment ex ante. Hence, Lindahl's cumulative process describes in this case the traverse between two stationary states (cp. ibid., pp.180-183). Interestingly enough this implies that the money rate could on its own determine the stationary state and the 'real' rate has to follow suit, in the sense that the capital stock is enlarged to such an extent that the expected rate of profit becomes equal to the money rate. However, the cumulative process is in this case base on inelastic price-expectations while Lindahl considers elastic expectations to be "a more realistic assumption" (Lindahl 1930, p.47; cp. Lindahl 1939C, p.186). The case described above is therefore "theoretically quite feasible, but ... in the real world, it would present great difficulties"

----
19 Lindahl must here assume that the entrepreneurs start to save during the period when they realize that their income is increasing, although this is contrary to the use of temporary equilibrium, and the aggregated result at the end of the period is equal to the increase in real investment. Once the Swedes started to use ex ante and ex post, they would rather suppose that the whole unanticipated income is saved, and it is therefore regarded as a windfall profit which will only affect the plans for the next period. However, savings ex ante are still dependent on the rate of interest.

(Lindahl 1939C, p.182).[20]

Lindahl's point with these two examples is to
show that the idea that savings <u>directly</u> determine
investment "is ... strictly speaking, not quite
correct, as long as monetary policy is autonomous"
(ibid., p.175). This is because his analysis shows
that at least when free currency is assumed, then the
direct link between savings and investment decisions
is severed, and the investment demand has the upper
hand. Therefore his purpose is in line with
Wicksell's as well as Keynes' analysis in the
<u>Treatise</u> of what happens when savings and investment
differ. Hence, the equilibrating mechanism is
different from the principle of effective demand,
since it is not the case that income is <u>the</u>
equilibrating mechanism independent of whether the
monetary policy is 'autonomous' or not. This has
already been shown above by the difference between
what is true during the cumulative process and what
is true for the stationary state itself. But we can
find further evidence which is even more directly to
the point, when Lindahl in 1939 analyses the
following question: "Is Saving or Investment the
Primary Phenomenon?" (Lindahl 1939B, p.131). After
describing a case similar to the cumulative process
he discusses <u>what is true in the long run</u>:

> "However, if we carry our reasoning one step
> farther [than the case with redistribution
> of income during the cumulative process], we
> must nevertheless admit the quintessential
> truth of the common opinion that savings on
> the whole are primary in relation to

----

20 After seeing this type of economic policy being in
use in the 1950s to increase real investment, Lindahl
took a definite stand against it:

> "In my view ... it is illogical to advocate
> a moderate inflationary process of this kind
> as a long-term <u>programme</u> for economic
> policy, for the result would be that the
> public tries to adjust itself to inflation"
> (Lindahl 1957, p.5).

investment. As a matter of fact, the amount of real investment planned for a certain period forward, is dependent,on the rate of interest and this rate might be regulated by the banks in such a manner that the planned investment corresponds to the planned saving. It is true that actual monetary policy shows many deviations from this rule and that the whole trade cycle phenomenon can be regarded as a demonstration of the manner in which the equality ex post between investment and saving is realized by means of unintentional saving and dissaving. But in the long run a certain tendency for the rate of interest to adapt itself to the amount of planned saving could probably be noticed" (ibid., pp.133-134).

The rate of interest seems here to have the same function as it has in Cassel's theory, namely, to restrict the demand for savings to the actual supply (cp. Cassel 1929, pp.76-77; p.109). Thus the rate of interest plays its traditional role and effective demand has no role to play.

3.3.2 - The role of quantity changes in the cumulative process.
Finally, we show what happens when quantity changes are incorporated into the analysis, which assumes that unemployed resources exist. Lindahl analyses a case where there are unemployed resources available in both sectors and it is also possible to transfer factors of production from one sector to the other. Increased real investment will then draw unemployed factors of production into the capital goods sector and nominal income will increase. This will lead to higher demand for consumption goods and thereby raise prices. The consumption goods sector will therefore also start to employ unemployed factors of production and the quantity of consumption goods (Q) will increase. It is now possible that "the supply of consumption goods during a certain period increases as much or even more than the money demand after these goods, whereby an equilibrium may ensue" (Lindahl 1930, p.44 n.1), which means that the

cumulative process will only describe an initial price rise before it comes to a halt when the production of consumption goods has caught up with the increase in demand. But in the English edition Lindahl only allows this to happen "for some time" (Lindahl 1939C, p.178). Thus it is only a temporary phase for sooner or later the price level will start to rise for the following reason:

> "Even if the volume of consumers' goods increases ... the transfer of productive forces to the capital producing industries will result in a still greater growth of the purchasing power of consumers, at least after a time" (ibid., p.179).

Hence, the inclusion of positive changes in employment and thereby in the quantity of consumption goods will mainly retard the price level increase. The only change that concerns the equilibrating mechanism during the cumulative process is that the total income changes are now made up of both nominal and real elements. But that is still not the principle of effective demand, since in equilibrium the interest rate resumes its orthodox role.[21]

From our point of view it is thus interesting to notice that the inclusion of unemployed resources and quantity changes do not necessarily entail any idea of effective demand. In fact, Keynes develops in the same way after the Treatise, when he explicitly incorporates quantity changes into the disequilibrium process, but that does not mean that he has started to determine the equilibrium level of output and employment (cp. Note 30 Ch. VI).

----

21 As late as 1957, we can find that Lindahl thought of this first phase where real income is changing as being explained by the Keynesian multiplier analysis, while the second phase was explained by Wicksell's cumulative process (cp. Lindahl 1957, pp.4-5). Hence, according to Lindahl both theories describe disequilibrium processes and they do not determine equilibrium situations.

4 - Lindahl's critique of Wicksell's conception of a normal rate.

We have seen that, to a great extent, Lindahl builds on Wicksell's ideas on macroeconomic theory (cp. above sect. 1:3), but he does not espouse Wicksell's notion of a normal rate of interest. In fact, he more or less discards the whole notion of a normal rate. However, it is crucial to expose that the abandonment of the normal rate implies a substitution of Wicksell's static method for temporary equilibrium. Furthermore, it is shown that the penetration of the meaning of the normal rate of interest spills over into a sequence analysis. Lindahl's analysis served later as an inspiration for Myrdal's Monetary Equilibrium, which is both a critique of Lindahl's position and an attempt to reconstruct Wicksell's version of the normal rate.

Despite the fact that Lindahl's analysis is based on Wicksell's idea of determining changes in the price level by looking at total demand versus total supply, he has not used the concept of a normal rate of interest, which plays such an important role in Wicksell's analysis. To provide a motive for this omission Lindahl offers the following:

> "We shall ... start from Wicksell's own definition, in order to analyse more exactly whether the concept 'normal rate of interest' can de defined so that it becomes of scientific value" (Lindahl 1939C, p.246).

Lindahl's exposition follows the three different characteristics of the normal rate and their interrelations a theme which was completely duplicated by Myrdal in Monetary Equilibrium.

For Wicksell the first characteristic of the normal rate corresponds to the real rate of interest. But it is only in a one-commodity world that the real rate could be determined independently, i.e. "purely by technical considerations, and thus independent of the price system [the loan rate is a part of the price system]" (ibid., p.247), and in such a world the loan rate has to correspond to the real rate. However, under more realistic conditions, i.e. in a multi-commodity world, it is impossible to compare input and output (unless the proportions are the

82   Chapter 4

same) without using a price system. Therefore
Lindahl redefines the real rate of interest in a
particular period as "the relation between
anticipated future product values (with appropriate
reductions for risk) and the values invested during
the period" (Lindahl 1939C, p.248).[22] It is then
evident that the loan rate influences the demand for
invested services and thereby their prices. Hence,
the real rate as here defined has now "a tendency to
adjust itself to the actual loan rate of interest in
every period" (ibid., p.249). To say that the loan
rate is the same as the real rate of interest and
therefore 'normal' has then no meaning, since it is a
part of the determination of the real rate.

Thus Lindahl interprets <u>the real rate as a
particular level of the loan rate</u>:

> "as the rate of interest on loans which
> emerges as a result of the pricing process,
> when equilibrium between the different
> factors, above all between the demand for
> and the supply of saving, has been attained"
> (ibid.).

In fact, this shows that a complete equation system
which includes the money rate (assuming that such a
system can be constructed) cannot be in equilibrium
unless the loan rate and the real rate, i.e. the
expected rate of profit, are the same. Consequently
in 1939 Lindahl makes the following assessment of the
independence of the investment schedule:

> "[it] will indeed have been influenced in
> various ways by the loan rate in preceding
> periods, but it can nevertheless be regarded
> as independent of the loan rate during the
> current period ... . However, the
> conclusion remains that it is impossible on
> the basis of this investment schedule alone
> to single out any definite real rate as
> having a decisive influence on the loan

----

22 This is exactly the same as Wicksell's sympathetic
description of Walras' theory of the rate of interest
(cp. Wicksell 1919, p.226).

rate" (ibid., p.262).

Henceforth, the equilibrium rate is the rate which equalizes supply (savings ex ante) and demand (investment ex ante) in the capital market. This is exactly the argument which Hammarskjöld voiced against Myrdal's version of the real rate as an independent entity in the determination of the money rate (cp. sect. VI:3:3). The new definition of the real rate has affinities with Wicksell's second characteristic of the normal rate.

Consequently the normal rate is the equilibrium point between supply and demand for savings, and the problem is then the following:

> "whether a particular rate of interest is necessary to bring about equilibrium between these two forces [net demand for saving and net supply of saving for a certain period]" (ibid.. p.250).

However, the savings paradox shows that if the future is not completely foreseen and frictional conditions exist, then the change in net investment for a certain period, due to a movement in the rate of interest, will <u>always</u> be balanced by a subsequent change in savings brought about through changes in the income distribution via changes in the price level. This loan rate is normal in the sense that it fulfils Wicksell's condition that savings should balance investment, but that is not only true for 'a particular rate of interest' but for all rates, though in most cases the price level will now have to change. Lindahl has therefore made the following addition to the second characteristic of the loan rate:

> "What is intended by the definition in question is naturally that the equilibrium will be attained without the necessity for any shift in the price level such as would alter the distribution of incomes, and thence the supply of saving, and even without any tendency towards such a shift arising from the interest level itself ... .
> But fundamentally that is equivalent to the

statement that the rate of interest is
neutral in respect to the price level"
(ibid., p.251).

This passage gives us the third characteristic of the
normal rate, namely, that it should be neutral in
relation to the price level; but that only implies
"such a development of price as is in accordance with
the expectations of the public" (ibid., p.252).
Hence, there are no reasons for the price level to
stay the same. However, 'under actual conditions',
i.e. imperfect foresight, individual anticipations
do not coincide, which has the following consequence
for the meaning of the neutrality of the normal rate:

"It is ... impossible to speak of a
generally anticipated future course of
prices. The price development to which the
loan rate is to be related must thus be
conceived as a sort of average of different
individual expectations of future prices.
Since a certain amount of arbitrariness can
hardly be avoided in a construction of this
kind, the concept 'normal rate of interest'
has some corresponding arbitrariness. This
brings to light a certain imperfection in
the concept. But it can hardly be
eliminated by any other interpretation of
its meaning" (ibid., pp.252-253).

Thus there is an arbitrariness in the definition of
the normal rate because of the difficulties in
defining the price level. There is also another
arbitrariness stemming from the side of the rate of
interest.
In this context Lindahl analyses the problem
with the differentiation of the rate of interest,
which was never included in Wicksell's analysis of
the normal rate. Therefore the normal rate does not
represent a single rate of interest but "a
combination of different rates for different types of
loans" (ibid., p.257), which means that it is possible
to think of "a number of combinations of long and
short term rate which will all be neutral in respect
to the price level, during a certain period" (ibid.,
p.258, italics omitted). Hence, the normal rate is

not uniquely defined, though the following
combination could be considered the most normal:

"Of the many possible combinations of short
and long rates which in a certain period
have no immediate effects on the price
level, the one that makes it possible to
maintain a stable price level, with the
smallest possible variation in interest
during future periods, has some claims to be
regarded as most 'normal'. ... . This
interpretation of the concept, however,
suffers from the weakness that it is only
possible to judge whether the rate for a
certain period was normal or not after a
considerable lapse of time" (ibid., pp.258-
259).

This passage is crucial since it shows that <u>Lindahl</u>
<u>is not analysing only a single period where the</u>
<u>notion of temporary equilibrium holds</u>, because that
notion would guarantee that for the initial period
the individual anticipations coincide and are
realized. Hence, 'a generally anticipated future
course of prices' will exist for this period and
Lindahl himself speaks about 'no immediate effects on
the price level'.

Lindahl must therefore refer to anticipations
over several periods, and for such a case the 'most'
normal rate should imply "a minimum of fluctuations
in the normal rate of interest during the forthcoming
periods" (Lindahl 1930, p.132; cp. Lindahl 1939C,
p.259). But it has already been noted that with this
definition of the normal rate, its normality could
only be judged 'after a considerable lapse of time'.
However, this problem could only be solved by a
sequence analysis exhibiting the development over
several periods [23], while the notion of temporary
equilibrium only determines the normal rate in
relation to the first period. This shows once again
that the notion of temporary equilibrium is not

----

23 Lindahl thus speaks of 'corrected long-term
equilibrium' in his additional note to <u>The Rate of</u>
<u>Interest</u> (cp. Lindahl 1939C, p.264).

really appropriate for the problem which Lindahl
wants to analyse.

Lindahl has thereby substantiated the following
proposition:

> "that the two first characteristics have
> under realistic assumptions broadly the
> same content as the third, and that the
> normal rate of interest may thus simply be
> defined as that which is neutral in relation
> to the price level" (ibid., p.246).

But, as has been shown above, even the identification
of the normal rate with the neutral rate will still
leave the concept suffering from certain weaknesses.
Lindahl's final decision is therefore not to use the
concept at all, and that the following is enough for
analysing the effects of the rate of interest:

> "that different interest levels, determined
> in respect of their average height and their
> differentiation, lead to different
> developments of the price level, when other
> conditions remain unaltered. For this
> analysis it is not necessary to denote any
> of these interest levels by the term
> 'normal'" (ibid., p.260).

We would argue that Wicksell, at least in Vol.II of
Lectures, would go along with Lindahl and say that
the normal rate should balance savings and investment
plans (cp. Wicksell 1935, pp.192-193), which was
later conceded by Lindahl (cp. Lindahl 1939C,
pp.262-263). Hence, Wicksell would consider that
this definition of the normal rate implies a neutral
rate in the sense defined by Lindahl above, because
incongruent anticipations related to the price level
will only lead to temporary disturbances since the
equilibrium is stable (cp. Wicksell 1935, pp.196-
197). This follows from Wicksell's allegiance to the
static method which excludes anticipations as a part
of the data determining the equilibrium position (cp.
sect. II:2).

Therefore Lindahl's inclusion of imperfect
foresight into the analysis of the normal rate has
lead to the substitution of Wicksell's static

equilibrium with temporary equilibrium. Hence, Lindahl, like the other members of the Stockholm School, found it necessary to break away from the static equilibrium approach in order to analyse a practical policy question like the definition of the normal rate under 'realistic' conditions, i.e. for an ongoing process in real time.

Appendix to Section 2:3a:2[1]

Commodities: nature $(q=1,\ldots Q)$, date $(t=1,\ldots T)$.
Numeraire $(Q,1)$, i.e. $P_{Q1}=1$.
The <u>discounted</u> price of commodity (q,t). The quantity of Q that must be given at date 1 to buy the right to one unit of the good q for delivery at date t:

$$P_{qt}$$

The own discount factor for good q:

$$R_{qt}=P_{qt}/P_{q1}$$

Put R_{Qt} equal to R_t so $R_t=P_{Qt}$.

The own rate of interest for period t (i.e. from date t to t+1), is r_{qt} and is derived from the formula:

$$R_{q,t+1}=[1/(1+r_{qt})]R_{qt}$$

By definition $P_{q,t+1} = [1/(1+r_{qt})]P_{qt}$

Put r_{Qt} equal to r_t:

$$P_{Q,t+1}=[1/(1+r_t)]P_{Qt}=[1/(1+r_t)][1/(1+r_{t-1})]P_{Q,t-1}$$

$$=[1/(1+r_t)][1/(1+r_{t-1})]\ldots[1/(1+r_1)]P_{Q1}$$

Put undiscounted prices at date t equal to $\bar{P}_{1t}$, $\bar{P}_{2t}$, $\ldots$ $\bar{P}_{Qt}$ they must be proportional to the corresponding discounted prices P_{1t}, P_{2t}, $\ldots$ P_{Qt}, and in addition $\bar{P}_{Qt}=1$.
It therefore follows:

$$\bar{P}_{qt}=\bar{P}_{qt}/\bar{P}_{Qt}=P_{qt}/P_{Qt} \text{ or } \bar{P}_{qt}=(1/R_t)P_{qt}$$

In equilibrium price equals costs of production. We

----

1 This is taken mainly from Malinvaud (1972) and Eatwell (1977).

can assume that the time unit is the production period. The equilibrium condition (for unit output) is then the following:

$$P_{q,t+1} \leq \Sigma a_{iq} P_{it} \qquad\qquad (i = 1,\ldots,Q)$$

a_{ij} are equilibrium inputs and include labour, current input of raw material etc. If inequality holds then q_{t+1} is not produced. [Terminal condition $a_{iq}^T = 0$ and output and date 1 is equal to zero] The profit of producing q for period t at <u>discounted</u> prices, i.e. in the numeraire P_{Q1}:

$$G_{qt} = P_{q,t+1} - \Sigma a_{iq} P_{it}$$

In equilibrium $G_{qt} = 0$.
Put g_{qt} as the rate of profit for producing q:

$$g_{qt} = (P_{q,t+1} - \Sigma a_{iq} P_{it}) / \Sigma a_{iq} P_{it}$$

In equilibrium $g_{qt} = 0$.
Now we want to compute the rate of profit for producing q during period t, evaluated in commodity Q for the same period:

(1) $[(P_{q,t+1}/P_{Q,t+1}) - ((\Sigma a_{iq} P_{it})/P_{Qt})]$

$\qquad / [(\Sigma a_{iq} P_{it})/P_{Qt}]$

$\qquad\qquad = P_{Qt}/P_{Q,t+1} - 1 = r_t$

This shows the general result, namely, that the rate of profit yielded by the production of commodities is uniform in terms of commodity Q for period t, which is used as a standard, and equal to the own rate of return on the standard. This is a necessary outcome of arbitrage.
Malinvaud reaches the same result for undiscounted prices:

$$\bar{g}_{qt} = \bar{P}_{q,t+1} - (1+r_t)(\Sigma a_{iq} \bar{P}_{it})$$

In equilibrium $\bar{g}_{qt} = 0$.
However, it is assumed that commodity Q is money in the ordinary sense of the word. Hence, Malivaud states that "r_t must have a central position in the

set of r_{qt} relating to the same date" (Malinvaud 1972, p.241). The 'central position' implies that:

(2) $[\bar{P}_{q,t+1} - P_{qt}]/\bar{P}_{qt} = (r_t - r_{qt})/(1 + r_{qt})$

Where r_t is some sort of 'average' for all the r_{qt}'s.

We can now analyse the effects of changes in the value of the standard:

$$\bar{P}_{Qt}/\bar{P}_{qt} \neq \bar{P}_{Q,t+1}/\bar{P}_{q,t+1} \qquad \text{for most q.}$$

By expanding the expression for g_{qt}:

(3) $(\bar{P}_{q,t+1} - \Sigma a_{iq}\bar{P}_{i,t+1}) + \Sigma a_{iq}(\bar{P}_{i,t+1} - \bar{P}_{it})$

$\qquad - r_t \Sigma a_{iq}\bar{P}_{it} = 0,$

where the first term shows the value of the net product and the second term the capital gain while the last term shows the interest on capital.

Chapter 5

A Critique of Static Equilibrium Theory
Lundberg (1930)

"My first article on equilibrium in E.T. 1930 was a part of my fil. lic. dissertation[1] under Bagge. It was written long before I started to work with macro-models (which was around 1932 in USA). The stimulus to this article came from German and Austrian economists (Rosenstein-Rodan, Schumpeter et. al.), but mainly from Ragnar Frisch and his mathematical formulations of dynamic theory. The article was isolated and became forgotten (even by myself)" (Letter from Erik Lundberg to the author, 14 February 1979).

Lundberg's article "Om begreppet ekonomisk jämvikt" (On the concept of economic equilibrium) published in Ekonomisk Tidskrift in 1930 has hardly been mentioned at all in the later works of the Stockholm School and it seems to have been almost forgotten by the author himself. However, we will show that this article has played a central role in the development of the Stockholm School. On the one hand, we have already seen that Lundberg's criticism of the dynamic methods developed by Myrdal and Lindahl may have been instrumental in changing their views (cp. sect. IV:4:2; VI:2:1). On the other hand, Lundberg joins hands with Lindahl in criticizing comparative statics for not explaining the traverse between two equilibrium situations (cp. IV:1:2).[2] Furthermore, Lundberg makes some suggestive remarks on the construction of dynamic methods which seem to

----

1 This degree is comparable to an Anglo-Saxon Ph.d.-dissertation.
2 Though he was possibly more influenced by Frisch, Lundberg also mentions that Lindahl and Åkerman had examined his article (cp. Lundberg 1930, p.135).

point forward towards the ideas developed in <u>Studies in the Theory of Economic Expansion</u>.

1 - Lundberg's purpose.
    Lundberg starts from the following view of the relation between statics and dynamics:

> "if the concepts are names of certain methods for attacking the economic problems, the static must be founded on certain simplifying assumptions, certain general abstractions from the reality. If it is a general demand that dynamic theory should be an extension and a complement to the static theory, it ought to constitute an abstraction which is not pushed so far as statics, a logical introduction of one or several of the real phenomena or relations, from which one abstracts in statics" (Lundberg 1930, p.134).

This is an explicit critique of Cassel's idea that dynamics is the concrete reality and it shows that Lundberg, like Myrdal, is interested in what constitutes a dynamic 'theory' (cp. sect. III:2). The idea itself had already been developed by Frisch, who differentiated statics from dynamics with respect to the <u>method of analysis</u>, which is something "characteristic for the mode of thinking of the human being itself" (Frisch 1929, p.321). Therefore it has nothing to do with any particular quality of the analysed phenomena.
    In this article the aim is not so much to build any particular dynamic method as <u>to show the limitations of statics</u>:

> "to expose the generally undeclared assumptions, which established the basis for the equilibrium concept[3], and consequently their limited possibilities for application" (Lundberg 1930, p.135).

This more restricted purpose is due to the fact that the implicit assumptions of static theory are not well defined and it is therefore important to know what the precise meaning might be. At the same time the article criticizes several attempts to dynamize the static theory. Thus, it is only after Lundberg has dealt with these problems that he sketches his own approach in less than two pages.

2 - A critique of static equilibrium theory.

We will only discuss Lundberg's critique of partial equilibrium theory, since, according to Lundberg, exactly the same critique is also valid for general equilibrium theory (cp. ibid., pp.140-142).

The partial demand and supply curve are generally given as $q^d=D(p)$ and $q^s=S(p)$ under ceteris paribus conditions. If demand and supply are equal then the price is supposed to be constant. However, the following proposition is the crucial one: if demand and supply differ then "a process will come into existence, which will tend to reestablish equilibrium" (ibid., p.136). This proposition rests solely on the assumption that if demand is greater than supply then the price will increase, which will set up an equilibrating process.[4] Hence, the following is taken for granted:

---

3 For Lundberg equilibrium theory is the same as statics (cp. Lundberg 1930, p.138).

4 A similar idea is expressed by Rosenstein-Rodan:

"The fundamental supposition that supply and demand are equal is a postulate and does not find expression in the equations themselves. It is outside the system of equations and ,is based on the assumption that the seller will put up his price as the demand increases. It rests, that is to say, on the assumption that demand has a specific effect on price - which cannot be expressed by the equations of the equilibrium theory" (Rosenstein-Rodan 1934, p.94).

"that the price 'in the long run' will
appear in the normal position, where demand
is equal to supply, and with every deviation
it will tend towards this position" (ibid.).

However, the demand and supply curves are not
functions of time and they could therefore only
"indicate alternative situations" (ibid., p.138) [5],
i.e. comparative statics. This implies that static
theory is 'time-less' in the sense that if one of the
demand and supply curves has changed, then they are
imagined to be "immediately brought into
correspondence with each other" (ibid.). Thus, a new
long run is instantaneously established, and the
actual price will at once tend towards the new
equilibrium level (cp. ibid., p.149).

The gist of Lundberg's argument is to show that
this theory must depend on very particular
assumptions concerning the 'velocities of
adjustment'. This term, which is taken from
Rosenstein-Rodan, signifies "the velocities, by which
the price affects demand and supply, and they affect
the price" (ibid., p.138). It is obvious that a host
of different assumptions might be made in relation to

---

5 This idea is probably taken from Frisch:

"The changes, which the static law aims at,
are in their nature not real changes in
time, but formal changes which arise when
one is comparing different more closely
specified situations which are thought of as
realized alternatives. ... . The analysed
changes are not changes with respect to
time, but variations with respect to certain
alternatives. In this sense the static law
is a timeless law" (Frisch 1929, p.322).

these velocities.[6] Therefore Lundberg's critique is directed towards the claim of static theory that it is able to determine the new equilibrium situation without taking the velocities of adjustment into consideration. Static theory basically ignored this problem, as is evident from the assumption that the transition process itself will not change the equilibrium level (cp. ibid., p.136; p.138). However, Lundberg is directly interested in finding a method by which to analyse this process, which he considers to be necessary for determining the forthcoming equilibrium situation.[7] From this idea follows Lundberg's general comment that "a dynamic analysis must precede the static analysis and not vice versa" (ibid., p.157; cp. p.154), which later became the methodological starting-point for Lindahl (cp. sect. IX:2).

3 - Lundberg's comments on dynamic method.

We have already looked at Lundberg's criticism of the methods used by Myrdal and Lindahl, but it is also interesting to try to find out his opinions, which are not very explicit, on other versions of dynamic methods.

----

6 Incidentally, the proliferation of business cycle theories is mainly explained by the the making of different assumptions about the magnitudes of these velocities, and "since no quantitative measure could be made plausible, almost every business cycle theory could appear as valid as any other" (Lundberg 1930, p.150; cp. p.159). This idea also lies behind Ohlin's discussions of 'what happens first', which plays an important role in his 'case-by-case' models (cp. sect. VIII:2).
7 Hicks had pronounced the same idea in the following way:

> "As soon as we face the problem of analysing a process, even its equilibrium values must be determined, somehow or other, in relation to the process" (Hicks 1965, pp.23-24).

3.1 - A system of differential equations.

Lundberg drops en passant the following remarks concerning the analysis of the traverses:

> "in the nature of things these transitional periods could not be made an object for static analysis. No equality between demand and supply is characteristic for such situations, ... The demand and supply become among other things dependent on the price change per unit of time, and we get a system of differential equations, which are extraordinarily difficult to grasp even under simplified assumptions. The unknowns of the system are no longer certain magnitudes (prices, demand and supply) but the corresponding curves as functions of time" (ibid., p.140).[8]

The solution to the system of differential equations will then show how prices and quantities are successively determined over time, and the solution depends on the form of the equations, which in their turn reflect the velocities of adjustments. Consequently Frisch writes of dynamics as determining a series of successive situations in time in contradistinction to statics which determine alternative situations (cp. Frisch 1929, p.322; cp. above Note 5). Therefore it seems that Lundberg has found a suitable method by which to exihibit the sequential character of the traverse. However, at the same time Lundberg contests the following proposition:

----
8 The meaning of this passage is perhaps easier to understand by refering to the following quotation from Frisch:

> "In statics 'an unknown thing' is simply an unknown quantity ... . In dynamics, on the other hand, an unknown thing is the same as an unknown curve, more specifically; an unknown timecurve" (Frisch 1929, p.331).

"The perpetual tendency towards determined
equilibrium situations, is an assumption,
whose real basis is extremely difficult to
make precise. The mutual connections
between the elements of price formation,
which should lead to perpetual
accomodations until the equilibrium
situation is reached, is not in agreement
with reality" (Lundberg 1930, pp.157-158).

Lundberg mentions the cumulative process as an
example to back up his proposition. But the solution
to a system of differential equations implies one
equilibrium situation towards which prices etc. are
tending all the time. Hence, it appears that
Lundberg does not really intend to use a complete
system of differential equations, and with hindsight
we know that it is also true for his later
constructions, i.e. the model sequences (cp. sect.
X:3). Furthermore, it is interesting to notice that
none of the members of the Stockholm School ever used
a system of differential equations, despite the fact
that they must have been familiar with Frisch's
works. In fact, it is only in Lundberg's Economic
Expansion that we can find an application of a
solution to a difference equation. However, at the
same time there is no explicit rejection of Frisch's
method; though, we could imagine that they found
Frisch's method rather unrealistic, in the sense that
it has to assume a steadfastness of behaviour over
the whole process, while most of the Swedes assumed a
constant behaviour only for a few periods (cp. sect.
II:5). Thus we have to look elsewhere for Lundberg's
positive proposals on how to develop a dynamic
method.

3.2 - A precursor to the model sequences.

We will first go back and specify what are the
particular abstractions which separate static from
dynamic theory (cp. sect. 1). Static equilibrium
takes certain factors as being fixed, e.g. demand and
supply functions, while other factors, the variables
like prices and quantities, have to accommodate to
the given factors. This idea, denoted as 'the method

Chapter 5   99

of argumentation within economics', must be based on the following assumption:

> "the velocities of adjustment for the variables should be relatively high compared to those of the constant factor" (Lundberg 1930, p.159).

Henceforth, the dynamic theory should refer to cases where velocities for the two types of factors are not too different, which implies that changes in the 'variables' may lead to mutual changes in the 'constant' factors. Thus, the distinction between dependent and independent factors is blurred.

However, Lundberg does not hold that the general equilibrium concept should be thrown overboard since this notion still has a role to play:

> "as an expression for the idea that the economic variables hang together and in reality they could not for a long time hold positions which strongly diverge from the former 'normal' positions, the conception is certainly indispensable for economic thinking" (ibid.).

That seems to imply that a new equilibrium position will generally be reached and it will be fairly similar to the old equilibrium position. The obvious economic phenomenon in the back of Lundberg's mind here is the business cycle.

Therefore it is not surprising to find that Lundberg holds that both statics and dynamics have a role to play in an analysis of business cycles. Hence, the following final remarks from Lundberg on the relation between statics and dynamics:

> "In reality the concepts of statics and dynamics could not be separated. One could say, that the two methods, which are called statics and dynamics, are always consciously or unconsciously used at the same time. As a rule the reasoning follows Marshall's pattern of fixing the tendencies at each particular point by giving the probable reaction to a given constellation of prices.

This reaction is determined in the form of a tendency to equalization, the direction is thus towards a partial equilibrium situation. But at the same time one takes into consideration, that before this situation has been reached other points have been disturbed by new tendencies, and through a suitable choice of the intervening time and the strength of the tendencies, one can give a statisfactory explanation of a business cycle" (ibid., p.160; p.156).

Thus, dynamics represents a movement while statics, or equilibrium theory, play a role in determining its direction. The dynamic method is therefore a <u>fusion</u> of static and dynamic elements, where the former refer to the fact that there is a tendency towards 'a partial equilibrium situation', i.e. it shows the direction, while the latter analyses the time and strength of the variables which make up this tendency. However, at the same time, the equilibrium situation towards which the actual prices are tending is very often disturbed, and these disturbances are not necessarily exogenous but they may also have an endogenous character. Hence, the traverse affects the equilibrium situation itself, which rules out the notion of 'perpetual accomodations until the equilibrium situation is reached' (cp. sect. 3:1). Therefore, it is not a question of <u>juxtaposing</u> a static method, which would once and for all determine the equilibrium position, with a dynamic method which would exhibit the path towards this position.
Since it is possible to make several assumptions about the velocities Lundberg comes up with the following suggestion for the construction of a dynamic method:

"Only by letting the processes actually observed in reality limit the possibilities [of the speed of the velocities of adjustment], could a dynamic theory be developed. The modern economic literature seems to point in this direction, and particular attention ought to be devoted to the lines of thought which have emanated from the American economists (Moore,

> Schultz, et. cons.). Here the equilibrium concept shows itself to be of great use, though not in its general form but in its specialization on a smaller number of variable factors" (ibid., p.160).

We shall see below (Ch. X) that this proposal points towards the model sequences, which is the method used in Economic Expansion of 1937, where there is a sequential relation between a few macroeconomic variables and where the notion of equilibrium still plays a well-defined role.

Lundberg himself took his own advice ('to devote 'a particular attention' to the American economists') seriously enough to leave for Chicago in the Autumn of 1931 on a stipend from the Rockefeller Foundation (cp. Lundberg's letter to Myrdal, 29 November 1931). There, among other things, he followed lectures given by Schultz and Knight and studied the works of Evans, Roos and Hotelling (cp. ibid.; Letter to Myrdal, 16 February 1932). The next academic year Lundberg moved to the Columbia University, where he met W.C.Mitchell, J.M.Clark and F.C.Mills. Hence, during these two years Lundberg obtained a good background knowledge of the theoretical and empirical parts of business cycle theory. Finally, it seems that in New York he started to work on what later became Studies in the Theory of Economic Expansion:

> "In regard of my own work, I have now settled down to work on business cycle theory" (Letter to Myrdal, 8 November 1932).

Chapter 6

The Disequilibrium Approach
Myrdal's Development of Ex Ante and Ex Post
(1931-1932)

"The first method of computation [ex post]
is 'book-keeping' about what has actually
happened during a completed period, the
second mode of computation [ex ante] is a
business calculation founded on what will
happen in the future" (Myrdal 1939, p.54).

Monetary Equilibrium was an attempt to make
a critical reconstruction of Wicksell's notion of a
normal rate of interest so it could be used for a
monetary analysis, and the starting-point was
Lindahl's analysis in The Rate of Interest and the
Price Level (cp. sect. IV:4). However, Myrdal's
most important contribution to the development of
dynamic method is not his version of monetary
equilibrium, which has some defects because of the
use of an 'instantaneous analysis', but the coinage
of the notions of ex ante/ex post, since with these
notions it is possible to undertake a disequilibrium
analysis. Myrdal shows the importance of ex ante/ex
post in his analysis of the equalizing factors
between savings and investment, which is much
superior to Lindahl's analysis of 1930. Furthermore,
his explicit analysis of the savings-investment
mechanism makes it an ideal vantage point for making
a detailed comparison between his analysis and
Keynes' principle of effective demand.

1 - The purpose of Monetary Equilibrium.
We will look at the purpose behind Monetary
Equilibrium both with regard to the prehistory of the
work and as it is presented in the work itself.

1.1 - The background to Monetary Equilibrium.

It is important to look at the background to Monetary Equilibrium in order to show that it started out as a short work on Wicksell's normal rate, and then came to include the meaning of equilibrium behind the use of that rate in monetary analysis. Myrdal finally added his comments on Lindahl's view of the same problem. In fact, it is possible to argue that the direction of Myrdal's whole venture was heavily influenced by his reading of Lindahl's book The Rate of Interest, which was printed in November 1930 (cp. Letter from Lindahl to Myrdal, 20 November 1930). Myrdal probably read the book during the following year, since a year later he describes the theoretical content of Lindahl's works in a letter to Seligman (10 November 1931).

In a letter to Hayek, Myrdal writes as follows:

"I would like to write a little article, but it is not written yet and it would have a very restrictive scope. It would be a critical discussion of the very conception of a 'natural rate of interest'" (Letter to Hayek, 4 September 1931).

Ten days later he is still planning "to write an article on the Wicksellian theory of a natural rate of interest" (Letter to Hayek, 14 September 1931). This article was already finsihed some days later, since on the 26th of September Myrdal writes to Hayek that "the little article" was "just finished". The article was originally intended for Journal of Political Economy (cp. Letters to Lundberg, 18 April 1932, and to Hayek, 25 May 1932), but Myrdal continued to work on it and extended its scope.

In April 1932, Myrdal speaks of the work in the following way:

"a half-finished manuscript on Wicksell's natural rate: I am trying to sort out the conception of equilibrium which lies behind it, i.e. immanent theorizing. Would also try such an exposition that it would give an introduction to the whole of this tendency of thought" (Letter to Lundberg, 18 April 1932).

Hence, at this time it seems that Myrdal still plans to publish the article in Journal of Political Economy, since it has an introductory character. However, a month later the following letter indicates that Myrdal has changed his plans:

"the article is getting too long and really too intricate to be in that journal [J.P.E.]. Its reading presupposes a rather intimate knowledge of Wicksell and his followers and you know well that most of the Americans (and even the English) do not have that knowledge. You see I originally wanted to give some sort of semi-popular introduction to the Wicksellian line of thought by way of taking up the central construction for analysis. But now, this analysis has grown too intricate and I would rather have it published in German ... In this situation, I ask you if you could still get place in your 'Sammelband' [the working name for what became Hayek 1933] for a treatise in German on the theory of monetary equilibrium involved in the Wicksellian construction. Most of it is already printed in the Swedish "Ekonomisk Tidskrift" but I would like to add some further notes on the discussion in Sweden since 'Geldzins und Güterpreise' and especially Lindahl's last and important contribution [must refer to The Rate of Interest]. My contribution would demand a space of, say, 35-50 pages" (Letter to Hayek, 25 May 1932).

Hence, from this letter it would seem that in the meantime " Penningteoretisk jämvikt" (Myrdal 1931) had been published.[1] But this is probably not correct, since the Swedish version contains a detailed comment on Lindahl. The article in Ekonomisk Tidskrift also amounts to 111 pages, so it would seem odd for Myrdal to estimate the length of

----

1 This article was published in Ekonomisk Tidskrift dated 1931, but the issue was actually printed during 1932 (cp. Landgren 1957, p.22).

his proposed contribution to Hayek's 'Sammelband' at 35-50 pages, if he had already seen the printed version of ""Penningteoretisk jämvikt". Furthermore, in two letters of June 1932 Myrdal writes that he has just finished a manuscript and was sending it off to the press (cp. Letters to Alf Johansson and Ohlin, both of 22 June 1932). It would appear that <u>this</u> manuscript is "Penningteoretisk jämvikt"; there is no reason to believe that the Swedish version of <u>Gleichgewicht</u> (Myrdal 1933) could have been printed before it was translated by G.Mackenroth.

After Myrdal had finished this manuscript he left for Germany and visited Mackenroth, who started to work on a translation of "Penningteoretisk jämvikt". However, in Germany Myrdal started to make changes in the version destined for Hayek's 'Sammelband':

"Reworked the whole treatise on money: it became much better and more direct in German" (Letter to Hammarskjöld, 18 July 1932; cp. letter to Ohlin, 29 August 1932).

By the end of August Mackenroth had translated everything (cp. Letter from Myrdal to Hayek, 27 August 1932), and the final corrected proofs of the German version was sent to Hayek at the end of the year (cp. Letter from Myrdal to Hayek, 31 January 1933). Thus, it was probably not possible for Myrdal to include Hammarskjöld's criticism of the relation between Wicksell's equilibrium conditions into the German version (cp. letters from Hammarskjöld to Lindahl, before November 1932; an undated manuscript sent to Myrdal by Hammarskjöld and answered by the former in 1932; sect. 3:3).[2]

The main difference between the Swedish version and the German and English ones is the two introductory chapters added to the foreign

---

2 Hammarskjöld's critique was finally published as an appendix to the article "Utkast till en algebraisk metod för dynamisk prisanalys" (Hammarskjöld 1932).

editions.[3]   (Of   course,   Myrdal   changed   his
theoretical argumentation between all three editions,
but these alterations will be dealt with in their
proper context.) In this dissertation we will mainly
quote the English version of 1939, and the quoted
passages are, unless otherwise is indicated, similar
to the corresponding ones in the two earlier
editions.

1.2 - Myrdal's problem.

Myrdal makes the following concise statement of
the problem he intends to analyse:

> "From the standpoint of the fundamental idea
> of Wicksell's monetary theory, what do the
> properties of a price situation in a non-
> stationary course of events have to be in
> order that this situation can be
> characterized as a position of monetary
> equilibrium?" (Myrdal 1939, p.42).

Thus the fundamental idea is monetary equilibrium and
the notion of a normal rate of interest is an active
factor in accomplishing such an equilibrium. Hence,
the subtitle to "Penningteoretisk jämvikt" is "A
Study of the 'Normal Rate of Interest' in Wicksell's
Monetary Doctrine" (Myrdal 1931, p.191). The fact

---

3 The most important changes between the English
edition and the German one are noted by Palander (cp.
Palander 1941, p.7 n.3). He describes the
difficulties in interpreting Monetary Equilibrium in
the following way:

> "This partly-revised English edition gives
> the impression that it is a presentation of
> what Myrdal of 1939 considers Myrdal of
> 1932, if this latter had thought correctly,
> ought to have considered that Wicksell ought
> to have thought in 1898, if Wicksell had
> then thought correctly and had possessed the
> theoretical apparatus possessed by Myrdal
> in 1932" (ibid., p.7).

that Myrdal was trying to sort out the implicit
notion of monetary equilibrium <u>behind</u> Wicksell's
normal rate made it necessary to use the procedure of
'immanent criticism'.

1.2.1 - Immanent criticism.

Myrdal's expository device of 'immanent
criticism' has the following meaning:

> "I accept for the moment the main line
> inside the Wicksell-Lindahlian theoretical
> explanation and the arguments are developed
> under the assumption that this explanation
> is fundamentally correct" (ibid., p.193; cp.
> Myrdal 1939, p.31).

However, in the German and English versions most of
the explicit references to Lindahl are deleted,
probably because Lindahl's works were not translated
by the time of the publication of the German version.
(Nevertheless, there are still several arguments in
both versions which could only be understood as a
criticism of Lindahl.) In the Swedish edition it is
explicit that Myrdal used Lindahl's <u>The Rate of
Interest</u> as a starting-point (cp. ibid., p.192). In
fact, Myrdal's main aim was to refute Lindahl's
critique and to show that Wicksell's ideas on
monetary equilibrium might, if properly developed,
still be used inside monetary theory (cp. ibid.,
p.193; cp. Myrdal 1939, pp.30-31).
Even if Myrdal pursues an immanent criticism it
is natural that he considers himself to have made
some <u>positive contributions</u>:

> "the main purpose of the subsequent analysis
> is to <u>include anticipations in the monetary
> system</u>" (Myrdal 1939, p.32; cp. p.131).

However, this 'main purpose' was not even mentioned
in the Swedish version, though it might have been
obvious for the Swedish reader that Myrdal was now
actually trying to apply the ideas from his
dissertation. It seems that Myrdal made this
addition in an attempt to differentiate his work from
Keynes' <u>Treatise</u> and Hayek's <u>Prices and Production</u>

and <u>Monetary Theory and the Trade Cycle</u>, but it does
not entail any critique of Lindahl. As a corollary
to the role of anticipations Myrdal estimates that
one of his chief contributions "is to have originated
the concepts <u>ex post</u> and <u>ex ante</u>" (ibid., p.47). But
these notions were first introduced in the German
edition, although they were already implied in the
Swedish version.

1.2.2 - The role of monetary equilibrium.

Myrdal studies the properties of an <u>actual</u> price
situation so as to determine, from a practical point
of view, whether monetary equilibrium prevails. This
illustrates the role of this notion as a <u>criterion</u>
for judging whether a cumulative process is going on
or not (cp. ibid., p.35). Consequently a cumulative
process is defined "as a departure from a position of
equilibrium" (ibid., p.34; cp. p.29; p.30). Thus, it
will come into existence and persist "<u>because</u> a
certain actual situation does not satisfy the
equilibrium condition" (ibid., p.35). This is the
reason why Myrdal insists that Lindahl implicitly
must adopt the concept of monetary equilibrium in
spite of his critique of the normal rate, because an
analysis of the cumulative process implies the
application of this notion (cp. ibid., p.31 n.2).

Monetary equilibrium also has an <u>instrumental
significance</u>, which is apparent from Myrdal's attempt
to find empirically measurable notions:

> "It must be our endeavour to formulate the
> condition of monetary equilibrium in such a
> way as to contain observable and measurable
> magnitudes. Otherwise any practical
> application of the theory to the analysis of
> an actual process is excluded or at least
> made very difficult" (ibid., p.47).

Hence, Myrdal considers it possible to gauge the
existence of monetary equilibrium by looking at
statistical estimates of the equilibrium conditions.
This is, of course, necessary if monetary equilibrium
is to be used as a norm for monetary policy.

But before using monetary equilibrium as a criterion it is necessary to understand the difference between monetary equilibrium and other equilibrium concepts. It is important to realize that monetary equilibrium is of an 'indifferent' type in Wicksell's sense, which means that it is unstable, and there is no tendency towards this type of equilibrium position once it has been disturbed (cp. ibid., pp.35-36).[4] Hence, <u>Myrdal is obviously not thinking of monetary equilibrium as a long run equilibrium.</u> Secondly, Myrdal points out specifically that monetary equilibrium refers to a

----

4 Wicksell analysed the difference between a <u>stable equilibrium</u> and a <u>neutral/indifferent equilibrium.</u> The former notion refers to the following type of equilibrium for relative prices:

"Every movement away from the position of equilibrium sets forces in operation - on a scale that increases with the extent of the movement - which tend to restore the system to its original position, and actually succeed in doing so, though some oscillations may intervene" (Wicksell 1936, p.101; cp. Wicksell 1935, pp.196-197).

While the latter concept is related to the equilibrium level of the absolute money prices:

"The general price level ... is, on the assumption of a monetary system of unlimited elasticity, in a position of, so to speak, an indifferent equilibrium ... if forces of sufficient strength to drive it from its position of equilibrium are brought into play, it has no tendency to resume that position, but if forces which set it in motion - i.e. in this case the difference between the normal or real rate and the actual loan rate - cease to operate they will remain in a new and also indifferent position of equilibrium" (Wicksell 1935, p.197; cp. Wicksell 1936, p.101).

price situation 'in a non-stationary course of events'. If a stationary economy is considered, then the conditions for monetary equilibrium as well as some additional conditions are fulfilled "ex hypothesi" (ibid., p.39) and the specificity of monetary equilibrium vanishes. Thus, <u>the notion of the cumulative process and thereby monetary equilibrium must be related to dynamic conditions</u>:

> "Wicksell's theory ... is an attempt to analyse a <u>dynamic</u> process and it therefore necessarily contains the idea that it is possible to test whether monetary equilibrium is ruling <u>at any moment</u> of such a process which process, of course, is not, and cannot be, stationary" (ibid., p.39).

However, in order to understand the meaning behind the statement that 'monetary equilibrium rules at a point of time' we have to look at the dynamic method used by Myrdal.

2 - The dynamic method.

2.1 - The instantanenous analysis.
According to Myrdal, monetary equilibrium implies the following dynamic method:

> "the concept of monetary equilibrium always concerns the <u>tendency of a situation at a particular point of time</u>. The quantities involved must be defined <u>ex ante</u>" (ibid., p.116).[5]

The crux of Myrdal's argument is to find the conditions which these tendencies have to fulfil for monetary equilibrium to hold. This is in fact the same as determining the content of monetary

----

5 Sections 14 and 15 in Chapter 5 are added to the German edition and such a clear statement of Myrdal's dynamic method is not to be found in the Swedish version (cp. Myrdal 1931, p.195).

equilibrium, which Myrdal considers to be "the primary task of monetary theory" (ibid., p.41). Given the instrumental character of monetary equilibrium it should then be possible to characterize every actual situation with reference to these equilibrium conditions, which is obviously of great advantage since monetary equilibrium implies "a definite programme of monetary policy" (ibid.).

The dynamic method proposed by Myrdal looks akin to Lundberg's discussion of finding the tendencies at each point in time (cp. sect. V:3:2). Furthermore, in a direct critique of Myrdal's treatment of anticipations in his dissertation, Lundberg put forward the following idea on how to incorporate anticipations:

> "As a starting-point there appears a given price situation with inherent discrepancies and tensions as a motivation for a certain determined way of acting by each individual" (Lundberg 1930, p.156).

This sounds similar to Myrdal's construction, where the tendencies are represented by ex ante plans ruling at a point of time. But Myrdal makes no reference to Lundberg's article so it is difficult to gauge Lundberg's direct influence on Myrdal. However, we know that Lindahl sent an offprint of Lundberg's article to Myrdal (cp. Letter from Lindahl to Myrdal, 16 February 1931), and it is certainly possible that Myrdal read this article before he started to work on Monetary Equilibrium in the autumn of 1931.

Myrdal denotes his dynamic method as an 'instantaneous' analysis (cp. Myrdal 1939, p.43) and it stands in the following relation to what he calls 'the real dynamic problem':

> "The dynamic problem proper of the movement during a period can be discussed only if one starts with the tendencies which exist in a certain price situation, tendencies which are determined by the anticipations dominant in this situation" (ibid., p.121; cp. pp.41-42; p.43).

Hence, the instantaneous analysis has to be developed prior to the proper dynamic problem, and this relation between the two methods is identical to the one between the two dynamic methods analysed in Myrdal's dissertation (cp. sect. III:3). Furthermore, it is possible to see a connection between the instantaneous analysis and the dynamic method developed in the dissertation, because both methods analyse relations at a point in time. However, there is one major difference: <u>the dynamic equilibrium defined in the dissertation determines a long run position while monetary equilibrium determines an 'indifferent' position.</u>

Myrdal focuses his attention on developing an instantaneous analysis, and he thinks that he can avoid discussing a sequence analysis. However, if monetary equilibrium is to be used as a criterion for determining whether any given situation will develop into a cumulative process, then a sequence analysis is necessary. That is, it is not enough to say that the actual situation does not fulfill the conditions of monetary equilibrium because even if disequilibrium rules for the first period, it is still necessary to have some idea about the formation of anticipations for the next period in order to show that the process is cumulative and not just a temporary disturbance.[6]

If we compare Myrdal's instantaneous analysis with the dynamic methods developed by Lindahl before the publication of <u>Monetary Equilibrium</u>, then his method bears a certain similarity to Lindahl's notion of temporary equilibrium. This is because Myrdal's second equilibrium condition shows that monetary equilibrium is only determined for the coming period despite the fact that the income concept used spans several subsequent periods (cp. sect. 3:3). Hence, even if monetary equilibrium rules for the first period that does not imply that it will rule for the

----

6 It is conspicuous that this problem was carefully analysed by Lindahl, who asserted that a cumulative process with inelastic expectations may end up in a new stationary equilibrium while elastic expectation would lead to a crisis (cp. Lindahl 1939C, Ch.II sect.7).

forthcoming periods. This means that a _latent disequilibrium_ may exist in exactly the same manner as with temporary equilibrium (cp. sect. IV:2:3b). At the same time, Myrdal has made a great advance on Lindahl, since via the introduction of the notions of ex ante and ex post he can even analyse a disequilibrium for the initial period. Therefore, Myrdal does not have to use an equilibrium approach as was pursued by Lindahl.

2.2 - Ex ante and ex post.

In this context Myrdal introduces the famous ex ante/ex post calculus, which has the following meaning:

> "The first method of computation is 'bookkeeping' about what has actually happened during a complete period, the second mode of computation is a business calculation founded on an estimation of what will happen in the future [i.e. a relation between realized and anticipated results]" (Myrdal 1939, p.54; p.46; p.124).

Even if the ex ante anticipations are the driving force in the dynamic process, the ex post results do still play a role, since "as a basis for the ex ante calculations, the ex post recorded experiences may regularly be decisive" (ibid., p.55).[7] Hence, compared to the dissertation Myrdal has now arrived

----

7 Myrdal in fact already refers to an ex post notion in his dissertation. He states there, that when an enterprise or a single investment is accomplished, it is possible to estimate "a result ... in the sense of the _difference_ between realized incomes and costs" (Myrdal 1927, p.47; cp. p.67; pp.117-118). But it is not necessary to await the end of an enterprise for estimating the result, since it is possible "to include on the credit side the capital value of the firm at the point of time" (ibid.), which seems to be a straightforward ex post notion where there is always an equality ex post and the balancing factors are profits and losses.

at a better understanding of the foundation of ex ante anticipations, and it is no longer the notion of "future changes exercising effects on the economic process long before they actually take place" (Myrdal 1927, p.9). Thus, Lundberg's critique has been taken ad notam (cp. Note 11 Ch. III).

The dynamic method is constructed in such a way that there is always an ex post balance. However, from the point of view of monetary analysis, the interesting problem is to analyse "the very changes during the period which are required to bring about this ex post balance" (Myrdal 1939, p.121; italics omitted). These changes must be the result of anticipations which are mutually inconsistent, or due to exogenous changes during the period. However, this is never explicitly stated by Myrdal since "the intervening changes" are simply referred to as "the deviations from earlier expectations" (ibid., p.122).[8] The intervening disturbances lead to changes in the anticipations, which then determine the ex post formulations in respect of the outgoing period. Thus the analysis has first to localize the cause of the disturbance, which is to be found among the ex ante anticipations, and then to analyse the elements which make up the changes in the ex post anticipations (cp. ibid., p.46; p.116).[9] It is important to notice that the ex post notions also contain anticipatory elements relating to forthcoming periods, but the results of the changes in anticipations cancel out in the ex post calculus (cp. sect. 4:3:1). Therefore the intervening changes are only made up of realized changes during the period, and these changes are deduced from the differences between ex ante anticipations and ex post (realized) evaluations of the same phenomena.

----

8 We have already seen in the analysis of Myrdal's dissertation that he never stated that an equilibrium situation required congruent anticipations and that a disturbance of an existing equilibrium must be considered as an exogenous change (cp. sect. III:3). 9 We are here excluding exogenous disturbances during the period since this type of disturbance can not be anticipated, and it has therefore no influence on whether monetary equilibrium (ex ante) exists or not.

It was precisely the insufficient analysis of these changes in Lindahl's method, without mentioning Lindahl's name in the German and English editions, that was criticized by Myrdal, since by "dividing time into a number of short equilibrium periods during which no changes occur" (ibid., p.122) the intervening changes can not even be comprehended (cp. sect. IV:2:4). Myrdal (and Lundberg) had thereby hit the weak point in Lindahl's method, even if Myrdal gives no details (i.e. that intervening changes like the savings paradox can not really exist if temporary equilibrium holds). Hence, the development of the notions of ex ante and ex post, and the concomitant analysis of the intervening changes, made it possible to come out of the strait-jacket of the equilibrium approach implied by the notion of temporary equilibrium.

3 - Myrdal's analysis of Wicksell's three conditions for monetary equilibrium.

It is necessary to make a detailed analysis of the conditions of monetary equilibrium so as to discover the precise meaning of this concept and its corollary, the normal rate of interest. Without such an analysis we can not come to grips with Myrdal's discussion of the equilibrating mechanism between savings and investment in a cumulative process, since Myrdal then actually applies his version of monetary equilibrium. We will also see that the debate between Lindahl and Myrdal on the validity of the normal rate in a monetary analysis shows that none of them had yet developed a dynamic method which could really solve the problem of the normal rate.

We will first reconstruct the protracted, and sometimes opaque process which Myrdal follows in his reformulation of Wicksell's first condition for monetary equilibrium. The analysis of the second equilibrium condition shows the manner in which the first equilibrium condition has to be determined in relation to the second condition. Finally, Myrdal demonstrates that the third condition implies definite price relations, which are deduced from the first two equilibrium conditions.

3.1 - A response to Lindahl's critique of the normal rate.

Having seen the importance which Myrdal gives to the notion of monetary equilibrium, and bearing in mind the method of immanent criticism, it is easy to see why Myrdal based his exposition on an analysis of the three equilibrium conditions implied by Wicksell's analysis of the normal rate of interest.[10] Wicksell's normal rate contains according to Myrdal the following three conditions:

> "Wicksell ... defined the equilibrium position by specifying the level of the 'money rate of interest' which brings about monetary equilibrium. This equilibrium interest rate Wicksell calls the 'normal rate of interest' and determines it with reference to quantities in three different spheres of price formation: 1. Productivity of the roundabout process of production; 2. Conditions in the capital market; 3. Conditions in the commodity market. The 'normal rate of interest' must now, according to Wicksell, (1) equal the marginal technical productivity of capital (i.e. the 'real' or 'natural' rate of interest); (2) equate the supply of and demand for savings; (3) guarantee a stable price level, primarily of consumption goods. Wicksell assumes that these criteria for the normal rate of interest are equivalent - i.e. never mutually inconsistent; but he cannot prove it. His formulations are, indeed, too loose and contradictory for this

---

10 Palander has given the following apt description of Myrdal's book:

> "He also tests the usability of each of the definitions of equilibrium, with or without reformulation, as well as the possibility of their identity, and this takes up the central point of his book" (Palander 1941, p.8).

purpose. In the following I will prove that they cannot be identical: Only the first and the second of the equilibrium conditions are even consistent; they are interrelated in such a way that the first is conditioned by the second and otherwise not determined. They both correspond to the main argument which is implicit in the whole theory ... With respect to the commodity market, however, the fulfilment of these two monetary equilibrium relations means something quite different from an unchanged price level" (Myrdal 1939, pp.37-38).[11]

Thus, <u>Myrdal's purpose is a critique and restatement of the relations between these three equilibrium conditions.</u> His aim is therefore identical to Lindahl's analysis of the normal rate of interest in <u>The Rate of Interest.</u> In fact, the idea that the normal rate implies three different equilibrium conditions was first put forward by Lindahl. Hence, it is not unjustifiable to view Myrdal's whole work as a refutation of Lindahl's criticism of Wicksell, which of course is partly conceded by Myrdal in his use of the method of immanent criticism.

3.2 - The first condition of monetary equilibrium.

3.2.1 - Myrdal's reformulation of Wicksell's first equilibrium condition.

----

11 In the Swedish version the proposition was formulated in a different way:

"only two of Wicksell's equilibrium conditions, namely the first and the second, are identical." (Myrdal 1931, p.194).

We will later come back to the importance of this difference (cp. sect. 3:3).

Wicksell's first condition states that the normal rate of interest should be equal to the 'real' rate of interest. Myrdal's critique of the applicability of this condition is basically a reiteration of Lindahl's reasoning as to why it is not fruitful to use the real rate (cp. ibid., pp.49-51; sect. IV:4). Hence, the notion of the real rate can only be used in a realistic monetary analysis if, as in Lindahl's analysis, it is replaced by the notion of "an exchange value productivity" (ibid., p.51, italics omitted).

We will now analyse in detail the steps which lead to Myrdal's reformulation of the first equilibrium condition, since his arguments are not very clear. Myrdal denotes the exchange value productivity (y_1) as the yield of real capital, which is calculated at a point in time and extends for a period of time (cp. ibid., p.54). From the point of view of the cumulative process it is the ex ante yield which is the interesting factor, since it is the expected profit which spurs the investment decisions. The expected yield is estimated in the following manner:

"the ratio between the net return of a particular capital good and its capital value in order that it can be compared with the money rate of interest - which is necessary in Wicksell's theoretical structure. This net return [(e) for a unit period] must, for the same reasons, be calculated in such a way that the property value, represented by the capital value, remains constant. Otherwise the net return contains not only an amount corresponding to interest but also an item of amortization" (ibid., p.55; cp. Myrdal 1931, p.201 n.6).[12]

Hence, it is implied that any ex ante calculation must take into consideration anticipated changes in the value of capital, i.e. appreciations and depreciations, which are added to or subtracted from the net income in order "to make net returns (=income) by definition congruent with the notion of interest" (ibid., p.97; cp. p.56). The calculation of this term (d) is done "most simply by taking the difference of the capital values at this point and the next point of time" (ibid., p.57; cp. p.58).[13]

Thus, the expected yield of real capital is formulated as follows: $y_1=e/c_1$.[14] The capital value for existing real capital is now defined as "the discounted sum of all future gross incomes [b] minus operating costs [m]" (ibid., p.62):

$$c_1 = (b_1-m_1)/(1+i_1) + (b_2-m_2)/[(1+i_1)(1+i_2)] + \ldots$$

$$=\Sigma\ (b_{1+t}-m_{1+t})/[\ldots(1+i_t)(1+i_{1+t})]\ (t = 0,\ldots,T).[15]$$

Anticipated depreciation for the forthcoming period is $d_1=c_1-c_2$, where

$$c_2 = \Sigma\ (b_{1+t}-m_{1+t})/[\ldots(1+i_t)(1+i_{1+t})]\qquad (t = 1,\ldots,T)$$

i.e. $d_1 = (b_1-m_1)-i_1c_1 \Rightarrow i_1c_1 = (b_1-m_1)-d_1$

----

12 In the rest of his argument Myrdal does not refer to a paricular capital good, since any net investment always becomes tied up with the existing real capital of the firm and mosts costs and revenues have therefore a joint character. He takes instead the firm itself as the smallest unit of price formation, since "price formation within a firm does not exist and imputation is indeterminate" (Myrdal 1939, p.74).
13 Capital gains and losses are excluded since by definition they represent deviations from the currently hold anticipations and "can therefore have influence only on the estimate of the yield which is made after their occurrence" (Myrdal 1939 p.56; cp. pp.59-60).
14 c_1= the value of existing real capital at the time of calculation.
15 i_t= the money rate of interest in period t.

But e is defined as equal to $b_1-(m_1+d_1)$ so $e=i_1c_1$ => $c_1=e/i_1$ and $i_1=y_1$. Therefore, Myrdal reaches the disturbing conclusion:

> "the capital value is thus equal to the capitalized value of a perpetual net return of the size of the net return of the next unit period ... The capital value from this standpoint is in other words only a price reflection of the two magnitudes: Net return and 'market rate of interest' ... This means among other things that there is always and necessarily a conformity between the yield thus defined and the interest rate in the market; for capital value and net return are defined in such a way that they must constantly fulfil this equation" (ibid., pp.62-63).

However, this seems to endanger the whole idea of the cumulative process, as this process is started by a difference between the normal rate and the money rate of interest. But the arguments above are, according to Myrdal, related "only to the real capital already existing" (ibid., p.64). This is evident from the Swedish version where Myrdal starts to discuss the yield ex post for didactical reasons (cp. Myrdal 1931, p.200), and also from such expressions as: the net return for the period should be defined so "the property value ... remains constant" (Myrdal 1939, p.55), or "the value of the principal remains unchanged" (ibid., p.62).[16] On the other hand, in

----
16 By 'unchanged property value' or 'constant value
of the principal' it must be understood that we look
for a net yield for the period, e_t, which is such that
if it is paid out every year for an indefinite
period, its capital value will be the <u>same</u> as the
capital value of the actually anticipated returns for
all periods, b_t-m_t t=1 ... T. That is to say, the
latter, which could vary and perhaps only last for a
definite period of time, is simply transformed into a
constant payment which lasts for ever (cp. Frisch
1935, p.14):

$$e_t/(1+i_t) + e_t/[(1+i_t)(1+i_{t+1})] + \ldots \text{ ad infinitum}$$

$$= (b_t-m_t)/(1+i_t) + \ldots + (b_{t+T})/[(1+i_t)\ldots(1+i_{t+T})]$$

$$= c_t$$

and if: $i_t = i_{t+1}$, etc.; then $e_t/i_t = c_t$.

$-e_t+(b_t-m_t)=d_t$ is set aside to a sinking fund. The
same result is thus arrived at from the way we have
defined depreciation. That means that unchanged
property value is <u>not sufficient</u> for always having
$i_t=y_t$, while the definition of depreciation is
<u>sufficient</u> and it also implies that the property
value is constant.

The idea of a constant property value is also used by
Hicks in his definition of income:

> "The purpose of income calculations in
> practical affairs is to give people an
> indication of the amount which they can
> consume without impoverishing themselves.
> Following out this idea, it would seem that
> we ought to define a man's income as the
> maximum value which he can consume during a
> week, and still expect to be as well off at
> the end of the week as he was at the
> beginning" (Hicks 1946, p.172; cp. p.174).

Myrdal's definition of (e) corresponds to what Hick's
denotes the 'standard stream' (cp.ibid., p.184).

Wicksell's theory the effect of the difference between the two rates "is precisely that it stimulates investment, i.e., construction of new capital" (ibid., p.64). In calculating the yield it is not therefore the existing real capital which matters but "plans for new construction" (ibid., p.65). We have therefore to look at the yield of planned investments (y_2) [17], which is defined in the following way:

"the ratio between the net return on the projected real investments and the cost of their production" (ibid., italics omitted).

The net return on the planned investment is defined in the same manner as above, i.e. $e=i_1c_2$, while the cost of production (r_2) "means the cost as anticipated at the moment in question" (ibid.). Hence, $y_2=e/r_2 \Rightarrow y_2=(i_1c_2)/r_2$. Monetary equilibrium signifies that $i_1=y_2$ which implies that $c_2=r_2$ and this is a genuine conditional relation. Myrdal's reconstruction of the first equilibrium conditions amounts in the end to the fact that the anticipated capital value of the investment must be equal to the

---

[17] y_2 no longer relate to the expected yield in the second period, but from now on refers to the planned investment. In the same manner c_2 now refers to the expected capital value of the new investment.

anticipated cost of the new investment.[18] This reconstruction is not really a critique of Lindahl's formulation of the first equilibrium condition, but it has more the character of a development of Lindahl's argument, which takes into consideration the problem of depreciation.

So far the analysis has only discussed the yield for a single firm or a specific investment, but "an important general assumption implicit in the Wicksellian theory is that the natural rate of interest is the same for all firms in the economy" (ibid., p.67). Furthermore, the entrepreneurs start to invest as soon as there arises a difference between the real rate and the money rate. Hence, in equilibrium the yield of all planned investments must be the same and equal to the loan rate of interest. Myrdal considers this to be a 'generous' interpretation, but it is obvious that this is Wicksell's intention, since it is a necessary

---

18 Shackle has proposed that what was wrong with the first formula was not that Myrdal was considering existing real capital instead of planned investment, but that he was trying to compare "capital value with itself instead of with the construction cost of the equipment; that same equipment which, when it has been constructed, possesses or will possess this capital value" (Shackle 1967, p.108). However, one must obviously compare capital value with itself when it is a question of keeping the value of the real capital, or its property value, intact at the end of the period, which is not an investment decision but an estimation of what can be taken out during the period, i.e. the net return, and what has to be added, i.e. depreciation, to a sinking fund which gives interest. Therefore Shackle is wrong in asserting that "the notion of depreciation, or value change, is needless and out of place in the sort of calculation that Myrdal really seeks" (ibid., p.105), since in this first instance of Myrdal's argument it is a question of keeping the property value intact. Though Shackle is partly correct, it seems to be a meaningless detour, in which Myrdal probably landed because in the Swedish edition he started to discuss the yield ex post.

condition for having an equilibrium in a marginal analysis. This shows on the contrary Myrdal's weakness in working with average quantities for c_2, r_2 etc., while in a marginal analysis the assumption of profit maximization gives a determinate volume of investment, i.e. where the marginal yield is equal to the rate of interest (cp. Palander 1941, pp.27-29).

3.2.2 - Practical considerations concerning Myrdal's reformulation.

The relation above gives the theoretically precise formulation of the first equilibrium condition, but for practical reasons, like the insurmountable difficulties in measuring the planned yield (cp. Myrdal 1939, p.69), Myrdal now wants to reformulate this condition in the following way:

> "to replace the net return on the planned investments by the net return on the existing real capital. We have then also to replace the cost of production of the planned investments by the cost of reproduction of existing real capital" (ibid., p.66).

The equilibrium condition then boils down to an equality between the capital value of the existing real capital (c_2) and the cost of reproduction of the same capital (r_1). The only difference between the two formulations is that the anticipated cost of production of the new investment does not have to be estimated in the new formulation, instead we have to calculate the cost of reproduction of existing real capital. However, even this last term is an ex ante conception (cp. ibid., p.71) so there does not seem to be any obvious advantage in this reformulation. Myrdal now gives an additional backing for his claim that the new formula is more practical, namely, that the problems of the money rate and the net return are "adequately represented by the actual capital values" (ibid.). This is true if the 'actual capital values' are easier to gauge, and Myrdal consequently assumes that they have "a market value" (ibid., p.73), i.e. a price on an existing market, while the expected value of new capital exists "only in the calculations of the entrepreneurs" (ibid.).

In the Wicksellian theory the new more practical formula will, according to Myrdal, have the following consequences for the whole economy:

"that in equilibrium there would be an equality between c_1 and r_1 in all undertakings and that in disequilibrium the difference between the two magnitudes would everywhere be the same. Neither of these two statements holds true" (ibid., p.72; cp. p.76).

However, the first proposition is true within Wicksell's marginal analysis. The second is to the best of our knowledge neither explicitly nor implicitly stated by Wicksell. A corollary of this, according to Myrdal, is Wicksell's idea "that the entrepreneurs' activity commences immediately a difference in the interest rate appears, however small it may be" (ibid., p.76). But in the formal example in Interest and Prices the reaction is not immediate, since there will only be a tendency to increase investments (cp. Wicksell 1936, p.143).

3.2.3 - Wicksell's first condition and a dynamic economy.

Myrdal's critique of Wicksell as outlined in the section above plays an important role in his argument. It is his belief that the same profit margin (q), i.e. c_1-r_1, in different firms leads to different amounts of investments. It is even possible that positive and negative profit margins for different firms may exist in equilibrium (cp. ibid., pp.76-77), which, incidentally, shows that Myrdal is once again not following a marginal analysis. Hence, the equilibrium condition for the economy as a whole is not just a simple summation where the profit margins for all firms add up to zero, but a summation where the so-called 'coefficients of investment-reaction' function as

126   Chapter 6

weights.[19]

---

19 These weights are defined in the following way:

> "the ratio between the amount of net <u>new</u>
> investment ... which it decides to
> undertake during a unit period and the
> amount of prospective invest-profit (c_1-r_1)
> necessary to induce this investment"
> (Myrdal 1939, p.78).

(Note continued on following page).

Myrdal should therefore have criticized Wicksell not
for having made inaccurate statements but rather for
making impractical ones. In the Swedish version the
critique is only related to Wicksell's "untenable
abstract assumption for empirical use" (Myrdal 1931,
p.262).

Palander is right in criticizing Myrdal for his
confusing use of the formula $Q=\sum (c_1-r_1)$:

> "it is hard to understand how the same
> mathematical expression, Q, can be at one
> and the same time an expression for the
> oppurtunity or _inducement_ to invest and an
> expression for the _investment_ actually
> arising out of this inducement. As a matter
> of fact, Q is nothing other than the
> investment obtaining in a certain
> situation" (Palander 1941, p.26; cp. Myrdal
> 1939, p.80).

Although this problem could be solved by taking
Myrdal's investment function for an individual firm
as $r_2^i =f^i(q^i)$ (cp. Myrdal 1939, p.64; p.78; p.83), and
for the whole economy it is obviously $R_2=\sum f^i(q^i)$,
Myrdal wants to formulate the latter as $R_2=f(Q)$,
where $Q=\sum q^i$, i.e. an aggregate investment function.
Since "monetary theory takes a summary view of the
whole price system, we had then to bring these
different profit margins together into an expression
for the profit situation in the system as a whole"
(ibid., p.80). Now Q happens to be the same thing as
the value of the aggregate net new investment, since
the weights are defined as $w^i=c_2^i/q^i$, i.e. $w^iq^i=r_2^i$,
and the whole idea of weighting seems to be a detour,
because we just end up aggregating net investment for
all firms. However, in this context, Myrdal is
discussing _practical_ problems with a theoretical
formula, and it seems from the remarks on p.79 that he
was actually groping towards a formula, where it
would only be necessary to know the weights for "a
number of ["important", Myrdal 1931, p.263] branches
of the economy" (ibid., p.79) for calculating the
aggregate new investment.

Even if we use Myrdal's reformulation of the first equilibrium condition as a weighted summation, in Wicksell's discussion it would still imply that "aggregate net new investment must be zero" (Myrdal 1939, p.80). This is because the basic idea underlying Wicksell's formulation of the equilibrium condition is the assumption that the new net investment is zero when there is no profit margin, which means that "the entrepreneurs are just exactly replacing the old outworn real capital but do not endeavour to make new investment" (ibid.). At the same time, since Wicksell's analysis is supposed "to furnish an analytical instrument for studying what happens in a dynamic system subject to all sorts of changes" (ibid., p.81). Hence, it is necessary to enquire what a 'dynamic state' implies for the first equilibrium condition. The most important change is that "in a dynamic state new saving cannot be supposed to be zero" (ibid., pp.81-82), and there is even "no reason why in monetary equilibrium saving should be zero" (ibid., p.82). If zero net investment were now to correspond to the first equilibrium condition while net savings were still greater than zero, then the second equilibrium condition would obviously not be fulfilled. Therefore Myrdal concludes:

"the basic idea of identifying monetary equilibrium with a zero-profit situation cannot be upheld and that, consequently, even the equilibrium formula given last [Q=0] must be remodeled in order to correspond to the implicit function of the equilibrium concept in Wicksell's monetary theory, which throughout has been my criterion" (ibid., p.82).[20]

This remodelling of the first equilibrium condition leads to Myrdal's analysis of the second equilibrium condition, since the first condition has to be defined in relation to the second. However, this is an addition to the Swedish and German editions where the second and third conditions "could only be accepted, if they completely coincide with or are consistent with the first one" (Myrdal 1931, p.207). The implication is that the real rate plays an independent role, which is a critique of Lindahl's position (cp. sect. IV:4). We will come back to the importance of this change between the editions in the next section.

3.3 - The second equilibrium condition.

Wicksell's second condition relates to the capital market. The money rate of interest is said to be 'normal' if investment is equal to saving. We will first look at Myrdal's definition of saving, net income and investment, before discussing the second condition itself.

Saving is defined "as a part of income, namely that part which is not used in the demand for consumption goods" (Myrdal 1939, p.90, italics omitted). This definition is used in conscious opposition to the idea of 'real' saving, which implies that the decision to save means a direct transfer of factors of production used for consumption goods to the production of investment goods, and the 'real' saving is by definition equal to real investment and Wicksell's problem can not even

---

20 There is a snag in Myrdal's critique of Wicksell, since in Lectures the latter in his analysis of the cumulative process takes positive net investment and net savings into consideration (cp. Wicksell 1935, pp.11-12; pp.192-193). In fact, Myrdal has once again misunderstood the marginalist character of Wicksell's analysis, since in a dynamic analysis Wicksell would assume that net investment would continue until the expected value of the marginal net investment is equal to its costs of production, which corresponds to Myrdal's zero profit margin. There is thus positive intramarginal net investment.

arise.[21]   Myrdal   therefore   concludes   that   "the
distinction [between savings and real investment] <u>has</u>
to be made since Wicksell's monetary theory deals
with an agreement or a discrepancy between the two"

----

21 Myrdal's discussion of the above definition is
based on his criticism of Wicksell's definitions of
savings and investment, since the latter "has never
really defined what he meant by saving and investing"
(ibid., pp.87-88). But this is definitely incorrect,
because there is no confusion on Wicksell's side with
his   definitions   <u>in   relation</u>   to   the   cumulative
process. However, in relation to other problems, for
example Wicksell's discussion of an increase in money
savings, it seems that savings are almost the same as
'real' savings. In this case he assumes that there is
hardly any friction in transferring resources from
the consumer goods sector to the investment goods
sector, i.e. he presupposes "an adaptability and a
degree   of   foresight   in   the   reorganization   of
production which is far from existing in reality"
(Wicksell 1935, p.193; cp. pp.11-12). In another
case, the confusion, for the non-attentive reader, is
due to the fact that he is discussing "credit as
between man and man" (ibid.) and not an economy with
organized credit.

Chapter 6   131

(ibid., p.89).[22]

Myrdal sets income equal to the net return (e) which depends on expectation of future prices and quantities. It is necessary to rely on expectations, in particular, because of the existence of durable goods whose income can only be estimated by some imputation method, i.e. the size of income must be an anticipated amount (cp. ibid., pp.93-95). Furthermore, it is necessary to use the imputation procedure to determine income "if one wants to understand by income something different from mere consumption" (ibid., p.93), which is identical to Lindahl's reasoning (cp. Note 18 Ch. IV).

Investment means here real investment. It is a gross magnitude, i.e. "includes 're-investment' as well as 'new investment'" (Myrdal 1939, p.98), since it is not possible to separate from total real

---

22 If this distinction between saving and investment is as crucial as Myrdal asserts, and he even elevates it to be "the essence of the modern monetary theory which starts with Wicksell" (Myrdal 1939, p.90; italics omitted), then he is bound to add that "it might seem strange that Wicksell did not emphasize it more explicitly" (ibid., p.88). Wicksell's lacuna might be explained by the fact that in his examples of the cumulative process the initial changes come either from the banks and influence the credit conditions or from the entrepreneurs because of changes in the real rate of interest. Nowhere does he mention the influence of ex ante changes in the amount of savings from individuals, and the examples in Interest and Prices show that an increased demand for money from the entrepreneurs is met by credit expansion of the banks and only later on is the expansion backed by increased deposits from the capitalists (cp. Wicksell 1936, pp.144-145). Hence, it seems that Wicksell did not find this relation between the amounts of savings and investment as important as the relation between the loan rate and the real rate (here the same as the expected rate of profit), since he assumed that equality between the two rates implies that the loan rate is normal. This was critized by Lindahl (cp. sect. IV:4), while Myrdal, in his turn, attacked Lindahl's position.

investment what is supposed to be new investment and what is re-investment when depreciation and appreciation are value-aggregates (cp. ibid.; p.81).

The second equilibrium condition is then formulated as follows:

> "The money rate of interest is normal if it brings about an equality between gross real investment on the one side and saving plus total anticipated value-change of the real capital, i.e. plus expected decreases in value minus increases in value of the existing real capital on the other side" (ibid., p.96; italics omitted).

As a formula it is written: $R_2=W=(S+D)$.[23] Myrdal has then a long and confusing discussion of the meaning of D (cp. ibid., Ch. V sect. 3 and 5), which is due to the fact that he never formulated the meaning of a perpetual net income as clearly as we did above (cp. Note 16). But it is also obvious that the supply of gross saving in each period is made up of S, which comes from the net aggregate income $\sum e^i$ and could be called net saving, and aggregate depreciation (D), where $d^i=(b^i-m^i)-e^i$. Therefore Myrdal is correct in remarking that free capital disposal is free in the following sense:

> "W, is 'free' from the standpoint of the private entrepreneur in the sense that, aside from the saved part of his income, and without selling or mortgaging his real capital, he can dispose of exactly such a part of the invested property value as corresponds to the amount of depreciation minus appreciation" (ibid., p.97).

But Myrdal is never explicit as to the meaning of 'dispose'. If we stick to his perpetual net income (e) we have to assume that D is saved for the sinking fund (cp. Note 16), if the property value is to

---

23 R_2= gross real investment.
   W= waiting.
   D= depreciation - appreciation.

remain intact. On the other hand if D is less than zero (i.e. an appreciation) then D has to be consumed, otherwise the property value will increase. This is hinted at in Myrdal's own analysis, since he speaks of S as "the increase or decrease of his property" (ibid.), which should imply that the function of D is to keep the property value intact.

Myrdal's chapter on the second equilibrium condition is rounded off in the Swedish and German version with an algebraic exercise, which shows that the two equilibrium conditions "in general correspond to each other" (Myrdal 1931, p.231; cp. Myrdal 1933A, p.431). Myrdal considered it to be virtually the most important result of his analysis "to have shown the assumptions which lie behind the correspondence between the first and the second equilibrium equations of Wicksell" (ibid., p.233). This could be accomplished because Myrdal had given an exact formulation of these equations. Hence, Myrdal has fulfilled one of the tasks he set up in the very beginning of Monetary Equilibrium:

> "From Lindahl's own starting-point a following up of Wicksell's ideas in relation to the 'natural' and the 'normal' rate should really have culminated in a more complete analysis and co-ordination of the profitability theory on the one side and the capital market theory on the other" (ibid., p.193; cp. p.194; p.213; p.222).

In Myrdal's construction an equality between the money rate (i) and the yield of planned investment (y_2) implies that waiting and gross real investments are equal and vice versa. Thus, there is a normal real rate, namely, that value of y_2 which is equal to the money rate. Therefore Myrdal is right in his critique of Lindahl, in so far as we can interpret the yield of planned investment as an investment demand curve which is independent of the current money rate, which was later conceded by Lindahl (cp. sect. IV:4). But that would still not prove, as was shown by Hammarskjöld (cp. below), that the first equilibrium condition could imply the second one, although the converse is true. Furthermore, no particular real rate could be taken as starting-point without having a money rate to compare it with.

In the English version Myrdal changed his mind. He now found that the first condition is "indeterminate per se, having a definite meaning only when determined by inference from the second formula" (Myrdal 1939, pp.115-116; cp. p.87; p.203). The exact formulation of that 'inference' is then the following:

"The profit margin which corresponds to monetary equilibrium is ... the complex of profit margins in different firms which stimulates just the amount of total investment which can be taken care of by the available capital disposal" (ibid., pp.82-83; italics omitted).

But the first formula still plays an important role, since it gives "the more intensive discussion of the causes - in terms of profitability - of the quantity of investment" (ibid. cp. p.84; p.132).

Myrdal probably changed his mind because of the critique of Hammarskjöld in Ekonomisk Tidskrift (1932). Hammarskjöld puts the relation between Wicksell's first two equilbrium conditions in a succinct form:

"To Wicksell, the normal rate must have appeared as being among other things an ordinary equilibrium price, which could be determined graphically as the point of intersection between the curves for the supply and the demand for loan capital at a given moment of price formation. The demand curve, judging from Wicksell's general starting-point, would have been conceived by him more or less as a line, with every interest rate on the price axis corresponding to a point on the quantity axis at which the marginal investment had a degree of remunerativeness equal to the .interest rate in question. When looked at in this way, the question of the relation between the interest rate that brings equilibrium on the capital market and the remunerativeness of investment disappears;

the latter factor is not on the same level as the former as a determining factor for the normal rate, and still less can the capital market condition be deduced from the condition of remunerativeness. The importance of the latter for the determination of the rate of interest is limited to deciding the form of the demand curve. Typically enough the condition of remunerativeness, seen marginally, is fulfilled wherever the point of intersection between the two curves may lie, i.e. whatever rate of interest may be normal from the point of view of the capital market" (Hammarskjöld 1932, pp.172-173; as quoted in Lindahl 1939C, pp.262-263 n.2).

If we retain Wicksell's idea of the natural rate as the primum movens (cp. Wicksell 1898, p.82), or Myrdal's version of the profit margin as constituting "the driving force in the dynamic system" (Myrdal 1939, p.108), then it is obvious that both proposals could be explained by a volatile investment demand curve disturbing monetary equilibrium. Hence, in the cumulative process the primary change "in the causal succession of Wicksell's theory is the profit margin ... determining the relation in the capital market between investment and free waiting" (ibid., p.179).

By using Hammarskjöld's formulation as an ex ante analysis it is now possible to reconcile Myrdal's position with Lindahl's position of 1930. Myrdal seems to imagine a situation where the real rate is different from the money rate at the outset, and he then criticizes Lindahl for assuming a more or less immediate tendency for the real rate to accomodate to the money rate (cp. Myrdal 1931, pp.204-209; Lindahl 1939C, p.249). But Myrdal's argument makes no sense in a marginalist analysis based on profit maximization where there is an immediate tendency for the investment plans to accomodate to the money rate at the transition point to the initial period, i.e. they take on such a value that the marginal expected profit is equal to the money rate. Lindahl could then have argued that every money rate could be considered normal, even if in several cases a change in the price level will be involved before savings are equal to investment. However, we have already shown that temporary equilibrium cannot handle an unanticipated change in the price level (cp. sect. IV:3:3:1). Instead, we would follow Myrdal and denote the normal rate as that money rate, set at a transition point, which will induce such plans for savings and investment that they balance. In fact, applying Myrdal's ex ante and ex post analysis within a temporary equilibrium framework makes sense, despite its equilibrium assumption, since Myrdal implicitly used a one-period analysis. This procedure entails that Lindahl's problem about defining a 'neutral' rate will disappear, since an ex ante equality between the plans implies not only that the price level is constant but also that it is expected to stay constant. However, we will see in the next section that Myrdal is only ahead of Lindahl as long as we look at a single period analysis.

3.4 - The third condition of monetary equilibrium.

Wicksell's third condition relates to the commodity market. The normal rate of interest is then the money rate which keeps the absolute price level of finished goods stable. Wicksell accepted this condition as giving a practical criterion for the analysis of ongoing situations (cp. Myrdal 1939, pp.128-129; Wicksell 1908, p.212; Wicksell 1966B, p.vii). However, Myrdal's formulation of the third condition takes into consideration his development of the other two conditions, and the proper construction of the third condition is then as follows:

"What does a development of the price system, in which the profit margin is kept continuously at such a level that the condition $R_2 = W$ is fulfilled, imply as to the tendency of the 'price level'?" (ibid., p.132).[24]

Myrdal's answer takes a long detour over the cases of perfect price-flexibility and complete anticipation. But here we will jump directly to his final conclusion:

"in reality there is always uncertainty about the future data, and since all reactions of price formation take time, the equilibrium conditions [the first and the second] provide because of these two reasons a definite condition for the development of the price level ... . Inasmuch as our equilibrium equations require definite price relations, they further require, on account of the different reaction patterns of different prices, the condition that the price level under monetary equilibrium must have that trend which permits fulfilment of the equilibrium price relations with the least possible change of the sticky prices" (ibid., pp.135-136; cp. p.36).[25]

Hence, Myrdal must here imply that 'the development of the price level' or 'the trend of the price movements', i.e. changes between consecutive unit periods, is more or less unique and determined by the savings and investment plans, which are made at a particular moment and run for the same number of unit periods. This seems to boil down to the simple fact that consistent anticipations obviously encompass

----

24 In the Swedish version Myrdal asks the following question:

"What does the normal rate, defined in accordance with the first equilibrium condition ... imply for the height of the price level" (Myrdal 1931, p.235).

25 Myrdal regards wages as being the most important of the sticky prices and they play a very similar role in his theory as wages do in Keynes' General Theory, namely, acting together with other sticky prices "as a restraint on the price system (Myrdal 1939, p.134; cp. sect. 4 App. I).

determinate prices. Myrdal acknowledges this tacitly, when he says that the third equilibrium condition has a <u>theoretical significance</u> because of "the fact that it makes explicit the determination of the general development of prices, which the two preceding equilibrium conditions already contain implicitly" (ibid., p.137).

Myrdal has, however, no great faith in his reconstruction of the third equilibrium condition for analytical purposes, because <u>even if the sticky prices are stable that does not tell us very much about the nature of an actual situation, since the prices could be stable and a cumulative process might still be under way, but has not yet gained enough momentum to disturb the sticky prices</u> (cp. ibid., p.141). Myrdal therefore draws the following negative conclusion about the relevance of the third equilibrium condition:

> "It is only a corollary of the earlier equilibrium formulas in a <u>special</u> aspect, and in order to yield complete determination we must rely on these earlier formulas. <u>The equilibrium character of a situation cannot, in other words, be characterized sufficiently by a mere study of the general price movements</u>" (ibid., pp.141-142).

Hence, the first two equilibrium conditions are sufficient for determining monetary equilibrium and their fulfilment is also the only practical criterion. In fact, this shows that if Myrdal's analysis is correct, then Wicksell was not wrong because he dragged normative arguments into a positive analysis (cp. ibid., p.128), but because he did not pay due consideration to inflexible prices. Myrdal's analysis of the third equilibrium condition is superior to Lindahl's, in the sense that Myrdal can argue that the problem with the neutral rate drops out if savings ex ante and investment ex ante are equal. Lindahl took up the problem with the neutral rate partly because he realized that savings and investments were always equal ex post, but he did not mention that the equilibrium could be reformulated by looking at the ex ante plans. Therefore Myrdal seems to have shown that his

reformulations of Wicksell's ideas on the normal rate
have made this rate applicable for monetary analysis,
while Lindahl thought he had shown the opposite. The
only necessary assumption for practical purposes is
that it should be possible to gauge the actual ex
ante values of the plans for savings and investment.
However, Lindahl is ahead of Myrdal since he realized
that monetary equilibrium could rule for the
immediate period, but that that is no guarantee that
the situation would be the same for periods further
ahead, i.e. a temporary equilibrium. Myrdal just did
not mention this problem, since he thought that his
method only concerned the tendencies at a point in
time, while we have seen above that he implicitly
uses a one-period analysis. Thus, Lindahl's analysis
proved implicitly that a sequence analysis was
necessary for discussing the normal rate within a
dynamic framework. We can therefore conclude that
the whole debate on the different restatements of
Wicksell's normal rate points to the fact that it is
necessary to go beyond the methods used by Lindahl
and Myrdal, i.e. temporary equilibrium and
instantaneous analysis respectively, in order to find
a method which could give a proper meaning to this
concept.

4 - The savings-investment mechanism during a
cumulative process.
We will first look at the role of an increase in
savings in Myrdal's analysis, which, as in Lindahl's
and Keynes' analyses, has a direct effect on the
demand for consumption goods. Then there follows an
analysis of Myrdal's equilibrating mechanism and its
similarities with Keynes' principle of effective
demand.

4.1 - The cumulative process.
We will not give an analysis of Myrdal's view of
the stages in a cumulative process, except for the
following figurative description of such a process:

"We have here a race of different 'price
levels': Of prices for real capital, factors
of production, and consumption goods. In

the theory is implied not only certain causal relations between them but also a given order of sequence in their movements. As long as there is a positive difference between the interest rates, capital goods hold their lead, even if single consumption goods, and possibly even more, single factors of production, especially raw materials used in the production of real capital, increase more than proportionately. If the capital value did not lead, the 'natural rate of interest' would no longer exceed the money rate of interest" (ibid., pp.27-28).

The theory implies 'certain causal relations' which guarantee the cumulative character, i.e. the demand prices of capital goods depend on the price level for consumer goods. But these relations, in their turn, imply 'a given order of sequence in their movements', which means that the price of capital goods will always keep ahead, so there is a continuous shift to more roundabout methods of production.

4.2 - The role of savings in a cumulative process.

4.2.1 - The effects of increased savings.
We will first look at an example where savings is increased, which means that "the curve of savings changes so that total saving increases" (ibid.. p.106), in a situation where monetary equilibrium rules and the money rate of interest is fixed. Free capital disposal must then increase, since the anticipations are supposed to stay the same so there are no changes in depreciation or appreciation. Myrdal now states that a downward cumulative process must ensue:

"Real investment is not directly stimulated ... It is then obvious that the increased saving immediately brings about a rupture of the monetary equilibrium in the capital market; for free capital disposal has increased, but not real investment. A

downward Wicksellian process has thus been
started. Furthermore, it is obvious that
real investments not only do not increase
but must even decrease. For increased
savings, defined to mean decreased demand
for consumption goods, necessarily bring
about some decrease in the prices of
consumption goods. This fall in prices must
itself tend to lower capital values by
influencing anticipations ... which
naturally means that real investments will
decline. Equilibrium on the capital market
is, therefore, disturbed not only by an
increase in free capital disposal but also
by a simultaneous decrease of real
investment. A downward Wicksellian process
has thus been brought about by increased
savings, where, paradoxically enough, the
increase in savings continuously results in
a decrease of real capital formation"
(ibid., pp.106-107).

There is a small snag in Myrdal's argument, namely,
the decrease in real investment can not be
simultaneous, since the fall in the prices of
consumption goods is unanticipated and take place
during a particular period and the decrease must
therefore come one period later. Thus, Myrdal has
again overlooked the necessity for a period concept.
However, the important point in this proposition is
the fact that there is no direct link from an
increase in savings to an increase in investment.
Instead, the immediate effect is on the demand for
consumption goods. But the proponents of a link
between savings and investment might argue that
Myrdal's analysis is somewhat concocted, since the
assumption of a free currency severs the link between
savings and investment and the banks can therefore
satisfy any demand for credit at the fixed interest
rate. Myrdal himself adds to a similar example that
the result only holds ceteris paribus, which partly
implies "that the money rate of interest remains
unchanged" (ibid., p.108). He therefore passes over
to an example where this ceteris paribus assumption
does not hold.

4.2.2 - The effects of increased savings when 'free currency' is not assumed.

This example of an economy already in depression is aimed at the proposition that increased savings are a way out of depression. The proposition has as its foundation the idea that the increased savings could entail "easier credit conditions, especially lower interest rates, than would have been possible without increased saving" (ibid., p.109). The lower interest rates would then halt the fall in the capital values and the real investment. Myrdal concedes that this effect "might mitigate the depression" (ibid., p.110), but it will only be an indirect effect and the direct effect of increased savings is still an immediate fall in the price level of consumption goods etc.

Myrdal goes even further, since he wants to demonstrate that the indirect effect might imply not a mitigation but an actual hastening of the downwards process. In this process, although it is actually triggered off by excess savings and even if the total available capital disposal will diminish during the downward process, the amount of real investment will fall even faster, and the excess of free capital will then be maintained. Thus, the paradox is that a continuous plethora of capital disposal will not alleviate the credit market:

> "It is this paradox of surplus capital disposal existing at the same time as an insufficient liquidity of the banking system - or the fear of insufficient liquidity - which confuses the argument so easily. But this paradox is really only apparent. The lack of liquidity is connected with the losses which the banks have made and are still making on their old commitments, and even more with the capital losses which they expect in future. Furthermore, it is related to the increased demand of the business world for liquid assets, stimulated by similar losses. 'New saving' would in itself ease the credit market under these circumstances. But since saving in its character of decreased demand for consumption goods at the same time

intensifies the depression and adds to the
primary causes of illiquidity, it is
probable, or at least possible, that the
liquidity or the feeling of liquidity of the
banks, and consequently their ability and
readiness to increase and cheapen credit, is
impaired rather than improved" (ibid.,
pp.111-112).

It seems therefore that Myrdal has made a substantial
contribution compared to Lindahl's analysis of the
case of a non-autonomous credit policy, since the
latter never discussed the effectiveness of the
indirect link via changes in the rate of interest.
However, the argument about the illiquidity of the
banks had already been developed by Ohlin in May 1932
(cp. Ohlin 1932B, pp.139-140). Furthermore, it is
not to be found in the Swedish version of Monetary
Equilibrium but it is added to the German edition.
Hence, it is possible that Myrdal's embellishment of
Lindahl's analysis occurs basically under the
influence of Ohlin, who discussed a problem which was
very topical at that time.

4.2.3 - The effects of a varying savings ratio.
We will now look at a case where the savings
ratio is changing during the cumulative process in
order to investigate whether the process may end up
in an underemployment equilibrium. Myrdal's argument
starts from the following observation:

"it must now be noted that the total
purchasing power of the society, which forms
the demand for consumption goods, shrinks
significantly less than does total income.
This means, naturally, that total saving is
reduced, not only because of the reduction
in incomes but also on account of the
smaller fraction saved" (Myrdal 1939,
p.164).

This factor depends in particular on the individuals
in the upper income brackets who are able to save,
and they will now prefer to reduce or to live on
their savings rather than to succumb to cuts in their

living standards (cp. ibid., p.166). However, whatever the reason for this factor, the effect will be a fall in the fraction saved, which will have a _direct_ influence on the equilibrium relation for the capital market by reducing the saving, i.e. W will fall. But there is also an _indirect_ influence since the maintenance of the demand for consumption goods will hinder a fall in the price level of these goods. This will bolster the capital values, because of the assumed relation between the prices of consumption goods and capital values. This, in its turn, will prop up real investment (R_2).[26] Thus, there are factors working in opposite directions on both sides of the equilibrium relation $R_2=W$. Myrdal's conclusion is then that "the fixed consuming habits have an effect tending to maintain monetary equilibrium despite the tightening of credit conditions" (ibid., p.168).

However, according to Myrdal, these forces only _tend_ to restore equilibrium in the capital market. But Myrdal also constructs the following case where a new equilibrium condition is reached and the cumulative process brought to a halt:

"If the forces maintaining consumption are strong enough and if the reaction of total real investment to a shrinking profit margin is relatively small, then the effects of the credit policy [an increase in the rate of interest has started the process] will be neutralized ... Thus after a credit contraction the business situation can under certain conditions attain quite a fair stability, at least stability for a considerable time, so that the relations fulfil the equilibrium criterion, $W=R_2$. The new equilibrium position would be characterized by the following: A largely unchanged price level for consumption goods;

----
26 Myrdal's argument is the same in the Swedish version, though there it is also mentioned that the equilibrium relation between the money rate and the natural rate will be established (cp. Myrdal 1931, p.273)

capital values which will be sufficiently
lower to correspond to the higher interest
rate, or more generally, to the tighter
credit conditions; somewhat lower wages,
particularly in the capital goods
industries; some, perhaps quite
considerable, unemployment, especially in
the capital goods industries; a production
volume restricted generally but
particularly in the capital goods
industries, implying a shorter time
structure of production; saving
sufficiently reduced to make free capital
disposal correspond to real investment,
which, according to what has been said, is
restricted on the whole and has a less
roundabout arrangement of production to
maintain" (ibid., pp.168-169).

This looks very much like Lindahl's example where the
cumulative process is a traverse from one equilibrium
situation with more roundabout methods of production
to another equilibrium situation with less roundabout
methods, and the ensuing unemployment will, as in
Lindahl's case, be due to inflexible wages.[27] This
interpretation makes sense for at least two reasons.
First, Myrdal accepted the idea that there was a
relation between the rate of interest and the time
structure of production (cp. ibid., pp.25-26).
Secondly, Myrdal had the idea that more than 'normal'
unemployment during a downward process is caused by
increased monopoly pressure from the trade unions,

----

27 Lindahl analyses a case where the money rate of
interest is increased in a situation which is in a
stationary state. The end-result will then be a
stationary state, but now with less capital and a
lower price level (cp. Lindahl 1939C, p.181). If it
is then assumed that wages are not flexible, then
Lindahl shows that unemployment will ensue during the
traverse (cp. ibid., p.185). In the new stationary
state employment will probably be lower than in the
initial situation but this is due to the higher real
wage and it is therefore in no contradiction with an
orthodox mechanism.

thereby hindering a fall in the money wage level (cp. ibid., p.144; p.157). Thus, the fall in wages cannot "be as great as would be required for unchanged unemployment" (ibid., p.164). Therefore, it seems that flexible wages might imply unchanged employment, which also was Lindahl's idea in relation to the same case.[28]

However, there is a snag in this interpretation, since Myrdal does not really analyse situations which are stationary states but on the contrary aimed at applying the notion of monetary equilibrium to situations which quite explicitly were non-stationary. This is vindicated by the fact that in the cited passage he speaks about 'a business situation' which is stable for 'a considerable time', and in the Swedish edition he uses the word 'konjunkturläget' for 'a business situation', which means a position in a business cycle. Thus, it is more correct to interpret the situation which is mentioned in the quotation as a trough in a business cycle, and the cumulative process then describes the downward phase of the cycle. Thus, Myrdal's exercise has more the character of an explanation of the factors which could stop the downward cumulative process, i.e.the fixity of consumption habits will eventually stabilize consumer goods prices which will bolster capital values etc. As a part of cumulative process the income is falling, but a situation will sooner or later be reached where the proportion of income saved has fallen even more and this will

---

28 This is hinted at by Ellis, who otherwise considers Myrdal's theory as a serious challenge to the General Theory:

"The crucial difference between Keynes and Myrdal is simply this: whereas Keynes does not utilize the downward inflexibility of wages in his theoretical explanation of equilibrium but only as a cue to monetary policy, Myrdal bases his very theory of chronic unemployment upon this rigidity and derives his economic policy directly from the theory" (Ellis 1940, p.434).

eventually entail a stable price level, which in
Lindahl's terms means that the equation E(1-s)=PQ
holds ex ante and there is no tendency for P to move.
The main difference from Lindahl's analysis is that
Myrdal has applied the cumulative process to a
business cycle analysis where a varying savings ratio
plays an important role, while Lindahl's version of
the cumulative process is either a traverse between
two stationary states or it ends up with a crisis.[29]
But this is not yet a Keynesian underemployment
equilibrium.[30]

----

29 Cp. Hicks' final verdict on Monetary Equilibrium
in his review:

> "Professor Myrdal's essay may be taken at
> its face value, as a contribution of the
> first importance towards the control of the
> Trade Cycle" (Hicks 1934, p.483).

30 It is interesting to notice that Keynes' analysis
follows the same lines as Myrdal's in the former's
Harris Foundation lecture of June 1931:

> "Now [after a continuing fall in output due
> to a fall in fixed investment] there is a
> reason for expecting an equilibrium point of
> decline to be reached. A given deficiency
> of investment causes a given decline of
> profit. A given decline of profit causes a
> given decline of output. Unless there is a
> constantly increasing deficiency of
> investment, there is eventually reached,
> therefore, a sufficiently low level of
> output which represents a kind of spurious
> equilibrium" (Keynes 1973A, pp.355-356).

But this 'spurious equilibrium' or 'equilibrium point
of decline' is obviously the lower turning point in a
business cycle and it does not imply a stable
situation with unemployment.

4.3 - Why are savings always equal to investment ex post?

Before we look at the equilibrating mechanism in Myrdal's analysis we will see what type of factors may make savings equal to investment ex post.

4.3.1 - Different gains and losses.

The starting-point is that whatever differences exist ex ante between savings and investment there has to be a balance in the ex post accounts for the following reasons:

> "In a pure book-keeping calculus after the period one has obviously 'a correspondence' between waiting and real investment: Otherwise one would have to reckon with an upsurge of claims, which have no direct or indirect correspondence to the values of real capital ... An account is always 'balanced', independent of the lack of balance which has existed during the accounting period. The book-keeping balance for the society between waiting and real investment is brought to 'balance' through certain gains and losses, which are not incomes and costs in Lindahl's and my sense, but are so treated in accounting" (Myrdal 1931, p.230 n.2; cp. Myrdal 1939, p.116).

Myrdal always speaks of these balancing factors as income changes. From all his examples that seems to imply almost exclusively changes in prices and anticipations of prices, and the only exception is if unemployed factors exist at the beginning of an upward cumulative process (cp. Myrdal, p.26).

We shall now discuss the actual character of these gains and losses. First, there are capital gains and losses:

> "They arise out of changes during the period in the anticipations of the entrepreneurs in regard to future revenues and costs" (ibid., p.60; cp. p.117).

Since the income concept is subjective and forward-

Chapter 6   149

looking, these type of unanticipated changes will, at the same time, be counted in toto as ex post increases in savings since they are added to the ex post income, as well as an ex post increase in appreciation. Hence, they will cancel out in the ex post analysis of the second equilibrium condition and "cannot [therefore] represent compensation ex post for the difference ex ante between free capital disposal and real investment" (ibid., pp.117-118). Thus, all changes in ex post values are due to changes in anticipations relating to phenomena beyond the current period and they therefore play no role in the equilibrating mechanism.

Secondly, there are gains and losses in revenues and costs:

> "They arise directly from the fact that the entrepreneurs realize different gross revenues and gross costs [during the period] than they have anticipated [at the beginning of the period]" (ibid., p.118; cp. p.61; p.117).

These gains and losses are parts of the costs and returns for the period and they are consequently part and parcel of income and saving ex post.

Thirdly, there are investment gains and losses which are divided into two groups:

> "(1) the difference between the anticipated cost of production of the real capital and the actually realized cost, (2) the difference between its capital value and its actual cost of production" (ibid., p.120).

It is evident that the first part is of the same character as gains or losses in revenues and costs. The second part has no direct effect on the ex post balance between savings and investment, since it affects both sides of the equation, and if such a difference is "added to the income of the period, the ex post saving is thereby increased by the same amount as the additional value of the investment" (ibid., p.121).[31]

4.3.2 - The equilibrating mechanism.

We will now look at an example of the functions
of gains and losses during an upward cumulative
process:

> "the gains of this kind [in revenues and
> costs] regularly exceed the losses, and in
> so far as they do not bring about a change
> in the demand for consumption goods, they
> have to be calculated ex post as saving.
> Therefore this saving in the ex post
> calculation is greater than that in the ex
> ante calculation by an amount which covers
> the difference between free capital
> disposal ex ante and (in this case) the
> greater invested capital disposal ex post"
> (ibid., p.118).

If the demand for consumption goods changes because

----

31 This notion is given an almost contradictory
definition on p.65 in Monetary Equilibrium. The
confusion is due to the fact that the version on p.65
of the last type of gains and losses does not refer
to an ex post analysis but to an ex ante analysis. In
its proper context it should be defined as the
difference between anticipated capital value for the
planned investment and its anticipated cost of
production, which is in line with the usage in the
dissertation (cp. Myrdal 1927, pp.46-47; pp.121-125).
This variety of investment gains and losses is of
fundamental importance for the ex ante calculation of
the entrepreneur, since it acts as a spur for the
investment plan (cp. Myrdal 1939, p.64). However,
the definition on p.61 and pp.119-120 of these gains
and losses refer to an ex post analysis and it is
then a difference between the capital value of the
investment goods when they are already constructed
(that is to say their realized construction costs,
which are akin to capital gains), and losses and this
difference therefore plays no direct role in the ex
post analysis.

of a variation in the savings ratio, then smaller gains and losses are required to realize an ex post balance on the capital market, since the savings ratio will rise in this case (cp. ibid., p.119), which in a Keynesian framework means that the numerical value of the multiplier is smaller.

Thus, in this case changes in nominal income due to gains or losses (unless unemployed factors exist) will act as a balancing factor. The mechanism is very similar to Lindahl's analysis (cp. sect. IV:3:3:1), and in both cases the changes in nominal income and the distribution of income will be brought about by an alteration in the price level. But it has also been shown that Lindahl could not analyse the intervening changes within temporary equilibrium, since this method presumes an equilibrium approach. Therefore, Myrdal's specific contribution to the analysis of the equilibrating mechanism is the notions of ex ante and ex post, by which it is possible to make a formal analysis of a situation where the initial ex ante plans are not consistent. Hence, the equilibrating mechanism itself is more or less the same as in Lindahl's case, i.e. income changes (made up of different gains and losses) due to changes in the price level, but by applying ex ante and ex post Myrdal showed his originality, since he used a method which could handle these intervening changes in a consistent way. Thus, he laid the foundation for the disequilibrium approach.

Myrdal does not explicitly mention how the process will keep going, i.e. its cumulative character, but in the English edition he has added that the sum of gains or losses of revenues and costs could function as "a measure of the intensity of the tendency to deviate from equilibrium" (Myrdal 1939, p.123). A positive sum would then probably imply that the investment plans are increased, so the process would be kept going.[32]

4.4 - Myrdal and the principle of effective demand.
We will finally study whether some of Myrdal's findings analysed above might be considered akin to Keynes' principle of effective demand.

In Myrdal's analysis, as in the principal of effective demand, income changes, whether they are made up of prices or output, or a mixture of both, act as an equilibrating mechanism between savings ex ante and investment ex ante. However, Myrdal does not determine the equilibrium level of income, but at most the income changes necessary to bring about an ex post equality at the end of a period within a cumulative process, i.e. during a disequilibrium process. His mechanism for determining the changes in income is also different from Keynes' multiplier, though akin to the analysis in the Treatise where windfall profit is "the balancing figure" (Keynes 1930A, p.136).

For example if savings ex ante are greater than investment ex ante, $S_t = sE_t$ and $S_t > I_t$, then prices have to fall so as to bring forth losses until income ex post (E'_t) is such that there is an ex post equality between savings and investment $(S'_t = I'_t)$. Instead of using the multiplier, Myrdal, like most of the Swedes after him, usually assumes that the income changes $(E'_t - E_t)$ have the character of a windfall, which implies that all the additional income is either saved or dissaved. This means that the expenditure plans ex ante are always realized and there are thus no endogenous effects on consumption

----

32 On the other hand, we have seen in the section above that Myrdal speaks of anticipated investment gains as acting as 'the profit motive', which in this analysis would imply that an actual difference between the realized investment cost and the anticipated capital value at the same point of time, i.e. the actual demand price for the capital goods, and this difference will be expected to stay the same also for the coming period.

and investment plans.[33] In the next period investment ex ante will fall ($I_t > I_{t+1}$), because the fall in the price level during the outgoing period ($P_t < P_t'$) lowers the anticipated capital values for subsequent periods and thereby decreases the investment plans. But savings ex ante will also fall since a lower income is expected for the forthcoming period ($E_{t+1} = E_t' < E_t$, i.e. $S_t > S_{t+1}$ since $sE_t > sE_{t+1}$ and $S_{t+1} > I_{t+1}$ since $S_{t+1} \equiv S_t' = I_t' = I_t > I_{t+1}$) so there will still be an excess of saving ex ante and the price level will go on falling etc.[34] After a certain number (x) of periods the savings ratio starts to fall ($s > s_1$), which implies that ex ante savings will fall proportionally more than income $[(S_{t+x+1}/S_{t+x}) > (s_1 E_{t+x+1}/sE_{t+x})]$ and the fall in the price level and the investment plans will be dampened. Finally, a quasi-equilibrium could be reached, if the savings ratio falls to such an extent that saving is equal to investment ex ante and total demand for consumption goods equal to total supply, because then there is no tendency for the price level to move. We call this a quasi-equilibrium, since it seems to represent a phase of the business cycle (cp. sect. 4:2:3). Hence, it is not the same as Keynes' underemployment equilibrium, since in the latter case there is no tendency to move away from such a situation.

It is interesting to notice that if we take quantity changes into consideration, then, strictly speaking, the cumulative process should not even start, since the fall in income would be accomplished without any change in the price level ($S_t = sE_t > I_t$; $S_t' = sE_t' = I_t' = I_t$; $P_t = P_t'$ and $E_t - E_t' = P_t(Q_t - Q_t')$) and investments would be equal to savings ex ante ($I_t = I_{t+1}$ and $sE_{t+1} = sE_t'$ but $sE_t' = I_t' = I_t$ so $S_{t+1} = I_{t+1}$), so we would only have a one-step fall in real income.

----

33 This opens the way in later works of the Stockholm School, when the multiplier was well known, to use a unit period which is shorter than the period which it takes for the multiplier to work itself out (cp. sect. XI:1:3).

34 We assume that the anticipated income is equal to the realized income for the outgoing period ($E_{t+1} = E_t'$).

But it is unlikely that Myrdal would accept this strict interpretation. Instead, he might have assumed that the losses due to the fall in output would still entail a curtailment of the investment plans, so the process will be cumulative (cp. Note 11 Ch. VIII).

Therefore, Myrdal does not aim to find the principle for determining the equilibrium level of output, but to determine the factors which constitute the ex post equality between savings and investment in an ongoing cumulative process. Hence, Myrdal as well as Lindahl appear to be similar to Keynes only so long as we look at their analysis of a disequilibrium process of a cumulative character. But Myrdal differs from Lindahl, since he never gives an explicit example to show his opinion on the role of the rate of interest in the stationary state or a long run equilibrium (cp. sect. IV:3:3:1).

Chapter 7

Profit as a Link between Consecutive Periods
Hammarskjöld (1932-1933)

"the equations of the system determine
unambiguously the strategic factor chosen
for linking up the successive periods ...
this role is played by the profits in the
final stage of production, which are
transferred as a given factor to the
following period and so in accordance with
the reactions presumed determine the
sequence of events" (Lundberg 1937, p.84).

In this chapter we will consider two of
Hammarskjöld's works, his article "Utkast till en
algebraisk metod för dynamisk prisanalys" (A Sketch
of an Algebraic Method for Dynamic Price Analysis) of
1932 published in Ekonomisk Tidskrift, and his
dissertation Konjunkturspridningen (The Transmission
of Economic Fluctuations) for which the oral
examination took place in November 1933. The
dissertation is made up of a methodological and
analytical part (around 50 pages) and an applied part
(around 200 pages). The former part is almost
identical to the article, and we will therefore
follow either the article or the dissertation
depending on which gives the clearest account of
Hammarskjöld's ideas.

His views on dynamic method are of the utmost
importance in the development of the Stockholm
School, since he gives the first algebraic
formulation of a link between consecutive periods,
i.e. a continuation analysis. As an adjunct to his
discussion of the connection between the periods
Hammarskjöld has to analyse the length of the period.
In this context he gives the first definition of a
unit period, which is related to the fulfilment of
plans. However, there is a flaw in Hammarskjöld's
construction as being the first representation of a
sequence analysis, since he explicitly conducts an ex
post analysis. Due to this analytical weakness, we

Chapter 7   157

would consider that Lindahl, in his "A Note on the Dynamic Pricing Problem" of 1934, is the first one to develop sequence analysis proper.

It is interesting to notice that besides the methodological points mentioned above, the main part of Hammarskjöld's macroeconomic theory was neither adopted nor commented on by the other Swedes.[1] There are probably two interrelated explanations why it so happened. The first is that they did not find Hammarskjöld's analysis useful, because of his unrealistic assumptions (cp. sect. 3:1). The second is that his thesis is by far the most complicated work which has emanated from the Stockholm School. Myrdal likened "the extraordinarily complicated nature of the thesis" (Myrdal 1933B, p.6) to "a crossword where the reader has to try to find the implicit assumptions, which have to be assumed if the author's conclusion should be accepted" (ibid.; cp. Yohe 1958, p.347). However, that might imply that we belong to that group of economists, whom Hammarskjöld sullenly described in the following way:

> "I have the impression that you [Lindahl] are fairly alone in your view of my opus; at the University [Stockholm] one seems to be so confident in monetary theory, that one, if one does not understand anything, draws the conclusion that there must exist a mistake" (Letter to Lindahl, 16 January 1934).

1 - Hammarskjöld's purpose.

Hammarskjöld's point of departure is 'the truism' that "every analysis of the general development of prices ... during a given period of time" (Hammarskjöld 1932, p.157) has to be based on the idea that total disbursements are equal to total value of transacted goods and services. The quantity theory is a particular version of this analysis where MV has substituted total disbursements. Hammarskjöld

---

1 The only exception is Lundberg's Economic Expansion (cp. Lundberg 1937, pp.77-88).

now wants to overcome the deficiences of the quantity
theory by taking the following approach:

> "if one does not avoid substituting the
> monetary phenomena [MV] for the sum of all
> disbursements and instead tries to work with
> a partition of these, thus one should reach
> an analysis of the mechanism of the price
> movements" (ibid., pp.157-158).

He therefore concentrates on "the functions of the
different disbursements and their mutual
connections" (ibid., p.158), and he looks in
particular at the disbursement on consumer goods,
i.e. like $E(1-s)$ in Lindahl's analysis.

The aim is then to construct a formula for the
price level of consumer goods, which he denotes as
"the analytical tool" (Hammarskjöld 1933A, p.34) that
would show the determinants of the price level for an
expired period. This far Hammarskjöld's intentions
look identical to Lindahl's and Keynes' formulations
of the price level for consumer goods.[2] But
Hammarskjöld now goes one step further since his
formula should also show "the mechanism - that is,
the ways and means by which given changes in prices
and purchasing power are transmitted [to the next
period]" (Lundberg 1937, pp.77-78). Hence,
Hammarskjöld's formula should explicitly exhibit how
two consecutive periods are related to each other,
and in his theory it is the profit earned in one
period but transferred to the next one, which will
function as a link (cp. sect. 3:2). Hammarskjöld is
thereby the first within the Stockholm School, to
give a formal explanation of the way in which two

---

2 This is not very surprising since Hammarskjöld has
the following opinion of the influences on his own
construction:

> "a combination and development of the
> constructions, which in connection with
> Wicksell has been used by Lindahl and
> J.M.Keynes in their works on monetary
> theory" (Hammarskjöld 1932, p.157 n.1).

periods are connected in a disequilibrium process. It has to be remembered that although Myrdal analysed the ex post equalization factors for one period where disequilibrium existed ex ante, he gave no formal account how these factors influenced the plans for the coming period. However, it is obvious that both Lindahl and Myrdal held, with greater or lesser clarity, that unexpected changes in the price level and the concomitant income changes would keep the process going, but their formulas, i.e. $E(1-s)=PQ$ and $R_2=W$ respectively, had no formal connections with plans in subsequent periods. The same is true for Keynes' fundamental equations where on the one hand, profits are said to be "the mainspring of change in the existing economic system" (Keynes 1930A, p.126), but on the other hand the algebraic formulation of these equations gives no account of how profits will influence the outcome in a forthcoming period.

It is possible that Hammarskjöld got the idea of using profit as a link between consecutive periods from Keynes' Treatise (cp. ibid., pp.125-126; pp.141-142). But Hammarskjöld could as well have taken up an idea which was already developed by Wicksell in the formal example of a cumulative process in Interest and Prices, where the profit for the current period is realized at the end of the period and it can only influence the activities of the subsequent period (cp. Wicksell 1936, p.142; cp. Hammarskjöld 1933A, p.12 n.1). There is just one explicit fact which gives a hint that the algebraic construction of a sequence of periods might have come from Robertson, who already constructed such a sequence in Banking Policy (cp. Robertson 1926, p.60f.); Hammarskjöld has namely a methodological appendix to Chapter II of the dissertation with the following quotation from Robertson:

> "The internal mechanism, so to speak, of a
> process of inflation are almost as hard to
> visualize as those of the atom, and seem to
> require the same kind of hypothesis of
> discontinuous motion" (Hammarskjöld 1933A,
> p.53).

If that is the case Hammarskjöld has been particularly influenced by the idea of analysing a process as a discontinuous motion. However, the same idea is also to be found in Lindahl's period device of 1929 and 1930 (cp. sect. IV:2:2).

2 - The dynamic method.

Time is divided into successive periods, as with Lindahl, and what is happening during these periods is "afterwards registered and summed up in equations" (Hammarskjöld 1933A, p.12; cp. p.53). This is an _ex post formulation_ which Hammarskjöld considers to be akin to the quantity theory and Keynes' _Treatise_. It is by design that Hammarskjöld does not apply the ex ante analysis of Myrdal and Lindahl, since that analysis is supposed to be a _causal_ analysis, while Hammarskjöld is just giving a _mechanism_ which is not supposed to imply any particular causality (cp. ibid., p.53; Hammarskjöld 1932, p.158). He seems to give two different meanings to a causal analysis. On the one hand, it is related to the influence from the registered profits of one period on the ex ante plans for the next period (cp. ibid., p.54 n.1). On the other hand, it implies that the registered profit for one period has no influence on the acts for the same period (cp. ibid., p.55). The first meaning seems at first sight a little odd, since Hammarskjöld himself assumes that the profit is transferred as purchasing power for the next period, i.e. the mechanism. That makes it possible "to follow determined causal chains [i.e. sequence analysis] during a longer period of time" (ibid., p.53). Lundberg thus considered this mechanism "a very special case of causal relationship" (Lundberg 1937, p.86). In fact, Hammarskjöld's analysis must presume that the plans for the subsequent period are unaffected by the transferred profit, which is then just added to the consumption plan.[3]

However, his second meaning of a causal analysis leads to a crucial finding for the sequence analysis. Profit for a period is now defined as the difference

----

3 Incidentally, Johansson's contribution is to have stressed the importance for the nature of the process of the assumptions concerning the way the profit is spent (cp. Johansson 1934, pp.121-123).

between revenues and disbursement for the same period and it is a windfall profit. Therefore, it follows that the size of the profit would be indeterminate if the profit could be spent during the period, since that would influence the amount of the revenues and thereby the size of the profit itself (cp. Hammarskjöld 1933A, p.13; Hammarskjöld 1932, p.159).[4] Thus, Hammarskjöld defines the length of the period in the following way:

> "that the entrepreneurs' profits are registered at the end of the respective period - or, as it could be expressed, that each period comprises the time from one registration of profits to the next one - and it therefore represents purchasing power first during the next period" (ibid., p.13).[5]

This is actually the first time within the Stockholm School that someone not only shows that the definition of the length of the period is a theoretical problem (cp. sect.IV:2:2), but also hints at the relation between fixed plans and the length of the period. After Hammarskjöld, it was almost always

----

4 This discontinous registration of profit is not considered to be unrealistic when it is applied to a single agent. However, when a group of agents are analysed then it is necessary to assume "an absolute simultaneous registration of all partial net amounts" (Hammarskjöld 1933A, p.55), while a continuous registration appears to be more natural (cp. ibid.). But Hammarskjöld never elaborates what this implies for his analysis.

5 This definition seems to be akin to Dennis Robertson's notion of a 'day':

> "I assume the existence of a period of time, to be called a 'day', which is finite but nevertheless so short that the income which a man receives on a given day cannot be allocated during its course to any particular use" (Robertson 1933, p.47).

assumed that the length of time for which the plans are unchanged determines the length of the unit period. Furthermore, without this assumption a sequence analysis is not possible, since such an analysis presumes that the development during the period, i.e. the ex post result, is completely determined by the ex ante plans, and that there is a fixed relation between the ex post result for the current period and the plans for the next period. That implies in Hammarskjöld's analysis that the size of the windfall profit is known at the end of the period and it is then transferred to the next period and used in toto for consumption.

3 - The formula for the price level.

3.1 - Assumptions.
Payments (E) for productive services during each period are supposed to be constant both in their value and their quantity component. At the same time productivity is supposed to be unchanged. These assumptions imply that nominal contractual income and real output are fixed for all periods, which shows with utmost clarity that Hammarskjöld only wants to determine changes in the price level, or as he puts it: "the mechanism of the price movements" (Hammarskjöld 1932, p.158).

These payments are looked upon as contracts determined at the beginning of the period and running for one period. This applies also to 'normal profits', i.e. the entrepreneurs' income "in their capacity of owners of productive services" (Hammarskjöld 1933A, p.13). Thus the changes in the price level for consumer goods and the concomitant windfall profit are the only unanticipated factors for the period. The idea of fixing the payments for productive services for the forthcoming period is later taken up by Lindahl in his "A Note on the Dynamic Pricing Problem" of 1934.

Investments (I) are outlays for productive services for a particular period whose result will mature during the subsequent period, and the entrepreneurs do not anticipate any profit. Furthermore, it is assumed that productivity will not increase even if "the result of the used up services will mature after the ends of periods, during which they have been used" (Hammarskjöld 1932, p.159). This last assumption seems to imply that the investment is just a storage of consumption goods for one period, and it could be looked upon as an entrepreneur's particular sales plan. Hammarskjöld is therefore probably using Marshall's market period, since once the investment decision is taken Q is determined and this amount is also sold whatever the price it will fetch.

3.2 - The formula.

We start from the 'truism' that the value of sold consumption goods is equal to realized purchases:

$$P_n Q_n = E + D_{n-1} - S_n \qquad ^6$$

The profit during a period is defined as the difference between the stream of outlays for consumption goods and productive services, i.e. cost of production, respectively:

$$D_n = (E + D_{n-1} - S_n) - (E + I_{n-1} - I_n)$$

Hence, in this formula the profit is fully determined for the current period. It is then transferred to the next period, where it influences the price level and the profit for that period as shown in the formula. In fact, <u>this is the first time that we have a formal exposition of sequence analysis within the Stockholm School, which shows algebraically not only how the unknown for the current period is determined, but also how this period determines the outcome in the next period.</u> That is to say, we have both a single-period and a continuation analysis. Thus,

---

6 P_n: price level for consumption goods for period n.
  Q_n: the amount of consumption goods sold.
  S_n: that part of E not used for consumption during the period.
  D_{n-1}: the production of profit from period n-1 and part of the disposable purchasing power during period n.

Lundberg has described Hammarskjöld's system in the following way:

"the equations of the system determine unambiguously the strategic factor chosen for linking up the successive periods ... this role is played by the profits in the final stage of production, which are transferred as a given factor to the following period and so in accordance with the reactions presumed determine the sequence of events" (Lundberg 1937, p.84; cp. Yohe 1959, p.10 n.19).

However, there is a drawback with Hammarskjöld's formulation as a single-period analysis, and that is the fact that his formulas exhibit ex post results. But we have already seen that Hammarskjöld's 'mechanism' assumes that the ex ante plans are independent of the transferred profit. Hence, we can interpret the ex post values of Q_n, E_n, S_n and I_n as being the same as the ex ante plans, while the price level (P_n) and the current profit (D_n) are unanticipated ex post results (unless $S_n=I_n-I_{n-1}$ in which case there is no current profit).[7]

It is obvious that the inclusion of profit from the previous period is the main difference between Hammarskjöld's formula on the one hand and Lindahl's and Keynes' formulas on the other hand, and Hammarskjöld has also noticed this difference:

"the construction ... deviates from Keynes' ((first fundamental equation)) by the way in which the outgoing net proceeds during a a period is transferred to the price formula for the next period" (Hammarskjöld 1933A, p.56).

----

7 This shows that an unexpected change in the price level will not influence the payments for productive services for the next period and thereby real output, which is another example of Hammarskjöld's peculiar assumtions. However it may influence the amount of goods put on the market (Q_n).

Thus, even if is possible to reinterpret their equations as well as Hammarskjöld's formula as ex ante formulations, Lindahl and Keynes would still not have shown an explicit connection with earlier periods.[8]

---

8 However, in determining the price level for consumption goods Hammarskjöld uses the value of investment, while Keynes applies the cost of investment (I') for the same equation, and the value of investment in Keynes' set up is a factor in the equation which determines the price level for output as a whole (cp. Keynes 1930A, pp.121-124). But it is possible to incorporate this factor in Hammarskjöld's formula. The physical amount of total output produced during the period (O_n) is defined as $O_n = Q_n + (I_n - I_{n-1})/P_n$. This does not involve any valuation problem if $P_n = P_{n-1}$, since investment is storage of consumption goods. I'_n the cost of new investment goods is equal to $E[[(I_n - I_{n-1})/P_n]/O_n]$. Then it is true that: $E + D_{n-1} - S_n = E/O_n[Q_n + (I_n - I_{n-1})/P_n] + D_{n-1} - S_n = EQ_n/O_n + I'_n + D_{n-1} - S_n$. Hence, the formula for the price level could be written as follows: $P_n = E/O_n + D_{n-1}/Q_n + (I'_n - S_n)/Q_n$.

Chapter 8

Autonomous Changes in Consumption Demand
Ohlin (1932-1934)

"Ekonomisk Tidskrift 1933, No.2. On the
Problem of the Exposition of Monetary.
BERTIL OHLIN. The author attempts to
construct a simple and more practical
apparatus than that of neo-Wicksellian
theory. It is necessary to clarify the
ambiguities in current definitions of
income, saving, and investment before we can
apply statistical data. The description
given by Wicksell, Lindahl and Hayek of the
cumulative process is based on the
assumption of a spontaneous lowering of the
rate of interest and of the stickiness of
wages and the demand for consumption-goods;
but a rise in prices need not necessarily
involve an increase in the demand for and
relative price of production-goods. The
relevance of the Austrian theory of capital
and of the time-structure of prices to
monetary theory is stressed, for the
exchange structure and time-sequence of
prices is at the core of monetary problems.
Finally, the neo-Wicksellian account of the
equilibrium rate of interest and price-
formation is stated to be inadequate"
(Ohlin's report to "Recent Periodicals and
New Books" in the Economic Journal December
1933, pp.732-733).

It will be argued that Ohlin has made no direct
contribution to the development of dynamic method, on
the contrary, he shows a certain lack of
understanding of the ex ante approach, although his
stress on 'what happens first', which means that the
character of a sequence will depend on the speed of
reaction of the different factors, leads him to adopt
a 'case-by-case' approach, which varies the ceteris
paribus assumptions according to the actual case

under consideration, and in this sense it is akin to Lundberg's model sequences from 1937. Ohlin's main contribution lies instead in macroeconomic theory, where he pointed to the possibilities of autonomous changes in the demand for consumption goods, which was a step forward from Myrdal's and Lindahl's concentration on the relation between savings and investment. Ohlin's analysis of the equilibrating mechanism is only superior to Myrdal's and Lindahl's analyses in the sense that he explicitly incorporates quantity changes. But at the same time it is inferior since he has not understood the difference between equilibrium conditions and ex post identities.

We will concentrate our attention on Ohlin's article "On the Formulation of Monetary Theory" published in Ekonomisk Tidskrift in 1933. The manuscript was sent to the editor D.Davidson in the end of May 1933 (cp. Landgren 1960, p.165), but Steiger has shown that an almost identical draft of the article already existed in the autumn of 1932 (cp. Steiger 1976, p.353). During the winter of 1932-1933 this draft was circulated "among some of Ohlin's colleagues in Sweden, notably Lindahl, Myrdal and Hammarskjöld" (ibid.).

Ohlin's report to the Unemployment Committee (Ohlin 1934) was published in April 1934 (cp. Landgren 1960, p.198 n.4), though judging from Hammarskjöld's memorandum from August 1933, the report, or at least the theoretical parts, must have existed in a fairly final shape by the summer of 1933. However, the report will only be used when it gives a more distinct version of Ohlin's ideas or where it shows a new development, since the report contains an introductory part which is very similar to the article in Ekonomisk Tidskrift, except for an inclusion of ex ante and ex post. The report is best characterized as an application to economic policy of the ideas from "On the Formulation".

1 - Ohlin's dynamic method.

Ohlin's object is "to describe price changes over time" (Ohlin 1933C, p.359) via an analysis of the relation between total demand and total supply. This induces him to ask the following type of questions:

> "Under which conditions, one may ask, will the system maintain a certain stability characterized by specific relations between the situation at one time and that at a later time? Under which conditions will the price system be moving upward or downward?" (ibid.).

These questions seem to be related to the cumulative process and therefore in line with, for example, the problems analysed by Myrdal in **Monetary Equilibrium**.[1] But we will see below that Ohlin had some additional ideas on the active forces behind a price change (cp. sect. 3).

The dynamic method used by Ohlin to analyse the development of demand and supply (in particular the former) is a peculiar mixture of ex post and ex ante:

> "Along with a description of changes in supply, a description of the generation of demand for various goods must lie at the heart of every analysis of price changes. ... such a demand analysis must be based upon an investigation of the composition of gross revenue reasoning backwards in time, as well as upon an investigation of prevailing notions of profitability computed forward in time. That is the only way to explain changes in demand. Quite simply, the task is to record transactions period by period, relating them to one another, thus illuminating why they came into existence" (Ohlin 1933C, pp.358-359; cp. Ohlin 1934, pp.5-7).

----
1 However we can find no discussion of a cumulative criterion until Ohlin's report to the Unemployment Committee (cp. Ohlin 1934, p.32).

This method does not have a purely ex post character like Hammarskjöld's analysis (cp. sect. VII:2), which only describes the outcome of the period, since Ohlin also tries to explain what has been going on during the period by looking at the ex ante plans ruling at the beginning of the period. However, the ex ante factors, e.g. 'the prevailing notions of profitability', are estimated at the end of the period, which means that it is an ex post reconstruction of the ex ante plans. It is important to understand why Ohlin chose this method, since he certainly considered that profit anticipations play a crucial role (cp. ibid., p.367; p.385).

To use an ex post method was a conscious choice on Ohlin's part, and it implied, according to him, that Myrdal's problem with a capital market equilibrium "simply does not arise" (ibid., p.354; cp. p.379), since saving is always equal to investment. But Ohlin only gives a few hints as to why he preferred his own method to Myrdal's ex ante analysis. First, he seems to hold that the notion of future plans is too vague and indeterminate and therefore that "a 'deep analysis'... [would] imply a very misleading rationalization of human beings' conceptual world" (Ohlin 1934, p.43; cp. Ohlin 1933C, p.358 n.4; p.377 n.26).[2] But even if individuals formed definite plans for the coming period, Ohlin could still not see "how such magnitudes, existing only in the human mind, could possibly lend themselves to statistical observation" (Ohlin 1933C, p.388). The last critical point is of the utmost importance for Ohlin, since one of his main aim is to construct an apparatus, which has "a form easier to handle and lending itself to an analysis of statistical data available, among other places, in business accounting" (ibid., p.383 n.30; cp. p.386). Hence, Ohlin's critique of Myrdal and Lindahl is mainly based on practical considerations. This is eloquently exemplified in his characterization of their concept of income as not only 'mystical' but also "inapplicable in any statistical analysis" (ibid., p.383; cp. 1933D, p.76). However, Ohlin must to a certain extent face the same type of problem within his own method, since he attempts to investigate "prevailing notions of profitability computed forward in time" (ibid., p.359), unless he thinks that it is easier to estimate these ex ante

---

2 In relation to the same problem, Steiger makes the following interpretation:

> "Ohlin, in his monetary approach, not only included expectations about future events but also stressed the fact that these anticipations were uncertain or as he expressed it, 'indefinite', i.e. changeable and therefore capable of influencing the present economic outcome (cf. his 1933 essay, esp. ... nn.4 and 26)" (Steiger 1978, p.444).

This seems to imply that Ohlin was criticizing the probablistic approach of Lindahl and Myrdal. Thus, Ohlin's ideas would be similar to the ones in the General Theory (cp. ibid., p.429). But we would argue that Ohlin's use of the word 'indefinite' has the same meaning as the word 'vague' or 'hazy', in the sense that individuals do not make specific plans for the forthcoming periods, which is his reason for not using an ex ante approach.

notions at the end of the period.

Despite this critique of what he calls the 'neo-Wicksellian approach'[3], Ohlin ends his discussion on the problem of the stability of the price system with the following idea, which he explicitly equates with "the core of Myrdal's formulation of monetary theory" (ibid., p.362 n.10):

> "one must allow for planned investment and consumption demand as well as for available factor supply, for such plans could indicate pending price changes. The question is to what extent a certain state of the price system carries in it the seed of more or less violent and significant changes to come" (ibid., p.362).

Ohlin has also understood that in Myrdal's analysis savings could differ from investment because they are plans "ahead in time" (ibid., p.359 n.7). However, it seems that Ohlin has not understood one of the crucial advantages of the ex ante analysis, namely, that an equality between planned investment and planned savings is an equilibrium condition. Indeed, without this, there would be no reason to examine monetary equilibrium. Ohlin speaks instead of the equilibrium implied by "ordinary price theory" (ibid., p.357) as referring to the identity between bought and sold quantities (cp. sect. 4:3). Had Ohlin understood that the equilibrium condition, including his own addition of the consumption goods sector (cp. sect. 3), implies that the plans for total demand are equal to the plans for total supply, then he would probably have seen the great advantage of the ex ante analysis, because this equilibrium condition answers the question posed at the beginning of this section, how the system may maintain a certain stability over a period of time.

There is further evidence, which shows that Ohlin did not really grasp all the intricacies of the ex ante analysis. He mentions cases where the

---

3 This refers at least to Myrdal, Lindahl and Hayek, but Hammarskjöld and Keynes are probably also included (cp. Ohlin 1933C, p.376; p.388 n.30).

anticipations and the plans change <u>during</u> a period:

> "In my book [Ohlin 1934] I use as a rule a
> longer period, during which the plans are
> adjusted" (Letter to Lindahl, 16 January
> 1935; cp. Ohlin 1933C, p.359; Ohlin 1934,
> p.28).

But in an ex ante analysis, at least after
Hammarskjöld's contribution (cp. sect. VII:2), the
adjustment of plans would signify that it is a new
period.

Therefore, we may conclude that in 1933-1934
Ohlin had not yet understood the advantage of an ex
ante analysis for both theoretical and practical
purposes. Thus, he can reject it solely on practical
grounds. It is only in his article for the <u>Economic
Journal</u> of 1937 that it is evident that he has
accepted the existence of plans based on expectations
concerning the future where the plans spell out the
actions to be undertaken (cp. Ohlin 1937A, pp.61-62).
Incidentally, much later Ohlin gives one of the best
accounts why the concept of plan has to be <u>precise</u> in
a <u>theoretical</u> analysis:

> "Many may feel that all this talk in
> quantitatively precise terms of 'planned
> savings' and 'planned investment' and so on
> is rather artificial. ... In the theory it
> is necessary to assume a certain
> quantitative precision instead of vague
> ideas. Otherwise, a theoretical tool of
> great practical usefulness would not be at
> our disposal" (Ohlin 1949, p.117).

<u>2 - 'What happens first' and the 'case-by-case'
approach.</u>

We have already seen that Ohlin attempts to
'describe price changes over time' which involve 'a
sequence', and in analysing such conditions Ohlin has
found "the <u>timing</u> of the various changes to be of
obvious significance" (Ohlin 1933C, p.368). The idea
of the importance of 'timing' leads to the following
central proposition:

"the effects of a given primary change will
differ widely if the secondary reactions
occur in one time sequence rather than
another" (ibid., p.369; cp. Ohlin 1934,
p.19; p.21).

Hence, everything depends on 'what happens first'
(cp. Ohlin 1933A, p.477).

The theoretical raison d'être for 'what happens
first' is the existence of frictions, which implies
that the price analysis has to be "an account of a
time-using process" (ibid., p.476). Ohlin gives the
following example to show the importance of taking
time into consideration:

"Assume that the demand for fish is suddenly
increased owing to a change in taste. The
reaction of the output and price of fish can
only be described in relation to the lapse
of time. The speed of the reactions or the
rate of change must be taken into account"
(ibid.).

This is basically the same thing as Lundberg's
velocities of adjustment (cp. sect. V:2), and the
ideas on frictions refer quite evidently to Myrdal's
dissertation (cp. sect. III:2). Therefore it seems
that Ohlin stresses a point which was known to the
other Swedes but had not yet been added to Lindahl's
or Myrdal's analysis.

In order to convey the meaning in a
macroeconomic context of 'what happens first' we may
take the following example of a general wage cut:

"In a depression imagine a general wage cut
of 10 percent in all industries, immediately
reducing labor's consumption demand. If at
the same time firms impressed with the
improved profitability prospects expand
their investment demand by the same amount,
aggregate demand will not fall. Then
average profitability will indeed improve
and may indirectly stimulate investment
demand. On the other hand, if no immediate
tendency to expand firm investment demand

arises, the wage cut reduces total consumption demand by as much as the cut in wage costs. Prices will tend downwards, and profitability will deteriorate" (Ohlin 1933C, pp.368-369; cp. Ohlin 1934, p.20).

Hence, in this case the outcome will depend on the speed with which the wage cut influence the demand for investment. Examples of this kind help to explain why Ohlin rejected attempts "to offer simple rules for the relative magnitude of price movements" (ibid., p.375). Ohlin's development of the aggregate demand approach (cp. sect. 3) could then be seen as a precursor to 'what happens first', since it gives a general formulation of the active forces behind a price change with the special intention of showing that the 'neo-Wicksellian' approach is too circumscribed. Thus 'what happens first' gives a particular explanation of the price movements at a given moment of time.

The importance of the notion 'what happens first', and the concomitant difficulties for any generalization concerning the explanation of price changes, explain why Ohlin adopts a so-called 'case-by-case' approach (cp. Ohlin 1933C, p.381; p.383; p.384). However, Ohlin gives no clear and concise description of this approach until his debate with Lindahl in 1941-1942, where he defends his approach against Lindahl's attempts to develop a general dynamic approach in "The Dynamic Approach" of 1939. In this context Ohlin describes his own procedure, which he considers to be analogous to Lundberg's model sequences (cp. Ohlin 1941A, p.172), as follows:

"to construct a series of typical cases, where the economic development can be described and predicted on the basis of certain assumptions concerning the speed of reaction and the strength of the tendencies" (ibid., p.171; cp. Ohlin 1941B, p.331)

But we would hold that Ohlin's critique does not really attack the core of Lindahl's dynamic method. In fact, Ohlin provides himself the proper answer, since he portrays Lindahl's method as "a conceptual system, so general that it could applied for studying all different typical cases" (ibid., p.172; cp. Lindahl 1941, p.237; Ohlin 1941B, pp.329-330; Lindahl 1942, pp.43-44). Hence, we consider 'what happens first' and the case-by-case approach as being contributions to macrodynamic theory. But these contributions do not in any way prove that a dynamic method is superfluous. Ohlin is therefore confusing a certain neo-Wicksellian proposition concerning macroeconomic theory with a critique of the dynamic method. This is all the more remarkable, since Ohlin, despite some misunderstandings (cp. sect. 1), seems to espouse this dynamic method in his works of 1933-1937. However Lindahl's use of the term 'dynamic theory' is to a certain extent responsible for this confusion, since he speaks of 'general dynamic theory' which in fact means 'dynamic method', while 'special dynamic theory' or 'real dynamic theory' relate to particular macrotheoretical propositions.

Ohlin's use of the case-by-case approach shows that by varying the ceteris paribus conditions in an almost infinite number of ways, he can reach a host of different macrotheoretical results. Nowhere is the reliance on the assumption of different ceteris paribus conditions shown more explicitly than in Ch. III of Monetary Policy, which is suitably titled "Different types of conditions for expansion", and where Ohlin analyses the effects of decreased costs, increased savings and decreased consumption demand etc.[4] Consequently, Ohlin ends this chapter by saying that a solution to the problem could only be found by "an analysis of the concrete cases" (Ohlin 1934, p.77).

3 - A critique of the 'neo-Wicksellians' or an autonomous change in the demand for consumption goods.

Ohlin wants to give a general answer to "the question of the driving force behind price movements" (Ohlin 1933C, p.384). His explanation is basically a restatement of an old Wicksellian idea:

> "rising prices in general imply that the demand for goods and services is rising more rapidly than the quantities supplied. One possibility is that so many entrepreneurs find immediate real investment profitable that investment is growing ... Another possibility is that demand for consumers' goods is rising. The necessary and sufficient condition for a process of rising prices is that the sum of those two kinds of demand is rising relative to output" (Ohlin 1933C, pp.373-374; cp. pp.385-386).

----

4 The impossibility of giving a general analysis of the causes of a credit cycle is of course true as well for the instruments of a monetary policy which are supposed to alleviate such a cycle:

> "it is impossible in a general argumentation to make more precise the possibilities of increasing employment and production in different situations of depression through influence on demand and prices. An infinite number of different cases could be imagined and the possibilities of reaching the desired result not only just temporarily but also in the longer run depend on the circumstances in the different cases" (Ohlin 1934, p.96).

Hence, 'the driving force' is made up of two forces, one coming from the side of investment and the other emanating from the side of consumption. Therefore an explanation of price changes must look at the factors influencing the demand and supply of consumption goods and investment goods respectively (cp. ibid., p.358; p.367; p.385; p.386).[5]

It is therefore not surprising that Ohlin finds the idea that the disequilibrium in the capital market represents the 'driving force', i.e. what he considers to be the hallmark of the 'neo-Wicksellian' approach, as being too narrow an explanation. This is particularly so when he can construct examples where a disequilibrium in the consumer goods market is the only factor behind a price movement or at least the initiating force (cp. ibid., p.368; p.374; p.380). His critique of the 'neo-Wicksellians' is aptly summarized in the following remark:

> "the development of price relations is far more varied than is claimed by neo-Wicksellian theory (Lindahl's, as well as Hayek's)" (ibid., p.376; cp. p.371; p.375).

----
5 Keynes makes the same extension of the fundamental equations of the _Treatise_ which only looked at I versus S:

> "The essence of the monetary theory of production ... can be expressed quite briefly, starting from the equation dQ=dI-dS or, as it may also be written
> dQ=dI+dF-dE or dQ=dD-dE where Q stands for profit, I for investment, S for saving, F for spending, and D for disbursement. For these equations mean that profit (for entrepreneurs as a whole) is increasing or decreasing according as the excess of investment over saving or (which is the same thing) of disbursement over earnings is increasing or decreasing" (Drafts to chapters 7-10 of the _General Theory_ from 1931-1932, Keynes 1973A, p.381).

Ohlin's extension of the Wicksellian approach is certainly a relevant one, but it still seems that his critique of Wicksell et cons. overshoots its target for two reasons. Firstly Ohlin analyses an <u>actual</u> situation <u>ex post.</u> In that case, it does not make sense to explain a price movement which has taken place just by "referring to the relative amount of credit" (ibid., p.386), since other factors might have been active as well, i.e. a concrete analysis is necessary (cp. sect. 2). However, Wicksell, and certainly Myrdal and Lindahl, generally pursued an ex ante analysis of the effects of a ceteris paribus change in the money rate, or the real rate, on the price level; although Ohlin is correct in stating that this means that "[one] merely succeeds in calling attention to the fact that a change in credit policy may produce a change in demand and price movements" (Ohlin 1933C, p.386). This points towards our second reason, namely that if Ohlin wants a general explanation of the possible factors behind price changes, then the following is obviously true:

> "it serves no good purpose to press the analysis of several kinds of demand changes into the straitjacket of seeing everything in terms of the relation between a 'normal' rate and the actual money rate" (ibid.).

It is true that Wicksell almost exclusively explained price changes by his ideas on the 'normal' rate, even if during his last years he started to consider other possibilities (cp. Wicksell 1925, p.201). But when we reach Lindahl and Myrdal, then it is explicit that they analysed changes in saving which <u>first</u> reacted on the prices of consumer goods and thereby triggered off the cumulative process (cp. sect. IV:3:3; sect. VI:4:2).

However, the important point is Ohlin's treatment of <u>autonomous</u> changes in consumption, which is in line with his mistaken critique of 'Wicksell and his followers' for assuming "wages, and with them consumption demand, to be rigid" (Ohlin 1933C, p.375 n.24). This seems also to have been Ohlin's own evaluation of his contribution to the development of the Stockholm School:

"Maybe it was no news in a purely logical
sense when in the years of the Great
Depression I pointed out intensively that a
process of inflation could be possible
despite equilibrium in the capital market.
But I myself conceived it as a news, because
the Swedish discussion to such a high degree
concentrated on the assumption that all
primary changes were shift of investments"
(Letter from Ohlin to Steiger, 2 September
1972, as quoted in Steiger 1976, p.356
n.22).[6]

---

6 Steiger is basically correct in the following
proposition:

"Ohlin to a certain extent held a pioneering
position [in relation to Myrdal and Lindahl]
by his early development of the aggregate
demand approach in the 1920's" (Steiger
1976, p.364).

However unlike Steiger, we can find no sign of this
approach until Ohlin's article "Den danska kronan
efter 1914" (The Danish Crown after 1914) from 1927,
where he speaks of disequilibrium in the capital
market as increasing the purchasing power and he
denotes this idea as a generally accepted theory (cp.
Ohlin 1927, p.122). Steiger mentions other works by
Ohlin before 1927 (cp. Steiger 1976, p.348), while in
his dissertation he starts with "Den danska kronan"
(cp. Steiger 1971, p.190 n.101). But it is only in
Ohlin's dissertation that there is a slight hint of
the aggregate demand approach; "Because of the
influence from the increase in total purchasing power
the home prices will rise" (Ohlin 1924, p.119).

(Note continued on following page).

But at the same time Ohlin summarizes his <u>empirical</u>
findings on the business cycle in the following way:

> "However, experience supports most closely
> the opinion that up to now the increase
> starts in general from the investment side"
> (Ohlin 1934, p.51).

In this light, Wicksell et al. were perhaps not so
mistaken to limit their ceteris paribus analysis to a
disturbance in the capital market, which was due
either to a change in the money rate of interest or
to a change in the expected profitability of
investments. Furthermore, Lindahl showed later on
that an autonomous change in demand for consumption
goods still appears as a disturbance of the
equilibrium condition that savings should be equal to
investments ex ante (cp. sect. IX:4:4).

It is only in 1932 that Ohlin mentions the
possibility of extending the analysis to the market
for consumption goods, but he does not develop this
approach (cp. Ohlin 1932A, p.16) since it "wurde
freilich zu weit führen" (ibid.). Instead he just
reformulates the equilibrium in the capital market by
taking <u>gross</u> saving and <u>gross</u> investment into
consideration (cp. ibid.; Ohlin 1931, p.22; Ohlin
1932B, p.131). Later on in 1932 Ohlin writes as
follows:

> "that the main push to an improvement <u>can</u>
> come from increased demand for consumption
> goods, whose producer will thereby order
> more capital goods" (Ohlin 1932C, p.23).

But the explicit analysis is still centred around a
balance or an imbalance in the capital market (cp.
ibid., p.24). Therefore we would argue that Ohlin
does not make an explicit analysis of autonomous
changes in consumption until the draft of "On the
Formulation" in the autumn of 1932.

4 - The equilibrating mechanism.

4.1 - Quantity changes.

Ohlin analyses a case where the saving intentions are reduced during a process of falling prices, which will have the following ex post consequences:

> "Rising consumption demand does not at all mean falling net saving, which equals new real investment. On the contrary. Aggregate demand and gross income will be rising _more_ rapidly than consumption demand. Consequently, gross saving will be rising while negative incomes are falling. Net saving, then, will be rising for a twofold reason" (Ohlin 1933C, p.380).

Income changes will thus lead to higher savings ex post. But it is not explicit whether the income changes are only made up of price changes or a mixture of price and quantity changes. However, in other examples Ohlin assumes spare capacity at the beginning of his analysis (cp. ibid., p.368; p.370; p.375)[7], and then it is obviously 'expanding output' which makes possible an increase in net savings ex

---

7 Ohlin's _Monetary Policy_ has in fact the following explicit aim:

> "an investigation of the effects of certain instruments of business cycle and labour market policy, which are effected during circumstances of widespread unemployment" (Ohlin 1934, p.3).

Hence, the full title of this book is _Monetary Policy, Public Works, Subsidies and Tariffs as Remedies for Unemployment._

post, even if consumption has risen (cp. ibid.).[8]
This is because in a case with idle capacity the
increased income and output stem from the following
factors:

> "more labour is employed, raising the total
> wage bill; for another, business income is
> up, both because of better utilization of
> durable capital goods and natural resources
> and because of a tendency of prices to rise"
> (ibid., p.370; cp. p.372).

Therefore, <u>Ohlin has stressed more than Lindahl
and Myrdal the importance of taking increased
production into consideration as a part of the
equalization mechanism.</u> However, in an analysis from
more or less the same period, Myrdal explicitly
mentions income changes which are due to increased
production. The starting point is a situation where
unused resources exist, such as in the trough of a
depression. We will look at Myrdal's comments
concerning the credit market:

> "it is on the one hand obvious, that the
> increased production and consumption
> require disposition of capital. But at the

----

8 A similar idea is already mentioned by Ohlin in his
article "Prisstegringens problem" (The Problem of
rising Prices) of August 1932. In a situation with
unused capacity in the capital goods industries:

> "the real saving which is necessary for the
> increased production, arises from a better
> utilization of the productive machinery, so
> the production is growing more than
> consumption" (Ohlin 1932C, p.28).

However the explanation is not really a theoretical
one, but based on an empirical generalization:

> "all the facts support the idea that net
> saving is low during depressions and grows
> in paralell with the upswing" (ibid.).

same time the income of all social classes are increased, with the result, that an increased amount of capital disposition in the form of new savings is also brought about in a sufficient amount" (Myrdal 1933C, p.23; cp. p.25).[9]

Myrdal considers this to be the normal state of affairs during the recovery from a depression (cp. ibid., p.24). Lindahl, who had studied a draft of this memorandum, puts forward the same ideas in a speech from November 1932:

"the capital which is absorbed by the public works is financed by the increase in societal production, which is the direct or indirect result of these works ... it appears probable that this condition is fulfilled when there ... is a large unused capacity in the private firms. In such a case the increased production could be so big that the accompanied increase in the national income could give rise to the saving which is necessary for the financing of the public works" (Lindahl 1932, pp.136-137).

Myrdal's and Lindahl's ideas should therefore be compared with Ohlin's statements in "On the Formulation".

Hence, it is very difficult to find out who was the first to expound these ideas. From the correspondence between Lindahl and Myrdal, we can see that Myrdal's appendix already existed as a draft at the beginning of November 1932, since Lindahl asks Myrdal to send him the memorandum, which he had already seen (Lindahl to Myrdal, 12 November 1932; Myrdal to Lindahl, 14 November 1932). However, we do not know how extensive this draft was. Thus, there is no way of telling the influence between Myrdal and

----

9 This pamphlet of March 1933 is a reprint of Myrdal's appendix to the budget for 1933, which is always presented at the first session of the Parliament in the beginning of January.

Lindahl. Ohlin, on the other hand, although he was present when Lindahl delivered his speech and supported Lindahl's thesis, probably precedes both Lindahl and Myrdal, since he had already put forward the same ideas in a very sketchy form in August 1932 (cp. Note 12).

4.2 - An example of the equilibrating mechanism.

The most formal account of the equilibrating mechanism is to be found in Monetary Policy (cp. Ohlin 1934, p.27). Here Ohlin draws a straightforward analogy between the supply and demand analysis for one good and the same analysis for all goods. In his example the income anticipations are unchanged as well as the will to save, which means fixed plans for consumption and savings. A decrease in the rate of interest will now lead to an increase in planned investment which is like an outward shift in the total demand curve, and as a result "volume of production, realized demand, measured in money, and perhaps prices will rise more or less" (ibid.). If it is assumed that the supply curve is completely elastic because of spare capacity, then it is obvious that an increase in investment leads to the same increase in real income $(dI=P(Q'-Q))$. Consequently, Ohlin draws the following conclusion:

> "the increase of investment purchases implies that at the end of the period the incomes show themselves to be bigger than what was formerly expected [PQ was expected], i.e. they have given a 'surplus'. As the consumption purchases have been unchanged this increase in income has been saved. The saving [realized] has increased due to the decrease in the rate of interest" (ibid., pp.27-28).

Hence, the whole increase in income is saved, and is

equal to the increase in investment.[10] In this type
of analysis we would have exactly the same effects on
prices and quantities if the demand curve shifted out
because of higher income anticipations, and then
planned demand for consumption goods would increase
even if planned investment were equal to planned
savings (cp. ibid., p.27). This is a formal proof
that the aggregate demand approach is superior to the
analysis of Myrdal et al., who looked mainly at the ex
ante balance between savings and investments. But as
we have already mentioned, that only implies that we
have to add the plans for demand and supply of
consumption goods to Myrdal's formulation of monetary
equilibrium.

In the example above the whole increase in
income is saved as a windfall, or as 'residual income'
as Ohlin calls it (cp. Ohlin 1934, p.28 n.1). This
is similar to Myrdal's analysis, and this increase
will only affect the plans for the next period as was
shown by Hammarskjöld (cp. sect. VII:3). However,
Ohlin also adds that during such a process "even the
income anticipations will increase during the period
and thereby the consumption purchase" (Ohlin 1934,
p.28), but even in this case certain income changes
will have a windfall character. It is probable that
Ohlin here refers to something like a multiplier, and
he actually mentions Kahn's article (cp. ibid., p.103
n.2) for the first time in any Swedish work. But in a
period analysis there can of course be no changes in

---

10 This mode of analysing is similar to Kahn's
analysis of the fundamental equations in his
multiplier article (cp. Kahn 1931, pp.9-10). Kahn
shows that for a closed economy the increase in the
cost of investment (I' in the Treatise) is exactly
balanced by an increase in saving, if the supply of
consumption goods is perfectly elastic. However he
assumes that (I'-S)/R stays the same after the
increase in investment, and I' is thus still smaller
than S. Hence, the new situation is not an
equilibrium situation since the price level is
different from the cost of production and where the
latter represents the long run equilibrium, i.e.
$P \neq (E/O)$ (cp. Keynes 1930A, p.122; p.137).

the anticipations 'during the period'.[11] Hence, either the income anticipations are correct and then they include the effects of the multiplier, or the multiplier might have a lagged character, a la Dennis Robertson, where the difference between the realized income for the previous period and the current period is saved. However, there exists a further problem in grafting the multiplier onto Ohlin's analysis, namely whether Ohlin thought of these equilibrating changes as leading to an equilibrium situation, as in Keynes' application of the multiplier (cp. sect. 2 App. I), or just to positions in an ongoing disequilibrium process.

4.3 - Equilibrating mechanism or ex post identities.

Ohlin often seems to confuse an equilibrating mechanism leading to an equilibrium situation of one sort or another with an ex post identity at the end of the period during a disequilibrium process. His entanglement is well exemplified by the following quotation:

"The new savings are produced by those, who for the time being have an increased cash holding" (ibid., p.110; cp. p.39).

Hence, an increased cash holding of a temporary character is looked upon as savings. That is in line with his usage of the latter term as income which has not been spent, without taking into consideration saving plans or saving propensities, like (s) in Lindahl's price formula (cp. ibid., p.37; sect. IV:1:3). However, this is an offshoot to Ohlin's view of equilibrium as being just the ex post identity between bought and sold quantities. But that shows that he has not properly understood the capabilities of an ex ante analysis as developed by Myrdal, which

---

11 It is possible that Ohlin is already thinking at this stage in terms of a unit period which is shorter than the period which it takes for the multiplier 'to work itself out', and during the latter period endogenous changes will therefore take place (cp. sect. XI:1:3).

would define equilibrium as an ex ante equality among certain plans. From this point of view, the ex post equality would only represent an equilibrium if it implied that the ex ante anticipations have been fulfilled. Otherwise, it will serve as a basis for changing the plans, which may or may not lead to an equilibrium for the coming period. Therefore Ohlin's main mistake seems to be a mix-up of ex ante and ex post notions.[12]

We would therefore argue that Ohlin is not determining an equilibrium position via the principle of effective demand, even if his analysis of the process leading up to the ex post equalities has

----

[12] In August 1933 Hammarskjöld wrote a critical note on Ohlin's draft of the report to the commission of which Hammarskjöld was the secretary (cp. Steiger 1976, p.362). The note contains among other things an obscure critique of Ohlin's notion of savings (cp. Hammarskjöld 1933B, pp.4-5; p.14). But Hammarskjöld's points have actually arisen because of Ohlin's confusing use of ex ante and ex post notions without any proper equilibrium concept. However, Hammarskjöld can not resolve the problem. Therefore, we can not support Steiger's view of Hammarskjöld's critique:

"what Hammarskjöld attacks as a 'contradiction' was one of the most fruitful insights Lindahl, Myrdal, and Ohlin had developed - the ex ante/ex post perspective of macroeconomic variables - above all, that of saving and investment" (Steiger 1976, p.362).

It seems more likely that Ohlin at this time did not fully understand or accept some of Lindahl's and Myrdal's 'most fruitful insights'.

certain traits in common with Keynes' mechanism.[13]
But, according to Landgren, it is easy to reinterpret
Ohlin's analysis of the equilibrating mechanism as a
comparative static framework and then compare it with
Keynes' analysis (cp. Landgren 1960, p.171; p.299).
This is the basis for his proposition: "that Ohlin
carried out a 'Keynesian' revolution in Swedish
economics" (ibid., p.299). However, Ohlin, like
Lindahl and Myrdal, pursues a disequilibrium
analysis, which amongst other things involves changes
in real income. But it is not possible, without
further ado, to transfer propositions, e.g. the
equilibrating mechanism, from this type of analysis
to an equilibrium framework. In fact, Lindahl is the
only one who really says what he considers to be true
for stationary equilibrium (cp. sect. IV:3:3).
Incidentally, if Landgren's procedure were possible,
then Myrdal would have carried out 'a 'Keynesian'
revolution in Swedish economics', since he also
includes quantity changes if there are unemployed
resources at the beginning of the cumulative process
(cp. sect. VI:4:1). Landgren ends up in this
mistaken analysis, because he never looks at the
dynamic methods developed for analysing
disequilibrium processes with changes in the level of
income and prices. Instead, he makes a direct
analogy to Keynes' equilibrium framework for
determining the equilibrium level of income (cp.

----

13 Our analysis of the principle of effective demand
(cp. App. I) is slightly different from Patinkin's,
who emphasizes "a feedback mechanism by which changes
in output directly affect demand" (Patinkin 1978,
p.414). However, we consider that Ohlin almost had
this mechanism, but it was not used to determine an
equilibrium position. This difference is probably
due to Patinkin's refusal to accept that Keynes
determined a long run equilibrium position with
unemployment and Patinkin speaks instead of "a
dynamic theory of unemployment disequilibrium"
(Patinkin 1976, p.113). Anyhow, even if Patinkin's
interpretation of Keynes' equilibrium (as being a
short run equilibrium (cp. ibid., p.116)), our
conclusion would still hold since Ohlin does not
determine any type of equilibrium situation.

Chapter 8   189

sect. 2-3 App. I).[14] Brems has noticed the weakness in Landgren's interpretation:

"Landgren, no friend of dynamics, ascribes to Ohlin a rather un-Ohlinian static-equilibrium determination of income and output" (Brems 1978, p.410; cp. Steiger 1978, p.441).

But for Brems, that means that Ohlin's analysis of a variable physical output actually goes beyond the 'static equilibrium' of the General Theory since Ohlin supplies a dynamic analysis (cp. ibid., pp.398-399), which was later taken up by the followers of Keynes, e.g. Harrod and Samuelson (cp. ibid., p.411). However, it must be considered completely unfounded to compare Ohlin's disequilibrium analysis with Harrod's and Samuelson's formulations of dynamic equilibrium, since we have shown that Ohlin had no clear concept of equilibrium besides static equilibrium and later he even rejected the possibility of constructing a 'dynamic equilibrium' (cp. Ohlin 1937B, p.224; sect. XI:1:3).

Steiger has given an extra twist to these arguments since he states that Ohlin was not the only one to go beyond static equilibrium, because Keynes' "General Theory cannot be reduced to such an

---

14 This view is supported by Fernholm's critique of Landgren's dissertation and Yohe has later backed the former's standpoint (cp. Fernholm 1960, pp.176-177; Yohe 1978, p.450).

equilibrium" (Steiger 1978, p.443).[15] It is true that
Keynes does not discuss a static equilibrium, but
that does not imply that he does not use any notion
of equilibrium. We have thus shown that Keynes
constructed a particular notion of long run
equilibrium (cp. sect. 3 App. I). Hence, we would
still hold that the crucial difference between Keynes
on the one hand and Ohlin, Myrdal and Lindahl on the
other hand is the fact that in Keynes' analysis
changes in income constitute the equilibrating
mechanism which determines the equilibrium level of
income, while the Swedes only determine an ex post
equality.

It is instead more natural to look upon Ohlin's
analysis as geared towards business-cycle theory,
which explains the ex post equality between savings
and investment via changes in prices and quantities,
but it does not determine any particular equilibrium
level of aggregate income and employment (cp. Ohlin

---

15 Steiger adds an even further twist to his own
argument when he insists that the Keynesian
revolution implies not only the principle of
effective demand but also "the significance of
uncertainty for investment decisions" (Steiger 1978,
p.446); from this point of view both Ohlin, Myrdal and
Lindahl anticipated Keynes. However, Steiger says
earlier in the same article that "Keynes incorporate
the uncertainty factor in the General Theory by means
of the concept of liquidity preference" (ibid.,
p.444, italics omitted), which coincides with our
interpretation of Keynes (cp. sect. 3 App. I). But
this proves in fact that the Swedes did not
anticipate Keynes since their inclusion of
uncertainty leads to the construction of dynamic
methods, which do not necessarily attack the role of
the rate of interest in static theory, while Keynes
thought of his theory as a complete substitute for
orthodox theory.

1933C, p.379).[16] Most business cycle theories do treat physical output as a variable, but that does not necessarily imply the principle of effective demand, since the latter principle not only says that output is changing, but also that these changes are part and parcel of a mechanism which determines the equilibrium level of output and employment. As regards Ohlin's position on this problem, we can rely on his own comments to his report to the Unemployment Committee:

> "the very assignment given by the Unemployment Committee referred to the quantity of employment, and it would have been downright impossible not to consider the latter a variable and with it national income in terms of quantity side by side with the price level and income in terms of value" (Letter from Ohlin to Brems, 2 December 1977, as quoted in Brems 1978, p.410).[17]

In a business cycle analysis one could also describe, as a matter of fact, a situation which is characterized as "a deep depression in which everything price and cost relations is temporarily

----

16 That seems to be close to Yohe's characterization of Ohlin's analysis:

> "it is in the broad sense of the term that Ohlin's 1933 paper may be classed at all as 'monetary theory', i.e. a synonym for business-cycle theory" (Yohe 1978, p.451).

17 The same opinion had already been put forward by Lindahl in 1939:

> "It is very natural that the Commission should have devoted its attention principally to cyclical unemployment, since its work was necessarily influenced by the depression which came on during the time of its investigation" (Lindahl 1939E, p.351).

'frozen'" (Ohlin 1933C, p.362). This 'temporary'
situation might then be explained as follows:

> "when prices have been falling for a while,
> investment demand and consumption demand
> may stop falling and the price fall come to
> an end. The reason may be that consumption
> demand cannot easily contract beyond a
> certain point, and its resilience will check
> the tendency to declining investment
> demand" (ibid., p.379).

In fact, both the situation and the explanation of
its existence are identical to Myrdal's analysis in
Monetary Equilibrium (cp. sect. VI:4:2:3). Hence,
Ohlin's analysis, like Myrdal's, amounts to an
explanation of the bottom of a business cycle rather
than of an underemployment equilibrium.

Chapter 9

A Fully Developed Sequence Analysis
Lindahl (1934-1935)

"The new construction is supposed to replace
the somewhat strained construction used in
Penningpolitikens Medel, pp.31-31 [The Rate
of Interest, pp.158-160] as a series of
temporary equilibrium situations, by which I
tried to get a connection to the ordinary
static theory" (Letter from Lindahl to
Frisch, 23 October 1934).

This chapter will show that around the turn of the
year 1934 Lindahl had already laid the foundation of
sequence analysis, in the sense that he had given the
first proper algebraic formulation of a single-period
analysis plus a sketch of the problems involved in a
continuation analysis. At this time Lindahl had also
reached the conclusion that the construction of a
general dynamic theory should stand in the forefront
of economic theory, which implies that other dynamic
methods, like temporary equilibrium, can be derived
from sequence analysis.[1]
    Lindahl's development of sequence analysis shows
that he has incorporated some of the notions
developed earlier on by the Stockholm School, such
as, for example, ex ante/ex post and Hammarskjöld's
ideas about the length of the period. We can now use
his method to take a fresh look at some of the
problems and methods dealt with in the earlier
chapters, e.g. the effects of autonomous changes in
consumption on the capital market equilibrium and the
dynamic methods developed before sequence analysis.

----
1 This has also been the rationale in our analytical
framework for taking sequence analysis as our
starting-point in the classification of different
dynamic methods (cp. sect. II:1).

1 - The dating of Lindahl's contribution.

For the first time since the publication of The Rate of Interest (1930) Lindahl returned to the problem of theoretical dynamics in October 1934. That month Lindahl started to circulate a stencil with the title "A Note on the Dynamic Pricing Problem". It is difficult to say when he started to work on this note, but judging from the following letter it could not have been before the summer of 1933:

> "In recent years I have not had time to work with monetary theory. But it seems now to have become highly modern ... . This Summer I must myself take up this subject again" (Letter from Lindahl to Lundberg, 19 March 1933).

The note contains only the barest of outlines of a disequilibrium approach and a sequence analysis. Furthermore, Lindahl gives almost no hints of the 'vision' or inductive background to this approach, and such a background is not to be found until 1939 when Lindahl published "The Dynamic Approach to Economic Theory" (Lindahl 1939B). However, we have fortunately unearthed a draft to the first chapter of a book called "Monetary Policy and its Theoretical Basis" (Lindahl 1935), and judging from a letter to Hicks, this draft was finished sometime in February 1935 (cp. Letter to Hicks, 22 April 1935).[2] The draft is almost identical to sections 1-5 and section 9 in "The Dynamic Approach". The sections added in the latter work relate amongst other things to general ideas on planning, and it seems that these sections might have been influenced by Svennilson's dissertation of 1938. Thus, Lindahl had worked out his sequence analysis as well as the general 'vision' of his dynamic analysis during the autumn of 1934 and the very beginning of 1935.

---

2 This book was never published and judging from the table of contents it was planned as a fusion of "The Dynamic Approach" (Lindahl 1939B) and The Rate of Interest (Lindahl 1930).

2 - A general dynamic theory as a basis for all economic theory.

Economic theory has the following object according to Lindahl:

> "to provide theoretical structures showing how certain given initial conditions give rise to certain developments. The structures are to be used as instruments with which to analyse historical and practical problems. Economic theory has thus no end in itself; it is only a servant of those parts of economic science which are devoted to the treatment of concrete economic problems. But it is an indispensable servant. Even the arrangement of empirical material must be based on a system of concepts, elaborated by economic theory" (Lindahl 1939B, p.23; cp. Lindahl 1935, pp.1-2).

Hence, economic theory needs tools of 'a purely logical character', which even if they "do not in themselves contain any statements about the real world" (Lindahl 1935, p.2) are still necessary for pursuing a concrete analysis. However, economic theory had not yet developed these theoretical structures, which was the raison d'etre for Lindahl's research programme:

> "for the time being, there is an especial need for generalisation of the concepts and assumptions used by theorists" (ibid., p.6; cp. p.4; Lindahl 1939B, p.28; p.31).

But this research programme did not simply emerge from a particular situation within the development of economic theory, since Lindahl also espouses the following view of the relation between general and particular theories:

> "the systematic exposition of economic theory should begin with general dynamic structures and then proceed to more particular assumptions" (Lindahl 1939B, p.34; cp. p.25; p.27; p.33; Lindahl 1935,

p.8).

The general dynamic theory should thus precede the
more particular theories, e.g. static theory, and the
latter are in fact constructed from the dynamic
theory. We have seen above that Lundberg voiced the
same idea in 1930 (cp. sect. V:2), which lead him to
throw out some prescient remarks concerning model
sequences which he developed first in Economic
Expansion.
    Lindahl more or less sticks to his old ideas
concerning the difference between statics and
dynamics (cp. Lindahl 1935, pp.7-8; sect. IV:2:2).
Nevertheless, it is obvious that he has now discarded
the following method, which he used in "The Place of
Capital":

> "an attempt to approach gradually a
> realistic economic theory, beginning with a
> simplified static analysis and introducing
> successively more complicated assumptions"
> (Lindahl 1939A, p.10; cp. sect. IV:2:3a:3).

The Rate of Interest probably also belongs to this
approach, since the idea of an equilibrium for the
first period makes it possible to use the ordinary
static tools (cp. Lindahl 1939B, p.68). Lindahl's
new view on how to develop dynamic theory is thus a
conscious break with his earlier position.

3 - The vision behind the construction of a general
dynamic theory.

3.1 - The concept of plan.
    Economic theory mainly studies "human actions or
the results of human actions" (Lindahl 1935, p.10; cp.
Lindahl 1939B, p.35). But human behaviour could not
be explained in the same way as events in the
physical world, which implies that "we can not prove
that certain human actions will necessarily be the
result of a definite situation at a given point of
time" (ibid.; cp. Lindahl 1939B, p.35), i.e. to
determine a definite dynamic sequence. However, this
is only a problem for the empirical relevance of the

theory, but it does not show that the theory is inconsistent. The construction of a dynamic theory thus 'solves' the problem in the following way:

> "all inexactness can be avoided through explicit <u>assumptions</u> about everything that in the real world cannot be definitely settled. We can thus assume that individuals, under given conditions, do act in a certain manner, and the use of this assumption makes it possible to determine exactly what results will develop from any given situation" (ibid., p.11; cp. Lindahl 1939B, p.35).

To develop his general dynamic approach Lindahl needs only to rely on the following postulate:

> "one basic assumption about the behaviour of the acting individuals, namely that their actions, for a shorter or a longer period, only represent the <u>fulfilment of certain plans,</u> given at the beginning of the period and determined by certain <u>principles</u> that can be stated in some way or the other. These principles should in general imply that the plans are made for the attainment of certain aims ... and that they are based on the individual expectations concerning future conditions, expectations which in their turn are influenced by the individual conceptions of the past events" (ibid.; cp. Lindahl 1939B, p.36).

<u>The notion of plan had played a central role within the Stockholm School almost from its beginning, but here for the first time it is explicitly stated that</u>

this is the pivot for its dynamic method.[3] The
relevance of the dynamic method therefore hinges upon
the realism of this basic assumption.

Lindahl later discriminates between two phases
in the actual planning procedure:

"first the intellectual prognoses of future
developments under alternative assumptions
as to the actions of the individual making
the plan, now and in the future; secondly
the valuation and decision whereby a choice
between these alternatives is made"
(Lindahl 1939B, p.40).

Therefore, it is necessary to analyse why particular
plans are chosen. But it was Svennilson's particular
contribution, rather than Lindahl's, to construct a
theoretical scheme for analysing this choice (cp.
Svennilson 1938, in particular part two).

3.2 - The relation between plans and periods.
     If the economic process is supposed to consist
of actions derived from definite plans, then it is
obvious that it takes a certain amount of time to
realize these actions, i.e. a period of time is
involved (cp. Lindahl 1935, p.13). As far as changes
in plans are concerned, Lindahl assumes that these
are "related to definite moments, namely to those
points of time at which the economic subject makes
the decision to set in practice a new plan" (ibid.).
Hence, it is implied that a period is defined by
unchanged plans, which was already hinted at by
Hammarskjöld (cp. sect. VII:2).

----
3 It should be noted that 'actions' and 'plans' are
not the same thing, since the former are realizations
of the latter (cp. Lindahl 1935, p.12). Lindahl
therefore denotes the whole demand curve as a plan
while the actions depend on the actual market price
(cp. Lindahl 1939B, p.56 n.*). Svennilson later
makes the same distinction (cp. Svennilson 1938,
p.19), but Landgren erroneously reverses the
influence (cp. Landgren 1957, p.31).

Because of the fact that the plans are intermittently revised <u>the dynamic process will have a discontinuous character</u>:

> "the dynamic process as a whole is not a continuous one, but that, from a theoretical point of view, it consists of <u>two</u> types of movements: first the events during a certain <u>periods</u> of time, and, secondly, the events at the transition <u>points</u> between these periods. The determining of these latter <u>discontinuous</u> changes, that is, the alterations of the plans of production and consumption ... may be regarded as the central part of the dynamic theory" (Lindahl 1934, pp.210-211; cp. Lindahl 1935, p.13).

It seems likely that the stress Lindahl puts on changing plans and the concomitant discontinuous process may be the reason why he shows no interest in using difference equations, since this tool presumes that the behaviour is unchanged which implies 'mechanical dynamics' (cp. sect. II:5; Note 5 Ch.10).

3.3 - The upper and the lower limits of the length of the period.

Lindahl does not discuss this problem in any detail in "Monetary Policy" where he only states that the period has to be 'fairly short':

> "There is now in operation a great variety of plans ... . One cannot count upon all these plans being kept wholly unaltered during a longer time period. The attempts to realise the plans must very soon show, that they are more or less incompatible with one another. The actual course of events cannot correspond to all the anticipations that the individuals have made about each others behaviour. The result must therefore be a modification of some of the plans" (Lindahl 1935, p.19; cp. Lindahl 1939B, p.55).

This idea seems to imply that there is an <u>upper limit</u> to the length of the period which is related to the probable incompatibility of the plans. Hence, the definition given in "The Dynamic Approach":

"the explanation of an economic process is after a certain point dependent on the registration of what has happened ... . Such registration is necessary in so far as it must be assumed to influence the planning and future actions of the economic subjects" (Lindahl 1939B, p.54).

This definition of the upper limit is the same as Hammarskjöld's view, that the registration of the profit for the current period must not influence what is going on during the same period (cp. sect. VII:2). As the existence of profits in Hammarskjöld's sense show that the plans are inconsistent, it follows that the registration of profit is an acknowledgement by the individuals that the plans are incongruent and should be revised.

Lindahl is the first to explain why there must be a <u>lower limit</u> to the length of the period. The lower limit arises from the following 'imperfection of human knowledge':

"Man cannot continuously register all that happens around him. He can only take account of it <u>intermittently</u>, observing the total result obtained for certain time periods, or registering more important events that can be referred to definite points of time" (Lindahl 1939B, p.42).

However, it is obvious that the plans must be defined as having a lower limit for another reason, namely, that continuous alterations of plans would imply that nothing definite could be said about what is going to happen. Thus, the method would have no explanatory value. This problem is similar to the inclusion of time lags in Lindahl's analysis of the cumulative process, which guarantees that the process will not be an avalanche (cp. Lindahl 1939C, pp.172-173; p.251).

202   Chapter 9

The determination of the length of the period becomes more complicated in an _aggregate_ analysis, since the individual plans are not synchronized, that is to say the _individual_ plans are not changed at the same time (cp. Lindahl 1939B, p.54; Note 4 Ch.7). This problem has the following influence on the length of the period in an aggregate analysis:

> "the time interval during which the plans of all members are unchanged must of course be much shorter than the time interval during which the plans of a single planner are kept unaltered" (ibid., p.125).

But the length of the period should not disappear (i.e. become zero) as long as each individual plan has a lower limit. In fact the length should be the highest common denominator. There is, of course, no guarantee that the period is long enough for profitable application to empirical analysis. But Lindahl is optimistic on this moot point:

> "Our scheme can ... even from a strictly logical point of view, be directly applied, if only the time periods used are made _sufficiently_ short. It should further be observed that, when we have to apply our scheme to practical problems, it is a quite justifiable simplification of the problem to assume that the time periods that elapse between the alteration of the plans are not _impossibly_ short but long enough to be of practical use. This represents only a slight modification of what really happens, and it helps us to get a clearer insight into the nature of the economic development" (Lindahl 1935, p.20; cp. Lindahl 1939B, p.55).

4 - Sequence analysis.

We will here discuss Lindahl's "A Note on the Dynamic Pricing Problem" of 1934, which gives the first proper sequence analysis. Lindahl discusses in this short note (four pages) most of the problems involved in a sequence analysis, and it is only his remarks on the complete dynamic process which are insufficient. In fact, this essay may be regarded as a prototype for all sequence analysis even if, for example, Lindahl's "Algebraic discussion" in "The Dynamic Approach" obviously contains a much more extensive analysis (cp. Lindahl 1939B, pp.74-136). Furthermore, the latter work does not really add anything to the fundamental structure and the most striking difference is basically the inclusion of financial markets.

4.1 - The problem of single-period analysis.

At an arbitrary point in time, t, the plans for production and consumption are given for a certain period of time (t to t+1), which means that once the prices are known then the individual actions are determined and fixed for the period (cp. Lindahl 1934, p.204). It is assumed that at the point t+1 the plans are changed. The problem to be solved is then the following:

> "the analysis of what happens during the said period, that is, the determination of the situation at the point t+1 as it results from the situation at the point t. When this problem is solved, the situation at the point t+2 can in the same manner be explained as it results from the situation at the point t+1, and so on. The solution of this problem implies, therefore, (...), the solution of the whole dynamic problem" (ibid.).

The solution to this problem, i.e. the single-period analysis contributes to the 'whole dynamic problem' in the sense that the same method could also be employed for the period (t+1 to t+2) at point t+1. But it does not yet entail the proposition that the whole dynamic process (from t to t+1 and onwards) has

been determined at point t, since the solution to
that problem, i.e. continuation analysis, needs some
further assumptions (cp. sect. 4:5).

4.2 - The assumption.
    At the beginning of the period the expected
value of the goods to be delivered during the period
(PT) is by definition equal to the expected value of
the production costs (E+D).[4] This definitional
relation follows from the assumption:

> "that part of E that is contractual income
> is known by the entrepreneurs; the income
> expectations of the wage-earners are, for
> the period in question, thus equal to the
> sum that the entrepreneurs expect to pay as
> wages during this period" (Lindahl 1934,
> p.207).

    Judging by the way Lindahl proceeds in his
analysis, it is implicit that all net incomes to the
owners of factors of production have a contractual
nature, including what we call normal profit.
Lindahl has therefore taken over an assumption that
was already developed by Hammarskjöld (cp. sect.
VII:4:1). The costs are thus known beforehand by the

----
4 P: the average price of all goods and consumers'
     services that have been sold during previous
     periods for delivery during the present period,
     or which the producers expect to sell during the
     present period. The payment takes place on
     delivery (cp. Lindahl 1939B, p.74).
  T: the corresponding quantity of products,
     calculated in a unit that is in accord with the
     notation of P.
  E: the sum of all net incomes that the owners of
     the factors expect to receive, including
     expectations of profits.
  D: the expected depreciation of the capital stock,
     occasioned by the delivery of products during
     the period, minus the appreciation of the same
     stock that is expected to take place (cp.
     Lindahl 1934, p.206).

entrepreneurs, and any difference between E and E' [5] must consequently be due to deviations from the normal profit. Hence the extra profit has a windfall character, and it is reckoned ex post, as in most of the works from the Stockholm School as well as in Keynes' Treatise (cp. Keynes 1930A, pp.112-113, p.126).

Lindahl assumes that the supply prices are given during the period, so all changes in prices take place at the transition point between two consecutive periods, i.e. a fixprice method. (cp. Lindahl 1934, p.204). At the end of the period the value of the goods actually sold (PT') must then necessarily be equal to realized net income and depreciation (E'+D'). At the same time, PT' must be equal to the value of the actual purchases for consumption goods (E'-S') and capital goods (I'+D'), and it follows that $I' \equiv S'$.[6]

The latter identity was criticized by Haberler, who obviously used a Robertsonian idea of income, namely, that "income available for spending = income earned or realised during the preceding period" (Letter from Haberler to Lindahl, 1 November 1934). The critique gives an oppurtunity for Lindahl to state that his concept of saving is different from Robertson's but akin to Keynes', and he even holds "that a part of the objections that R. has brought against Keynes are refuted with my (and Myrdal's)

----

5 E', D' etc. are calculated at the end of the period, i.e. ex post magnitudes.
6 I: the investment, defined as the planned increase of the capital employed by a firm, to be realized either by the purchase of capital goods produced by other firms, or the increase of the stock of the firm in so far as the sum of these two items is in excess of the depreciation of capital.
   S: the total saving planned by the consumers at the beginning of the period. The definition of the concept must be in accordance with the definition of income, so that (E-S) is equal to the sum of what the consumers intend to pay for goods and services during the period (cp. Lindahl 1934, p.206).

distinction between planned and realized savings"
(Letter to Haberler, 6 November 1934). In fact, it
seems that Lindahl doubted that Keynes' formulations
in the Treatise were ex post formulations (cp.
Letter from Lindahl to Haberler, 20 November 1934;
cp. sect. 4:3:2).

4.3.1 - The ex post equality in a disequilibrium process.

To solve his problem Lindahl makes the following
important assumption concerning the spending plans:

> "the plans for production and consumption,
> existing at the beginning of the period,
> have been actualy realized during the
> period, as regards the amounts that the
> consumers have granted to their consumption
> and the producers to the provision of new
> capital goods to be delivered during the
> period" (Lindahl 1934, p.207).

The role of this assumption is to show that the
actions during the period "can be directly deduced
from the plans [once the prices are given] at the
beginning of the period" (Lindahl 1939B, p.92). It is
only because of this assumption that "the excess of
realized over expected sales appears as a logical
necessity" (ibid., p.127). Hence, the result of the
period is a necessary outcome of the ex ante plans
for the current period.
    It is implied that the purchasing plans for
consumer and capital goods are realized, i.e. E-

---

7 The indices a,b,c, ... n indicate the different
stages of the productive process. The stage (a)
contains the production of services and non-durable
goods which are sold to the consumers, the stage (b)
the production of capital goods which are sold to the
producers in stage (a), the stage (c) the production
of capital goods which are sold to the producers in
stage (b), etc.. In the last stage (n), no capital
goods are received from producers in other stages.

$S \equiv P_a T'_a$ and $I+D \equiv PT'-P_a T'_a$.[7,][8] These two identities could be summarized as $(E-S)+(I+D) \equiv PT'$, which could then be transformed into $(I-S) \equiv (E'-E)-(D-D') \equiv P(T'-T)$.[9] If for example $I>S$ then the following will happen:

> "income gains for the producers, that is, a positive value of the expression $(E-E')$, if that is not prevented by an increase of the depreciation term D'. In that latter case, the only immediate effect of the excess of planned investment over planned saving will be a decrease in the stocks of the producers" (Lindahl 1934, p.209).

Thus for the first time there is a formal example of how disequilibrium during a period, in the sense that not all plans are fulfilled, leads to an ex post equality via a change in income or stocks. This is basically the same argument as was put forward by

----

8 Bent Hansen makes the following comment on this assumption:

> "It is a typical assumption of a not insignificant part of the Stockholm School that purchase plans are always fulfilled without exception, but ... it turns out to be a wholly or partly untenable assumption when applied to the analysis of inflation – in any case so long as prices are fixed throughout the period" (Hansen 1951, p.29).

Lindahl et cons. must therefore assume that there are enough unemployed factors of production and sufficient stocks of consumer and capital goods (cp. ibid., p.30; p.45).
9 According to Steiger, Ohlin has, in a letter to Lindahl (7 December 1934), brought out "some tacit assumption" (Steiger 1976, p.360) which this identity presupposes. But Steiger does not mention what this 'tacit assumption' is supposed to entail, and as far as we can understand, Ohlin and Lindahl used the same assumption, namely, that planned purchases are realized.

Myrdal and to a certain extent by Ohlin, but now it is given a more explicit formulation. However, as was the case with Myrdal and Ohlin, there is no reason to interpret this ex post equality as a proof that Lindahl applied the principle of effective demand (cp. sect. VI:4:4; sect. VIII:4:3).

Lindahl does not discuss the actual length of a unit period except to say that it is equal to the time for which the plans are unchanged. However, since most income is contracted and paid out by the entrepreneurs there can be no change in income and consumption without changes in the production plans, and the time it takes to change these plans can therefore serve as a unit period. In this case Lindahl's analysis will coincide with Lundberg's choice for the unit period:

> "As a unit period we select a reaction interval, measuring the average distance between the rise in demand and the subsequent increase in production activity. On the condition that the plans as to consumers' outlay do not change independently of the operations of producers, the unit-period will also express the interval of time between changes in production activity ... . The unit-period will in this way constitute an expression for the fact that producers react with a certain inertia to changes in receipts and profits" (Lundberg 1937, p.187).

It is then likely that in the 'income period', i.e. the time for which the income contracts run, the sales plans and the fixed supply prices are linked to this unit period. However, the plans could be made up for a much longer period of time. But, the point is that they will not be revised until the end of the period even if the entrepreneurs start to have strong feelings during the period that the plans will not be fulfilled. Hence, all adjustments during the period take place through changes in stocks, which is a characteristic of the fixprice method (cp. Note 8).

4.3.2 - Lindahl on the fundamental equations.

Lindahl proves that his formula (I-S) will determine the total profit from Keynes' second fundamental equation (cp. Letter from Lindahl to Keynes, 7 November 1934, in Keynes 1979, pp. 122-123). Furthermore, it is shown that the value of investment in Keynes' formula is identical to Lindahl's realized investment, which implicitly demonstrates that Keynes' equations are ex post formulations. However, Lindahl has his doubts about this implication:

> "Only regarding one point I cannot understand you fully, namely that the difference between saving and investment not is a cause of losses but the losses themselves. Even if this should be a consequence of Keynes' definitions (which I doubt), it seems to me not in accordance with a sensible definition of the terms" (Letter from Lindahl to Haberler, 20 November 1934).

But we would argue that the terms in Keynes' equations are, strictly speaking, ex post quantities (cp. Keynes 1930A, p.126). However, with the help of ex ante and ex post Lindahl was able to give them 'a sensible definition', and then they were appropriate for the task they were supposed to solve, namely acting as "the mainspring of change" (ibid., p.141).

4.4 - Autonomous changes in consumption and capital market equilibrium.

By dividing the economy into different stages, an idea which was taken from Hammarskjöld (cp. Letter from Lindahl to Frisch, 23 October 1934), Lindahl demonstrates the following proposition:

> "the amount of planned saving is only of direct importance to the producers of consumption goods and services and that the investments terms only affect the producers of capital goods. If a positive value of (I-S) is ceteris paribus caused only by a diminished value of S, that is, an increase

of (E-S) in relation to the expectations of
the producers of the a stage expressed by
the term $P_a T_a$, then the whole gain will go
to these producers of consumption goods"
(Lindahl 1934, p.209).

This shows explicitly that a disturbance could arise
from the consumption side of the market only, as was
stressed by Ohlin (cp. sect. VIII:3). However, this
disturbance will still appear as a disruption of the
'neo-Wicksellian equilibrium' condition, namely, as
$I \neq S$. This is obvious if we look at the complete
equilibrium condition, which says that the purchase
plans for consumption and capital goods are equal to
the planned production, i.e. $(E-S)+(I+D) \equiv PT$, which
boils down to $I=S$, since by definition $E+D \equiv PT$ (cp.
sect. 4:2). Hence, it is important to notice that
under this assumption the equilibrium condition ($I=S$)
is not only related to the capital market, which was
Ohlin's standard criticism, but also to the market
for consumption goods, since the complete equilibrium
condition shows that ex ante savings (S) are related
to the market for consumption goods.

4.5 - The complete dynamic process or the problem of continuation analysis.

We have now been able to determine the ex post
results from the given ex ante plans at t. But this
does not imply that the ongoing process after t+1 can
be determined at t without further assumptions, i.e.
the problem of continuation analysis remains. The
crucial supposition concerns the relation between ex
ante plans for the forthcoming period and the ex post
result for the current period:

"this problem could only be dealt with
theoretically under the assumption that one
makes particular postulates concerning the
relation between the process of events
during a period and the ex ante concepts for
the next period" (Letter from Lindahl to
Ohlin, 31 December 1934).[10]

That this was a very conscious position on Lindahl's part can be seen from the fact that this letter to Ohlin was in reality a reply to the latter's grave doubts about the usefulness of this method:

> "The greatest difficulties might be met with the treatment of those parts of the development which you locate at the borders between the periods. Therefore, one should according to my opinion be aware of not having too great expectations concerning the usefulness of the conceptual apparatus, which is the result of the ex-ante and ex-post partition" (Letter from Ohlin to Lindahl, 7 December 1934).

Lindahl seems to make the following 'particular postulates', namely, <u>if the plans are fulfilled and there are no changes in the exterior events, then it is possible to postulate a simple functional relation between the ex ante plans for the consecutive period and the ex post result of the current period.</u> By using this assumption for several periods we reach the following result:

----
10 A.G.Hart gives a very succinct picture of Lindahl's view:

> "We can describe the rational adaptation of plans to anticipation, but not the rational adaptation of anticipation to events. I am in hearty sympathy with what is apparently your view, that we can proceed further in dynamic analysis only on the basis of special assumptions which enable us to bridge this gap" (Letter from Hart to Lindahl, 5 November 1934).

This gives in fact a glimpse of Harts' ideas on 'expectational' dynamics (cp. Note 5 Ch.10). However, Lindahl does not give any answer to this particular point in his responding letter to Hart.

"the whole dynamic process can be deduced
from the data [the plans at t are part of
the data], given at the beginning of the
first period" (Lindahl 1934, p.210).

Lindahl does not mention that if the functional
relations between the periods always have the same
form, then we can interpret the whole dynamic process
as a case of moving equilibrium. The equilibrium
character of the process would in such a case be
defined in the following way:

"The existence of equilibrium through time
... presupposes the existence of an
expectation function of constant form"
(Hahn 1952, p.804).

However, it was left to Lundberg to make an explicit
assumption of constant expectation functions.
Lundberg also leaves out the 'particular postulate'
that the plans have to be fulfilled within each
period. We will therefore distinguish between
equilibrium and disequilibrium sequence analysis,
where Lindahl is pursuing the former and Lundberg the
latter (cp. sect. II:1:5).

4.6 - The equilibrium concept.
    Lindahl has also a very puzzling and destructive
criticism of the 'neo-Wicksellian' equilibrium
condition:

"If the future were foreseen with certainty
by all individuals, then of course I must be
equal to S. In more realistic cases, the
equality between these quantities is
neither a necessary nor a sufficient
condition for an economic equilibrium,
supposing that the equilibrium is not
defined in such a way that the expectations
of the producers must be realized" (Lindahl
1934, p.209).

It seems that almost by sleight of hand, Lindahl has
without further comment thrown out the idea that an

equilibrium exists when the plans are fulfilled ex ante. We will now look more closely into Lindahl's argumentation.

I=S is not a <u>sufficient</u> condition for the following reason:

"I=S implies only that the sum of all expected deliveries must be equal to the <u>total</u> value of the transactions actually made during the period. But even if that is the case, there can be on the one side positive and on the other negative differences between the realized and expected selling values that can be characterized as disturbances not compatible with the equilibrium concept" (ibid., pp.209-210).

Hence, there may be disturbances, in several markets, which cancel out in the aggregate, implying that expected results will differ from realized results, i.e. that equilibrium has not been ruling during the

period.[11] <u>Lindahl is thereby the first to show that
the equilibrium condition (I=S) is not sufficient to
fulfil equilibrium, in the sense that expectations
are realized.</u> A sufficient condition has to ensure
that planned supply is equal to planned demand in
every market.

We can without any doubt accept Lindahl's
critique of the sufficiency of the equilibrium
condition. But his critique of the necessity seems
more intriguing. Lindahl's holds that it is possible
to imagine a state which is reiterated in every
period despite the fact that the producers constantly
make some losses (cp. ibid. p.209; Lindahl 1939D,
p.287 n*). However it is hard to imagine that such a
situation might be sustainable, unless Lindahl
believes that all that is involved is the question of
the expectations being "never perfectly realized"
(ibid.), i.e. there are <u>small</u> divergences. But that
would still lead us to consider equilibrium as

----

11 This point is further developed by I.Grünbaum in
"Inkongruente førventninger og begrebet monetaer
ligevaegt" (Incongruent Expectations and the Concept
of Monetary Equilibrium), where he includes the
labour market (cp. Hansen 1951, p.34 n.2). Grünbaum
takes into special consideration that anticipated
purchases and sales in the labour market are not
necessarily equal. We would then have have the
following equilibrium condition (where l_A is expected
sales of labour):
$I-S=P(T'-T)+w(l_A'-l_A)$
Grünbaum's main thesis is that if $I-S \neq 0$ the reactions
are different depending on whether $P(T'-T) \neq 0$ and/or
$w(l_A'-l_A) \neq 0$, for the following reason:

> "that for example the workers' anticipations
> are not realized in respect of their
> expected income, that has no <u>direct</u>
> influence on whether the production in the
> next period will increase or decrease, ...
> on the other hand the entrepreneurs'
> unrealized anticipations have a direct
> influence on the production" (Grünbaum 1945,
> p.102; cp. p.111).

Chapter 9   215

meaning that the plans are at least approximately realized, which means that small discrepancies are acceptable 'in more realistic cases'.

We may give a more favourable interpretation of Lindahl's point of view, if we take into consideration that his critique of the equilibrium notion comes before he mentions the continuation analysis. Therefore, the critique might refer to a single-period analysis and it is then similar to his critique of the existence of a normal rate of interest; the latter may guarantee price stability in the current period but there is no guarantee of what is going to happen in subsequent periods (cp. sect. IV:4), i.e. there is no continuation theory. Hence, Lindahl should have defined an equilibrium notion in relation to a continuation analysis, even if he considered this to be a dificult task:

> "A fuller discussion of this question [the conditions for monetary equilibrium] would necessitate a definition of the term "economic equilibrium" which seems, even from a purely monetary point of view, to be very difficult with regard to a society of non stationary character and with imperfect foresight of the future" (Lindahl 1934, p.210).

Furthermore, in the 1939 addition to The Rate of Interest, Lindahl mentions the notions of 'uncorrected' and 'corrected' long term equilibrium between saving and investment, which seem to refer to equilibrium and disequilibrium sequence analysis respectively (cp. Lindahl 1939C, pp.263-264).

5 - The disequilibrium method applied to the analysis of price movements.

Lindahl now uses his disequilibrium method to analyse problems which have always been in the forefront for the Stockholm School, namely, an explanation of price changes under dynamic conditions (cp. sect. IV:1:3).

5.1 - The fixprice method.

Lindahl gives the following background to his fixprice approach:

> "The pricing problem is often treated under the assumption of free competition, whereby the prices operating in a certain period can be regarded as the <u>result</u> of the operation of certain given demand and supply functions during the period. This construction is quite appropriate when used for the analysis of the <u>equilibrium</u> position of a price or a system of prices. But it is not always so appropriate when the pricing problem is analysed from a more realistic point of view. In an actual dynamic case, there is no necessity for equality of demand and supply. But the opposite concept of price as <u>continuously changing</u> under the influence of the demand and supply factors is equally not correct" (Lindahl 1939B, p.60).

Hence, <u>Lindahl is consciously giving up the equilibrium approach used in The Rate of Interest where the equilibrium price is determined as an outcome of the forces of demand and supply</u> (cp. sect. IV:2:1). Instead, he is applying a disequilibrium approach, though this term is first mentioned in "The Dynamic Approach". But to avoid the idea of continuously changing prices, which might be implied by the disequilibrium approach, Lindahl assumes that the supply prices are fixed at the transition point between consecutive periods and they are supposed to stay constant during the period (cp. Lindahl 1935,

p.21; Lindahl 1939B, p.61).[12] It is thus interesting
to notice that the idea of a disequilibrium method
goes hand in hand with the assumption of fixed
prices. It is assumed that supply prices will be
fixed by the sellers in accordance with their
anticipations of demand, and these anticipations, in
their turn, depend on what has happened to stocks and
orders in the foregoing periods (cp. ibid., p.23;
Lindahl 1939B, pp.62-63). The assumption of fixed
prices has the following obvious consequences for the
central pricing problem:

> "the determination of the prices offered by
> sellers and buyers is thus not directly
> related to what happens during the periods,
> but to the events, more difficult to
> analyse, that occur at the transition points
> between the periods" (bid., p.21; cp.
> Lindahl 1939B, p.61).

Despite the introduction of the disequilibrium
method, the aim is identical to the one discussed in
the earlier works. Hence, the purpose, both in The
Rate of Interest (cp. Lindahl 1939C, pp.141-142) and
in "Monetary Policy" (cp. Lindahl 1935, pp.27-28), is
to include the theory of the value of money in the
theory of relative prices in an attempt to explain
changes in the value of money. The end result is in
both cases, that the theory of relative prices should
be able to explain relative prices within the period
as well as the intertemporal price relations. This
means that the old distinction between the

----
12 Ohlin had a very high opinion of this idea:

> "I believe that the most important
> suggestion in your note [Lindahl 1935] is
> the method of considering fixed prices
> during each period determined by the
> entrepreneurs. It might be the most
> practical procedure and it is the one which
> in most cases comes closest to the reality.
> Thus a double merit" (Letter from Ohlin to
> Lindahl, 7 December 1934).

determination of relative prices and the determination of the absolute price level simply disappears, since "the problem of the general price level ... is related to the whole pricing process" (ibid., p.27).

5.2 - Disequilibrium vs. equilibrium methods.

In 1939 Lindahl compares his disequilibrium method for studying price movements with two versions of temporary equilibrium. The first version refers to Keynes' Treatise on Money, where it is assumed that all the goods produced during the period are sold irrespective of the price they will fetch, i.e. a completely inelastic supply curve. This assumption is not so unrealistic, if the transition point to the forthcoming period has been preceded by a dynamic process, which has led to the situation that "the sellers see no reason to alter under the prevailing conditions" (Lindahl 1939B, p.65). In this case the actual price is in a sense a dependent factor since it is "adjusted to the demand and supply factors as they appear currently in the market" (ibid.). The market price will of course affect the realized income for the period and it will thereby affect the behaviour for the next period. Although Lindahl is generally favourable to the Treatise, he still prefers his disequilibrium method since the other method has a particular drawback:

"the basic assumption that the quantity of consumers' goods sold is independent of the prices received for them. In reality this quantity can at least partially be adjusted to the price through changes in stock holdings" (ibid., p.68).

In the disequilibrium method coupled with the fix-price assumption, it is thus presumed that a deficiency or excess in demand will be met with changes in stocks (cp. Note 8).

The second version of temporary equilibrium is the one used by Lindahl himself in The Rate of Interest. In this case the equilibrium is characterized by an interdependence between prices and the demand and supply functions, in the sense that in the actual position demand and supply have been brought into equality via price changes, but there are also "income and cost relations (on which the curves are based) that agree with the current price" (Lindahl 1939B, p.66). Lindahl describes this method as a Walrasian equilibrium for only one period (cp. ibid.). Even if this method has "a narrower range of application to real conditions" (ibid., p.69) than the first version of temporary equilibrium, and consequently even more so in relation to the disequilibrium method, it still has one particular advantage:

> "the entire static apparatus may be employed in the analysis of a dynamic sequence. It thus bridges the gap between statics and dynamics. The cumbersome _ex ante_ and _ex post_ terminology becomes superfluous, for the individuals are assumed to have knowledge at the beginning of the period of all the transactions and of the relevant prices valid for the period" (ibid., p.68).

Hence, Lindahl still considers his version of temporary equilibrium as being valuable, at least, for analytical purposes, since it is possible to use the notions developed for static analysis.[13]

---

13 Hicks stresses the same point in his defence of temporary equilibrium (cp. Hicks 1946, p.127).

Chapter 10

Disequilibrium Sequence Analysis
Lundberg (1937)

"There is ... a difference in kind between
equilibrium processes where behaviour is
routine and non-equilibrium processes where
it is not. This has some bearing on the
setting up of dynamic models, which are not
equilibrium models in the sense that
expectations are being fulfilled. Given
available mathematical techniques, all
these models must be relatively simple, and
in fact all of them at present assume what
we called routine behaviour. Now it may be
sensible to imagine producers as changing
routine behaviour at discrete time
intervals rather than as continuously
taking new decisions. A routine is tried
for a certain period of time and if found
inappropriate replaced by another one. In
that sense, then, non-equilibrium dynamic
models of the type known to us must be
short-period models, that is the equations
must be taken to hold for certain discrete
periods of time only. From this, it follows
that it is not legitimate to use such models
to define long-period moving equilibria, for
unless expectations are being fulfilled, a
new model will have to be set up" (Hahn
1952, pp.805-806).

Our main aim is to present Lundberg's version of
the sequence analysis, and, in particular, to show in
what sense it has a disequilibrium character while at
the same time it employs a particular notion of
equilibrium. It is these two characteristics which
make Lundberg's analysis different from Lindahl's
method of 1934. We would also like to show that
Lundberg's development of the model sequences proves
that he is partly pursuing problems, which were
already dealt with in his article of 1930 (cp. Ch.5).

It is self-evident that in tackling these problems, he makes ample use of the earlier developments of the dynamic method within the Stockholm School. In the preface to Economic Expansion Lundberg also mentions that he has had the possibility of discussing his work with Lindahl, Myrdal, Johansson, Hammarskjöld and Svennilson (cp. Lundberg 1937, p.vi).

1 - The background to the model sequences.

Judging from the preface to Economic Expansion, Lundberg's general purpose is very similar to the one pursued in his article of 1930, namely, to show the limitations of static analysis, or equilibrium methods, in dynamic analysis:

> "Most of the concepts and methods of analysis employed in economic theory are related to various types of equilibrium. The conditions of an equilibrium can be exactly formulated so as to give the concepts a definite meaning, but then the methods are often transferred mechanically to a study of changes pertaining to a total economic system and embodied in a theory of money or of business cycles. As a direct confrontation with reality is not feasible, as a rule, the limitations of the conclusions drawn from such a widened application of equilibrium methods can best be judged by referring the concepts employed to a defined dynamic system. The object of this thesis is to investigate the conditions of a determinate sequence of economic changes from this point of view" (ibid., p.v).

The limitations of static analysis are thus ascertained by comparing it with 'a defined dynamic system', i.e. a Lundberg model sequence.

Before we discuss the basis of the model sequences, we will see that Lundberg has formulated his ideas as a critique of the application partial equilibrium analysis to macrodynamic problems.[1] His criticism is based on two different points, the aggregation of the partial equilibrium analysis which is then supposed to encompass the whole system, and the assumption of an unproblematic adjustment towards equilibrium (cp. ibid., p.20). The latter half of his critique is certainly in line with his critique in the 1930 article, namely, that the velocities of adjustment have to be taken into consideration in the analysis of an adaptation process (cp. ibid., pp.10-19; sect. V:2). However, this problem is now tackled by constructing a sequence analysis which explicitly shows the adjustment over time.

The first problem may be illustrated by looking at a partial sequence. Lundberg's example takes the current production of each consumption and capital good (q_i^s) as dependent on the profit from the former period (g_i^{t-1}) in the same line of production (g_i^{t-1}), and the profit is therefore the link between periods

----

1 Lundberg looks only at the method of partial equilibrium for the following reason:

> "It has proved practicable to make comparison with methods that apply only to a partial analysis ... . It is, after all, in this limited field, especially in the theory of price determination, that the analytic methods used in economics have been most fully worked out" (Lundberg 1937, p.1).

His critique does not therefore deal with a dynamized version of a general equilibrium scheme. Hence, Bryce seems to be correct in the following remark:

> "He fails to see that a general equilibrium theory (properly constructed) does not need to be supplemented by such aggregates, containing itself sufficient explanation, given its assumed data, and the use of aggregative concepts is merely a short cut to permit concentration on certain problems rather than an attempt to introduce anything new" (Bryce 1938, p.119).

as in Hammarskjöld's formulations (cp. sect. VII:2-3). What is produced is also supposed to be supplied so there are no stocks. The supply function for good (i) is then the following; $q_i^s = q_i^s(g_i^{t-1})$. The demand function for good (i) (q_i^d), being a consumption good, depends on the total purchasing power for the current period (E-S) and the current price of the good (p_i); $q_i^d = q_i^d(E-S;p_i)$. The price is then determined so the production-cum-supply is equal to demand. Lundberg speaks only of one equilibrium condition for this model, namely, that the profit is the same whatever the entrepreneurs are producing, i.e. $g_{i-1} = g_i = g_{i+1}$ etc. (cp. Lundberg 1937, p.20), which should probably ensure that there is no incentive to switch from one type of production to another. If we should have equilibrium over time, in the sense that the result of this period is reproduced in the subsequent period, then it is also necessary to assume that $g_i^{t-1} = g_i^t$ etc., which means that the entrepreneurs will keep their production unchanged.

The main thrust of Lundberg's argument is to show that a <u>partial</u> demand function like $q_i^d(E-S;p_i)$ cannot from a <u>logical</u> point of view be used in a <u>total</u> analysis, because the total purchasing power (E-S) is taken as given, i.e. a parameter, while it is obvious that it is the interrelation between all the markets which will determine (E-S). Therefore it is not a determinant but something to be determined.[2] Lundberg has formulated this conclusion in the following general way:

> "even if one is able to give a correct explanation of the development in <u>each</u> separate field of the whole economic life within the scope of the equilibrium concept, a sum of all these explanations <u>cannot</u>, logically, give an explanation to the total economic development" (ibid., p.4).

Hence, even if partial equilibrium analysis is valid

---

2 This implies in an ex ante language that these demand functions are only valid if the ex ante values of the purchasing power happen to be the same as the realized ones, i.e. ex ante is equal to ex post.

for each market, that still fails to imply that the aggregation procedure is valid. The crucial implication of this critique is that instead of taking the total categories as given, e.g. (E-S), we have actually to do the opposite:

> "when the analysis is extended to cover the whole field of variation possibilities within the partial systems, all at one time, the causes and effects of variations of the total categories become instead the primary problem. ... . The approach to the problem and the method of analysis must, therefore, through a monetary theory of some kind be directly focused on an explanation covering the interrelations of these total categories" (ibid., p.24; cp. p.1; pp.4-5).

Thus, Lundberg's starting point is to construct a sequence analysis made up of total categories whose interrelations should be taken from monetary theory.[3] It is important to realize, that the structure of the sequence analysis is partly taken from Wicksell's formal model of the cumulative process in Interest and Prices (cp. Wicksell 1936, p.136ff.), and it is for the first time within the Stockholm School that this model is put at the forefront of the analysis (cp. sect. I:3). But Lundberg was probably also influenced by Johansson's method which Lundberg in fact denotes as 'model sequences' (cp. Lundberg 1937, p.vii). The choice of variables, on the other hand, is based on current monetary theory and Keynes' Treatise in particular.[4] Lundberg thus summarizes his contribution in the following way:

----

3 The total categories are, as in the rest of the Stockholm analyses, simple summations of individual plans (cp. Lundberg 1937, p.191).
4 We do not think that the influence from the General Theory could have been very important, since Lundberg had only six months to digest that work (cp. Note 3 Ch.11).

"I should like to describe the positive part of this thesis as an attempt to apply the methods developed by Wicksell and his followers to the system of explanation formulated by Keynes" (Lundberg 1937, p.vi; cp. Lundberg 1960, p.199).

Even if Lundberg, as a part of his general purpose, critizes static equilibrium, that does not imply that Lundberg discards conceptions of equilibrium completely, since they "may turn out useful, when used in connection with the system of relations that is intended to explain the total development" (ibid., p.6). That shows that the notion of equilibrium may play a role in the model sequence, and Lundberg consequently concludes his introductory chapter by stating the following problem:

"The question is now to what an extent equilibrium constructions may be used in a sequence analysis which starts with total categories" (ibid., p.25).

This shows that Lundberg to a certain extent has followed up his own proposal of 1930 on how to develop a dynamic method, namely, by applying an equilibrium concept to a smaller number of variable factors (cp. sect. V:3:2). In fact, the equilibrium constructions play a fundamental role in the development of sequence analysis:

"we must assume that certain relations and interadjustments are valid even in the case of the 'deviation' from the general state of equilibrium which we call a sequence. If this possilibility is denied, it apparently is tantamount to saying that the sequence is not explainable at all. The first and foremost question is which equilibrium relations are bound to become disrupted in order to attain to a satisfactory analysis of a total sequence" (Lundberg 1937, p.27).

Hence, some equilibrium relations must hold even out of equilibrium, if a sequence analysis is to be possible. Our aim is now to find out in what sense an equilibrium concept may be said to be used in a sequence analysis, which is a process out of equilibrium.

2 - The equilibrium notion in a disequilibrium sequence analysis.

Lundberg constructs what he calls a 'neutrality condition for the general system', and it has a certain resemblance to Lindahl's complete equilibrium condition, which says that the purchase plans are equal to the production plans (cp. sect. IX:4:3:1). Lundberg holds that such a condition is "purely formal" (Lundberg 1937, p.163), since for given plans it will only show whether profits or losses will exist for the current period, that is to say a single-period analysis. But it is not possible to draw any conclusion concerning what is going to happen in subsequent periods, since "no causal elements have so far been introduced" (cp. ibid.), which implies a continuation analysis. This was already realized by Lindahl, when he said, that the formulation which gives the ex post results for one period does not yet imply the solution to the complete dynamic process (cp. sect. IX:4:1).

The 'causal elements' in a sequence analysis refer to "the causal connections over successive periods of time of plans and decisions" (Lundberg 1937, p.245; cp. pp.67-68; p.78; p.86).[5] That is to say, they show how the ex post results for an outgoing period influence the ex ante plans for the subsequent period (cp. ibid., p.49). Lindahl was also aware of this problem, since he realized that in the construction of a complete dynamic process it was necessary to make 'particular postulates' which determined these causal connections (cp. sect. IX:4:5). Svennilson holds that it is this causal mechanism, which gives sequence analysis its character of one-way causality in time in contradistinction to the interdependency of the

---

5 This term was already introduced by Hammarskjöld but his analysis was not very clear (cp. Lundberg 1937, p.78; pp.86-87; sect. VII:2).

equilibrium systems (cp. Svennilson 1938, pp.3-4; cp. sect. II:1).

Lundberg now goes beyond Lindahl, in the sense that he looks more closely at these causal elements while the latter just assumed that some functional relations between the periods had to exist if it were possible to determine the whole dynamic process. He assumes what he calls given response functions (cp. Lundberg 1937, p.172), which means that, for example, the current investment is functionally related to the profit for the outgoing period and the relation will have the same form independent of whether the expectations are fulfilled or not. This is an important difference from Lindahl's sequence analysis, since the latter considered it necessary to assume that the expectations were fulfilled (cp. sect. IX:4:5). We would therefore denote Lundberg's version of the sequence analysis as a 'disequilibrium sequence analysis', while Lindahl in 1934 pursued an 'equilibrium sequence analysis', though in "The Dynamic Approach" Lindahl has accepted Lundberg's version (cp. Lindahl 1939B, pp.57-58). This distinction is in line with Hahn's classification, which denotes a case similar to Lundberg's as belonging to non-equilibrium models (cp. Hahn 1951, p.805). Hence, the equilibrium notion is represented by the fixed response functions, since the latter implies routine behaviour (cp. sect. II:1), and at the same time the sequence analysis is a disequilibrium process in the sense that expectations are not fulfilled within each period (except when a stable equilibrium has been reached, cp. below Note

8).[6]

Lundberg gives the following background to his acceptance of given response functions:

"it is sensible to link actions with expectations only if the latter can be explained on the basis of past and present economic events. Total lack of correlation here would mean the complete liquidation of economics as a science" (Lundberg 1937, p.175; cp. p.143; p.147).

This may give the impression that Lundberg opts for 'mechanical' dynamics since he assumes that the

----

6 We therefore hold that Yohe has made an incorrect summary of the mature dynamic method of the Stockholm School:

"Swedish disequilibrium approach may be said to deal typically with progress toward short-run equilibrium while using an implicit period of shorter duration than the first equilibrium method; whether the process ever reaches such a position is another matter" (Yohe 1959A, p.242).

There is no evidence that the Swedish analysed a tendency towards any equilibrium in this sense. Thus, our main problem has been to find out what equilibrium notion they might still consider applying.

formation of expectations is 'endogenous'.[7]
Furthermore, his examples of model sequences show
that the development of the whole system could be

----

7 These terms are used by Hart in the following way:

> "If we assume that the framing of
> expectation is an 'endogenous' process -
> that expectations depend strictly on the
> previous sequence of economic-quantitative
> events - and that the pattern is stable,
> then any formal model will show events as a
> function of expectations, and expectations
> as a function of earlier events. In this
> case, events can be reduced to a function of
> earlier events. The result is a clearcut
> 'sequence analysis' in which anticipations
> need not appear explicitly - formally a
> mechanical dynamics, with an expectational
> dynamics between the lines" (Hart 1951,
> p.viii).

Bryce is also critical of this approach:

> "The behaviour of the entrepreneurs is based
> on the experience of only the preceding
> period. No consideration of expectations
> appears; the entrepreneurs do not attempt to
> anticipate. This leads naturally to a type
> of dynamic development where things which
> follow in logic are made to follow in time -
> a very dangerous means of approaching
> dynamic analysis" (Bryce 1938, p.121).

But Lange holds the opposite view:

> "Dr. Lundberg's expresses himself very
> definitely, and in the reviewer's opinion
> very righly, against the treatment of
> anticipations as independent variables ...
> . Unless anticipations are linked with past
> and present events no determinate time
> sequence would be possible" (Lange 1938,
> p.245).

summed up in a difference equation where the solution to the equation will represent a stable equilibrium (cp. ibid., p.195; p.201), which proves that it is basically mechanical dynamics. However, Lundberg is probably not as interested in showing the existence of a stable equilibrium, as in the fact that the model sequence explains the development from period to period where each period is determined by its predecessors. Nevertheless, the actual formulation and analysis of the model sequences give the impression that Lundberg is mainly interested in mechanical dynamics. But we will see below that his discussion of the general validity of the model sequences will give a different picture.

3 - The limitations of model sequence analysis.

    Lundberg is aware of the fact that the model sequences have a restricted value, since the assumption of given response functions, which plays such a crucial role in the construction of model sequences, will only be true "over a period of time by accident" (cp. ibid., p.243). He refers in particular to "the simple mechanical assumptions as to motivations and reactions, including their timing" (ibid., p.169), which have to be used for constructing a sequence analysis. The model sequence must therefore play a modest role:

> "According to this view it would not be worth while in a causal sequence to carry the analysis far at any point with respect to the sequels" (ibid., pp.5-6).

Hahn consequently calls such a model 'a short period model' since it is only valid "for certain discrete periods of time" (Hahn 1951, pp.805-806).[8] Thus, it seems after all that Lundberg has at least some doubts about the value of mechanical dynamics, which are further vindicated by his application of sequence analysis after 1937.

Despite the fact that the model sequences are

---

8 The same view is put forward by Hart:

"If we assume (which for many problems makes more sense) that expectations on the basis of a past sequence of economic quantities are powerfully influenced by politics, inventions, etc., then without bringing in 'exogenous' variables we cannot get a clearcut process-analysis sequence. We may assume we know expectations and plans at the outset; but after a few 'periods' the influence of revisions accumulates, so that any long sequence can only be illustrative" (Hart 1951, pp.viii-ix).

However, there is a possibility of a 'freak' case, namely, where the stable equilibrium, i.e. the solution to the difference equation, is reached within the few periods during which the routine behaviour is unchanged. In this case, the model sequence will of course be valid for ever, since once we are in equilibrium there is no endogenous reason why we should ever drop out of equilibrium, i.e. it represents a static equilibrium.

based on very restrictive assumptions [9], Lundberg considers them very apt for handling questions relating to economic policy, since by applying the model sequences we may "be able to discuss the effects of a certain monetary policy, of public works, or of a devaluation of the currency" (ibid., p.245). In fact, when Lundberg started to work for Svenska Konjunkturinstitutet (The Swedish Business Cycle Research Institute) [10], his works concentrated on the existing state of the business cycle and a prognosis one year ahead, which should give a basis for economic policy, i.e. a type of single-period analysis. Lundberg's first two reports are thus called The Situation of the Business Cycle in the Autumn of 1937 and The Situation of the Business Cycle in the Spring of 1938, and the aim of the analysis is quite modest:

"The investigation of a business cycle can go no further than to make intelligible the different risks in the existing situation

---

9 However Lundberg is adamant that a sequence analysis is less abstract than static equilibrium theory, because even if the sequence analysis could not be constructed, that would also limit the validity of the conclusion drawn from a static analysis. He therefore makes the following conclusive remark concerning the relation between sequence analysis and static analysis:

"The limited bearing of a static analysis can evidently just be proved by constructing alternative model sequences. The static analysis can only give results if the time discrepancies therein considered are shown to be without relevance" (Lundberg 1937, p.246).

This result looks similar to Samuelson's correspondence principle, which shows that a static equilibrium situation may be the stationary outcome of different dynamic models.
10 This institute was established in 1937 with Erik Lundberg as its research director.

which are judged with reference to the
preceding development ... . It may be
possible to say something about an increase
or decrease of the lability of the situation
and of the existing risks in comparison with
the immediately preceding survey period.
But the conclusion will always result in an
indication of a series of alternative
possibilities of the development" (Lundberg
1938A, p.8; cp. 121).

We can find no one more experienced, both from a
theoretical and practical point of view, to evaluate
the dynamic method developed by the Stockholm School,
than Lundberg, in his remarks in the preface to the
1953 edition of Economic Expansion:

"The critical attitude to more involved
types of sequence analysis which is taken in
this book has been verified so far by my own
experience in practical research as head of
the Swedish Business Cycle Research
Institute. It is clearly an advantage to
have theories of expansion and of the
possible course of expansionist processes
in the back of the mind and to use concepts
that can be fitted into a dynamic sequence.
But we have to be aware of the extremely
limited applicability of our more involved
models to an ever changing economic reality,
where it is precisely the changes in the
assumed coefficients that will often be more
important than the fixed relations. My
experience shows me that the more modest
approach to dynamics by way of the
disequilibrium method - that is, ex ante
discrepancies between plans made and
measures taken by different groups and
countries - in nearly all cases gives the
necessary starting point for dynamic
analysis. This disequilibrium approach
usually gives also a sufficiently good
account of potential tendencies for the
purpose of making decisions about economic
policy. It is a question of ambition and
perhaps also of taste how far and with what

intended degree of precision a disequilibrium approach should be followed up by a study of probable sequences of economic development. The intention of the present book is in fact to give a critical evaluation of these more ambitious methods of dynamics, by exposing the underlying assumptions in detail" (Lundberg 1937, p.iv).

Hence, it seems that Lundberg finally came down decisively on the side of 'expectational' dynamics, since the latter stresses 'changes in the coefficients'. Furthermore, 'the disequilibrium approach' advocated by Lundberg appears to be a single period analysis. In fact, most of the empirical works done by the Swedes during the 1940s belong to the category of single period analysis, like the analysis of the inflationary gap which was iniated by Keynes in his pamphlet How to Pay for the War of 1940 (cp. Hansen 1951, pp.60-62). We would therefore propose that the Swedes considered sequence analysis more as theoretical tool which could be used for analytical purposes than something which was directly applicable to an empirical analysis.

Chapter 11

The Immediate Response to The General Theory

We now examine the initial reaction of the
members of the Stockholm School to the publication of
the General Theory; that is to say, their reactions
before they had been influenced by the debate which
came to rage later. Only Ohlin and Lundberg gave an
explicit and immediate riposte to Keynes' General
Theory. Svennilson also mentions Keynes in his
dissertation of 1938 but mainly in a comparison
between the income concepts used by the Stockholm
School and Keynes respectively. Only in 1953 did
Lindahl write a long article on Keynes' economic
system for Ekonomisk Tidskrift, while neither Myrdal
and Hammarskjöld offered any direct interpretation of
the General Theory. Of the older generation both
Davidson and Cassel gave vent to their misgivings
about Keynes' message; the former wrote four articles
in Ekonomisk Tidskrift (1936-1937) while the latter
reviewed the General Theory for International Labour
Review (1937). Hence, our concern is only with
Ohlin's and Lundberg's contributions.

In this chapter we will particularily study
Ohlin's and Lundberg's methodological critique of
Keynes, plus some examples of their criticism of
Keynes' theoretical propositions which will help to
show that in fact they used a different method from
Keynes. It can quite often be shown that their
critique is misdirected, once one has accepted that
Keynes' theory moves within an equilibrium method.

1 - Ohlin on Keynes.

"Owing to a coincidence of circumstances,
already at an early stage of the depression
Swedish economists came to deal with the
problems of variations in employment, output
and prices by means of a theoretical
apparatus rather different from the price
theory in economic textbooks. There are
surprising similarities as well as striking

differences between that apparatus and the conclusions reached in Sweden on the one hand and Mr. Keynes' 'General Theory' on the other hand" (Ohlin 1937A, p.53).[1]

1.1 - The "somewhat 'revolutionary' flavour" of the General Theory.

According to Ohlin, The General Theory has "a somewhat 'revolutionary' flavour from the point of view of economic theory" (Ohlin 1937B, p.233) for the following reason:

> "he [Keynes] attempts ... to provide a theory for changes in total employment and price-levels, which can also be called the theory of processes of general contraction and expansion" (ibid.)

The 'revolutionary flavour' follows from the fact that Keynes has challenged the implicit assumption in value theory [2], namely, what Ohlin calls 'monetary stability' and which "eliminates changes in general price-levels, i.e. that kind of process which is commonly called inflationary and deflationary" (ibid., p.231; cp. p.235). However, the flavour is only 'somewhat revolutionary', since Keynes' proposition that there is no automatic nexus between saving plans and investment plans was already part and parcel of Wicksell's cumulative process, as well as the analyses pursued by Robertson and Hawtrey (cp.

----

1 The first part of the article (Ohlin 1937A) reached Keynes during January 1937 while the second part (Ohlin 1937B) came in the beginning of February, and late in March Keynes finally got the third part (Ohlin 1937C) which was never published (cp. Keynes 1973B, pp.183-186). It seems therefore that Ohlin had a longer time to digest the General Theory than Lundberg (cp. below Note 3).
2 Ohlin does not use the term 'value theory' and he speaks instead of 'theory of price and distribution proper' versus 'money and cycles theory' (cp. Ohlin 1937B, p.230 et seqq.).

ibid., p.234; Ohlin 1937A, p.55). But if this proposition is the basis of the <u>General Theory's</u> "'a somewhat 'revolutionary' flavour'", then already the <u>Treatise</u> would have had the same flavour, since the whole analysis of that book is based on the idea that savings and investment decisions are taken by different individuals (cp. Keynes 1930A, p.123, p.127). Hence, Ohlin seems to have missed Keynes' main point, which is not to provide a theory of change, i.e. to dynamize value theory as Ohlin aimed (cp. Ohlin 1937A, p.54; p.57), but, in the first place, to construct a theory which determines the equilibrium level of employment and output. Keynes' theory is therefore 'revolutionary' in the sense that it is a substitute for othodox value theory on its own grounds. Keynes would therefore discard Ohlin's contention that orthodox value theory should be kept, with its assumption of 'monetary stability', "as an introduction ... [representing] one of the most fruitful simplifications that are used in economic science" (Ohlin 1937B, p.232). Ohlin's viewpoint of traditional value theory and his misunderstandings of Keynes' claims are exemplified in the following quotation:

> "A coordination of the theories of price, money, and cycles [which according to Ohlin is the outcome of the 'theory of processes of general contraction and expansion' (cp. Ohlin 1937B, p.235)] does, of course, lead to something rather different from the orthodox theory of price and distribution. But this does not seem to justify a denial that this theory has given significant insight into certain aspects of the economic world. It should not be criticised for being unable to do what its authors never intended it to do but tried to accomplish in the theories of money and cycles instead" (Ohlin 1937C, p.31).

Ohlin has here identified his own critique of the orthodox theory as not being dynamic with Keynes' critique. However, the latter's point is that 'the orthodox theory of price and distribution' could not accomplish what it intended to do within its own framework, namely, to give a general theory of the determination of output and employment. Nevertheless, as we shall see below, Ohlin is not really attacking orthodox theory because of its assumption of full employment, but because of its inability to make an explicit analysis of dynamic processes (cp. ibid., p.231; p.235).

1.2 - 'The novelty' of the General Theory.

At the same time, the following remark by Ohlin seems to prove that he actually understood Keynes' main intention:

> "The novelty lies in his construction of an equilibrium, governed by the quantity of money, the propensity to consume, the marginal efficiency of capital, and the liquidity preference. These 'independent' variables determine the rate of interest, the volume of investment and, thus, the volume of employment" (ibid., p.236).

The novelty is thus the equilibrium construction for determining the level of output, since, even before the General Theory, most business cycle theories already explained changes in the level of employment by changes in the volume of investment.

Ohlin holds that this construction is fallacious since the multiplier is an ex post relation. This critique is based on Ohlin's interpretation of Keynes' marginal propensity to consume (MPC), or the consumption plans, as being too closely tied to the realized income of the preceding period. This implies that it does not take into consideration the fact that those plans are "determined by expectations, which often have only a loose connection with last period's realised income" (Ohlin 1937A, p.63). However, this critique misses the point that the MPC-schedule is a portmanteau-function, where all types of anticipations are incorporated including the size of future incomes far ahead in time. Therefore, it seems possible to interpret the multiplier in an ex ante/ex post framework, though, in the main, Keynes assumes implicitly that ex ante plans are realized, i.e. ex ante is equal to ex post (cp. sect. 2 App. I). Hence, we can not support Ohlin's conclusion:

"The equation above [Y=I/(1-MPC)] only expresses a truism [i.e. an ex post relation], showing that the definitions are consistent with one another, and explains nothing. The relationship in question does not throw any light on the question 'what determines the position of employment at any time', as Keynes claims his theory to do. Neither does it indicate an equilibrium position, towards which the economic system tends and which, if reached, will remain stable, in the absence of new changes in the independent variables. As a matter fact, this equation holds true for every period, even in the most unstable situations" (Ohlin 1937B, p.236).

However, Ohlin is correct in the sense that even in an ex ante/ex post framework the equation will ex post be 'true for every period'. But that overlooks the fact that as an ex ante construction the equation may express an equilibrium condition. If the ex ante plans are realized and net investment is different from zero, then the system will tend towards the short period equilibrium determined by the equation. This position may 'remain stable' in Ohlin's sense (i.e. static equilibrium, cp. sect. 1:3), if net investment is zero, that is to say a long run equilibrium (cp. sect. 3 App. I).
However, Ohlin also holds that if the equation is interpreted as an ex ante relation then "it is entirely wrong" (Ohlin 1937B, p.237) for the following reason:

"There is no reason why the planned investment plus the planned consumption should be equal to the expected total income for society as a whole. In other words, the planned investment will differ from the planned saving, unless they should happen to be equal by mere chance. Owing to this difference, expectations will not be fulfilled" (ibid.).

But it is essential in stating an equilibrium condition, which is Keynes' main problem, to assume that expectations are fulfilled. Hence, Ohlin's critique is really levelled against the use of equilibrium conditions as such.

Ohlin is adamant that if "by mere chance" (ibid.) planned savings and investment were equal, that "does not necessarily mean a stable situation" (ibid.). This is because even if the current period were in equilibrium, it is still possible "that the series of events during the preceding periods may well lead to a change in planned savings or planned investment for the next period" (ibid.). From this passage plus the rest of Ohlin's argument (cp. ibid., pp.237-238) it is clear that he equates 'a stable situation' with a recurrent situation, i.e. a static equilibrium. Keynes' short period equilibrium does not imply stability in this sense, but we will show in the appendix on Keynes that he also determines a long run equilibrium which has a stable character (cp. sect. 3-4 App. I). In his book _Employment Stabilization_ of 1949 Ohlin also tries to prove that Keynes is wrong even within his equilibrium framework. Ohlin's argument goes as follows:

> "Take a situation where there is a 'normal' development and interest level ... if people increased their willingness to save, a greater volume of investment and a lower rate of interest would be compatible with this normal economic development, for instance a stable price level. On the other hand, if people reduced their willingness to save, only a smaller volume of investment and a higher interest level would be compatible with this normal economic development. Thus, the central idea in orthodox interest theory, that savings and investment govern interest rates, seems to me to be essentially true" (Ohlin 1949, p.124).

This argument implies, in Keynes' framework, that we start from a given level of employment with a stable price level, i.e. 'the 'normal' development'. An exogenous shift in the willingness to save, i.e. a change in the value of the multiplier, must then be followed by such a change in the rate of interest, via a change in the money supply and/or a shift in the liquidity preference schedule, that just the right amount of investment is forthcoming (which may necessitate a shift in the MEC-schedule) to sustain 'the 'normal' development' for the new value of the multiplier. But this is hardly a proof of the validity of the orthodox theory of the rate of interest, since the rate has played no role at all in equilibrating savings and investment. Ohlin then immediately followed this argument with a straightforward Keynesian proposition:

> "The connection between savings and investment, on the one hand, and the rate of interest, on the other hand, is indirect and goes chiefly via the influence of the rate of interest on the volume of investment and the consequent effect on the size of income and savings, given a certain propensity to save" (ibid., pp.124-125).

How it is possible for Ohlin to hold these two positions at the same time? The clue seems to be that he has turned the Keynesian problematic on its head, which is shown in the following remark:

> "the height of the interest level and the volume of investment activity that can exist, if we want a certain economic development, depends on the propensity to save" (ibid., p.125).

Keynes' quaesitum the level of employment, is here the starting-point of the argument, plus the assumption of a particular consumption function, and the rate of interest and the volume of investment must then follow suit if an equilibrium is to exist. Hence, Ohlin is going backward in Keynes' scheme, since we start with a given level of income and if the propensity to save is given that gives us the volume of savings. In equilibrium savings are equal to investment so we also have the volume of investment, which reading backwards on the MEC-schedule determines the rate of interest. However, this does not show that 'savings and investment govern interest rates', but that in equilibrium the variables have to be compatible, i.e. a solution to a system of simultaneous equations.

1.3 - Keynes' 'old-fashioned' method.

Ohlin may be wrong in his critique of Keynes' macroeconomic theory when the latter is employed within an equilibrium framework. But his most interesting criticism, and which later became standard for the Stockholm School, is his attack on the 'old-fashioned' Keynes or his "exaggerated conservatism in method" (Ohlin 1937C, p.31):

> "it [Keynes' theoretical system] is ... 'old-fashioned' in the second respect which characterises recent economic theory - namely, the attempt to break away from an explanation of economic events by means of orthodox equilibrium constructions. No other analysis of trade fluctuations in recent years - with the possible exception of the Mises-Hayek school - follow such conservative lines in this respect. In fact, Keynes is much more an 'equilibrium theorist' than such economists as Cassel and, I think, Marshall" (Ohlin 1937B, pp.235-236).

His critique of the equilibrium method follows up the attack in 1933-1934 on the neo-Wicksellian conception of a normal rate of interest (cp. sect. VIII:3). However, in 1937 he has gone further in his aversion to equilibrium methods, since he not only holds that static equilibrium theory is no good for dynamic analysis (cp. Ohlin 1937B, p.223), which was a Swedish commonplace, but also that it is unlikely that it will ever be possible " to define a dynamic equilibrium in such a way as to make it useful for the analysis of practical problems" (ibid.. p.224). Hence, Ohlin rejects all references to any notion of equilibrium. In fact, we have only been able to find one positive reference to an equilibrium concept in the whole article:

"a process analysis in which not more of the
equilibrium idea is left than consideration
of more or less stable positions" (Ohlin
1937C, p.31).

Having in mind what Ohlin seems to mean by a stable
position (cp. sect. 1:2), this concept is probably a
process where savings and investment are unchanged
over several periods. It is also difficult in
Ohlin's later works to find any comment on a feasible
notion of equilibrium (cp. Ohlin 1941A, 1941B, 1949).
Ohlin's rejection of Keynes' equilibrium
approach is based on his espousal of the following
method:

"If we want to know the effects of a certain
reduction in the planned volume of
investment ... then one evidently has to
follow the process through a study of the
successive changes in expectations and
plans in actual events, in the differences
between them, and in the consequent
reactions of the new expectations, plans,
and actions, etc." (Ohlin 1937B, p.238; cp.
p.237).

It is evident that Ohlin is here referring to some
type of sequence analysis, or what he calls "a
Process Theory of the Stockholm Type" (ibid., p.235;
italics omitted). On the basis of this method Ohlin
now directs his criticism towards Keynes' attempts to
explain a complete business cycle with the help of
his equilibrium method. He holds it to be "absurd to
assume a relatively constant multiplier" (ibid.,
p.239). However, the idea of some normal multiplier
over the whole cycle is not his main critique, but
the following argument:

"The chief reason why the multiplier theory
can tell us little about the effects of a
certain increase in investment is not its
fluctuation, but the fact that it leaves out
of account the reaction of a certain change
in the volume of output and in the general
business situation on profit expectations

and the willingness to invest" (ibid., p.240).

In fact, this passage shows that Ohlin has misunderstood how Keynes would go about explaining the phases of a business cycle. Keynes would not assume a constant multiplier, but he would incorporate exogenous shifts in the consumption function during the transition between consecutive short period equilibria. In the same manner, he would take into consideration reactions which would lead to shifts in the MEC-schedule as well as the liquidity preference schedule, but like the Swedish sequence analysis no shifts take place during a period. Thus, a business cycle, or any process, is described by jumping from one short period equilibrium to another. However, even if Ohlin had properly understood Keynes' method, he would still not have considered it appropriate, since his aim was to show in advance how actual events during a period would lead to shifts in the functions for the next period and so on, i.e. a sequence analysis.

At the same time, this quotation is proof of Ohlin's intention to take into consideration changes in the investment plans during the period when 'the multiplier works itself out'. This shows that Ohlin is implicitly thinking of a shorter period than the one used by Keynes. In fact, this is a corollary to the critique of Keynes' equilibrium approach, since the period for 'the multiplier to work itself out' would only be equal to Marshall's short period in the case of the instantaneous multiplier (cp. sect. 5 App. I). Changes in investment plans during the period, or endogenous changes in the investment plans, i.e. induced investment, came back later on as a part of Ohlin's critique of Keynes:

> "If we are interested in the consequences of a certain increase in the volume of investment ... we do not want to know only how much more consumers will buy. We must know also how the profit expectations and investment purchases will be affected" (Ohlin 1949, p.149; cp. Ohlin 1977, p.159).

This passage also shows, that Ohlin looked upon the

246   Chapter 11

multiplier as a sequence analysis with endogenous
changes between each period. Therefore he could see
no reason why changes in investment should be
excluded. But we have to remember, that in Keynes'
equilibrium framework, the consumption plans are not
changed during the multiplier process, since they are
based on proper expectations of the income for the
current period (cp. sect. 5 App. I).

Brems has realized that Ohlin in his article of
1933 and the book of 1934 is already discussing
induced investment during a disequilibrium process
(cp. Brems 1978, p.399). That is one of the reasons
for Ohlin not to look at the static multiplier. Thus
"his multiplier approach is thoroughly dynamic"
(ibid., p.407; cp. p.403; p.411). This is taken as a
proof of "Ohlin's strong sense of realism" (ibid.).
However, Ohlin's 'realism', which is coupled with a
disequilibrium analysis without any equilibrium
concept whatsoever, leads to a concentration on the
practical difficulties of using the multiplier. He
thereby overlooks the fact that this concept is a
crucial part of a new theory for determining the
equilibrium level of output, which is a substitute
for orthodox theory.

2 - Lundberg on Keynes.

"Keynes' theories are here examined from the
point of view of the traditional methods of
approach inaugurated by Wicksell. I should
like to describe the positive part of this
thesis as an attempt to apply the methods
developed by Wicksell and his followers to
the system of explanation formulated by
Keynes" (Lundberg 1937, p.vi).[3]

----
3 It has to be taken into consideration that Lundberg
did not have much time to study the General Theory,
since he got the book in February 1936 and finished
his thesis in September 1936 (cp. Lundberg 1960,
p.196 n.1).

2.1 - A critique of Keynes' use of an equilibrium method.

Lundberg is positive towards the General Theory as long as it is used "[to determine] the degree of employment which is possible under given conditions" (ibid., p.34), where the latter are basically represented by Keynes' three psychological functions (cp. ibid., p.33). The criticism starts when "Keynes applies his equilibrium system in unmodified form to the analysis of a business cycle sequence" (ibid., p.36), since Keynes bases his proposition on the idea that the possible existence of an equilibrium situation also proves that the actual development will show a tendency towards this position (cp. ibid., pp.26-27; p.35).[4] However, the tendency towards an equilibrium can, according to Lundberg, only be proven by an explicit sequence analysis, which is continuation of his old interest in the 'velocities of adjustment' for an analysis of the adjustment process (cp. sect. V:2; X:1). In this context he opts for Wicksell's "method of combining states of disequilibrium over successive periods" (ibid., p.45 n.1). This is the reason, why the Swedes were always very favourable to the method used by Keynes in the Treatise, which they saw as an attempt, although perhaps an obscure attempt, to analyse how the discrepancies between plans for savings and investment plans develop into changes in prices and quantities (cp. Lundberg 1948A, pp.55-56; Lundberg 1948B, pp.163-167; Lindahl 1954, pp.169-170).

Hence, as the introductory quotation shows, Lundberg wants to fuse 'Keynes' theories' or 'system of explanation' with 'the traditional methods of approach inaugurated by Wicksell'. This reconstruction can, in fact, start from Keynes' three psychological functions and the only difference is that "the complete interdependence in a simultaneous adaption process has been eliminated" (Lundberg 1937,

---

4 Lundberg must rule out the possibility of describing the business cycle with a string of short period equilibria, since the business cycle is "characterized by unexpected profits or losses" (ibid., p.38).

p.45).[5] It is easy to grasp Lundberg's intentions
concerning the reconstruction if we look at his
critique of Keynes' notion of the marginal efficiency
of capital, which is taken as given for each period
and where the changes between periods are exogenous
(cp. ibid., pp.178-179). However, Lundberg now wants
to incorporate the effects of the investments in the
productive capacity (cp. Lundberg 1960, pp.200-201),
i.e. to go beyond the short period. The growth in
the capital stock will then serve as a link to
explain changes in the marginal efficiency of capital
(cp. Lundberg 1937, p.180). Therefore, it is not
surprising that Lundberg, in this context, comes up
with an equilibrium concept related to a growth path,
where investments balance the forthcoming savings as
well as guarantee a full utilization of the growing
capital stock (cp. ibid., pp.183-185). He finally
differentiates his own concept from Keynes' short run
equilibrium in the following way:

> "With the new investments given, Keynes
> tries to find the equilibrium position of
> employment and income. We wish to state the
> equilibrium in terms of a continued dynamic
> development and can not, therefore, assume
> investments as arbitrarily given" (ibid.,
> pp.185-186).

However, this dynamic equilibrium is only supposed to
serve as some sort of vague reference, since the
actual development is characterized by an inequality
between savings and investments, hence the need for a
sequence analysis (cp. ibid., p.186).

2.2 - A critique of Keynes' theory.
The introductory quotation shows that Lundberg
uses the sequence analysis as a basis for a critical
examination of Keynes' theory. The most important
case is Lundberg's construction of a particular model

----

5 We will show below that it is possible to give a
sequential interpretation of Keynes' system which
captures its particular causality (cp. sect. 5 App.
I).

sequence as "an example of the use of the classical conception about the relation between savings and investments" (ibid., p.221 n.1), i.e. savings and investments determine the rate of interest. However, a closer inspection of Lundberg's example proves that 'the classical conception' only holds for the case where income is changing. Thus, it does not refute Keynes' construction for the equilibrium case. This mode of argument drew the following critique from R.F.Kahn:

> "He [Lundberg] throws no light on the simpler question how, in his opinion, the rate of interest is determined at a time when to-day's income is equal to yesterday's ... the lack of any clear account of the fundamentals on which the author is basing his treatment, a constant exhortation to run before the reader is sure that he remembers how to walk" (Kahn 1938, p.267).

Hence, Lundberg has made the common mistake of criticizing the validity of Keynes' theoretical propositions outside their equilibrium framework.

We can conclude that both Lundberg and Ohlin criticize Keynes' equilibrium construction on the basis of a sequence analysis, since the latter could incorporate endogenous changes. However, this critique is mixed with an attack on Keynes' theory. But the latter criticism is misplaced if Keynes' equilibrium method is accepted, since then the plans are fulfilled and all changes have to be exogenous. Their critique is therefore valuable as a methodological exercise and it shows that the Swedish contribution is complementary to the Keynesian revolution.

Chapter 12

Summary

The aim of this final chapter is to summarize the findings. We will first look at the development of dynamic method and the Wicksellian influence on the Stockholm School. The School starts with Myrdal's dissertation of 1927 where the main contribution was the construction of the 'method of expectation'. This method includes anticipations as a datum in determining a long run equilibrium position, which was an innovation with respect to the current tradition. Myrdal's interest seems to have been aroused by the limitations of the static method as developed by Cassel, and his positive solution might have been influenced by Knight's treatment of anticipations.

The inclusion of anticipations as an independent entity among the data became an integral part of the later attempts to develop a dynamic method. However, Myrdal's dropping of the assumption of objective risk coupled with an equilibrium concept which is a long run normal proved to be highly problematic if not contradictory. Hence, the subsequent development may be characterized as an attempt to construct equilibrium notions which are different from long run equilibrium.

Under the influence of Myrdal, especially in respect of the role of anticipations, but also as an independent contribution, Lindahl constructed the notion of intertemporal equilibrium, which constitutes a break with the equilibrium notion of the traditional theory. Intertemporal equilibrium was developed as an answer to the shortcomings of comparative statics in handling the complication due to the inclusion of the time factor in production. Temporary equilibrium in its turn grew out of the failure of intertemporal equilibrium to incorporate imperfect foresight in a meaningful way.

Neither method is directly related to Wicksell's method in Interest and Prices. Furthermore, both are obviously different from Wicksell's notion of a.

static equilibrium, which is explicitly shown in Lindahl's treatment of Wicksell's normal rate of interest. However, Lindahl applied temporary equilibrium to the analysis of cumulative processes. In this context he took over Wicksell's theory for determining changes in the price level via the relation between total demand and total supply. This is the precise way in which Wicksell came to impinge directly on the further evolution of the Stockholm School, that is to say his macrotheoretical formula for changes in the price level was fused with the dynamic methods for the purpose of analysing dynamic processes. However, Lindahl's formula for determining the price level which opposes consumers' outlay for consumption goods with the production of consumption goods was also influenced by Hawtrey's Currency and Credit.

Lundberg and Myrdal criticized these methods, which are equilibrium methods, since they could not analyse the successive determination in an essential sequence. These shortcomings spurred the development of a disequilibrium approach.

Myrdal's Monetary Equilibrium was a landmark in this development since his notions of ex ante and ex post laid the foundation for a disequilibrium method. However, his instantaneous analysis was a misdirected attempt to avoid the problems involved in a sequence analysis.

Hammarskjöld's works of 1932-1933 filled an important gap in the disequilibrium approach, since he showed how consecutive periods could be linked to one another via the existence of windfall profit which falls out at the end of one period and is then transferred to the next. This procedure was later taken up by most of the other Swedes. Furthermore, Hammarskjöld's algebraic formulas were the first examples of a formal exposition of sequence analysis within the Stockholm School. However, these formulas were ex post constructions, which showed Hammarskjöld's connection with the earlier works of Lindahl and Keynes. In fact, from now onwards the Wicksellian influence on macroeconomic theory was mixed not only with Lindahl's and Myrdal's interpretations of Wicksell but also with Keynes' formulations in the Treatise.

Ohlin wrote many works during the period under consideration but none of them made any direct contribution to the development of dynamic method. On the contrary, Ohlin showed a certain lack of understanding of the approach developed by Myrdal and Lindahl, and his importance lay instead within the development of macroeconomic theory, where he stressed the importance of quantity changes as part of the equilibrating mechanism. However, his concentration on the role of the speed of reactions, which led him to adopt a case-by-case approach, had certain similarities with Lundberg's model sequences. Ohlin's inclinations may have been influenced by Lundberg's intervention in 1930 which stressed the role of the speed of adjustment. This is one of the few examples where foreign economists impinged directly on the methodological ideas of the Stockholm School, since Lundberg had come under the direct influence of Frisch, Rosenstein-Rodan and Lindahl in his critique of comparative statics and the stress on velocities of adjustment.

Lindahl's works of 1934-1935 put the notion of a plan as the basic notion of economic analysis. He built on Myrdal and Hammarskjöld when he gave the first proper algebraic formulation of a single-period analysis together with a sketch of the problems involved in a continuation analysis. It is interesting to note that the assumption of fixed prices was developed alongside the disequilibrium approach.

The development finally came to its close with Lundberg's construction of a disequilibrium sequence analysis. His distinctive contribution was to investigate to what extent an equilibrium concept could be used in a sequence analysis which is a process out of equilibrium in the sense that expectations are not fulfilled within each period. This concept is represented by fixed response functions, that is to say plans are related to the profit for the outgoing period but this relation will have the same form in each period independently of whether the expectations are fulfilled or not. When Lundberg discussed the dynamic problems he was the first within the Stockholm School who explicitly referred to the method used by Wicksell in Interest and Prices.

We will now look at the relation between the Stockholm School and the Keynesian revolution.

Lindahl studied cases where the difference between savings and investment is resolved by changes in the income distribution brought about by changes in the price level. This mechanism looks akin to Keynes' principle of effective demand as long as a cumulative process, which is a process out of equilibrium, is analysed. But Lindahl still considered that in the long run the rate of interest would play its traditional role as an equilibrating mechanism between savings and investment.

Myrdal's macrotheoretical analysis built on Wicksell's and Lindahl's analyses of the normal rate of interest, which is obvious from his procedure of immanent criticism. In this context Myrdal looked into the equilibrating mechanism between savings and investment, and this analysis, like Lindahl's, appears on the surface to be similar to Keynes' principle of effective demand. However, this similarity is misleading since Myrdal only determines the factors which constitute the ex post equality between savings and investment in an ongoing cumulative process. Thus, it is not a principle for determining the equilibrium level of output. But this analysis was not identical to the principal of effective demand, since Ohlin, like Lindahl and Myrdal before him, pursued a disequilibrium analysis which amongst other things involved changes in real income. Ohlin's analysis as well as Myrdal's are better characterized as belonging to business cycle theory. It is then possible to explain the bottom of such a cycle, but this is not the same as an underemployment equilibrium in Keynes' sense.

Lindahl's algebraic analysis in his A Note of 1934 shows with the utmost clarity that the equalization between savings and investment has the character of an ex post equality and is not a matter of determining an equilibrium position. Furthermore, he partly used his analysis to sort out certain problems connected with Keynes' fundamental equations, which shows his concentration on analysing changes in the price level.

The immediate reaction in 1937 to Keynes' General Theory from Ohlin and Lundberg is a proof of our main contention that the Stockholm School can not be understood without a thorough understanding of the dynamic method involved. Hence, their critique was mainly directed towards Keynes' equilibrium method. But at the same time their criticism of Keynes' principle of effective demand is misplaced once Keynes' equilibrium method is accepted. Furthermore, it has been shown above that the Swedish method could be grafted on to Keynes' theory.

We would therefore conclude, following Hicks, that one can speak of two revolutions in the 1930's:

> "To pass from one pure method to the other flex-price to fix-price is quite a revolution. It is a revolution that is mixed up with the so-called 'Keynesian Revolution'; but I do not think that it is accurate to identify them. Though the 'methods' that are used in the Treatise on Money and in the General Theory are different, neither of them is a pure method ... . There is, however, no question that, as between his two works, Keynes was moving in the direction of the new method ... the direction of movement is one that is very widespread in contemporary economics, both through the influence of Keynes and otherwise ... . A corresponding change was occurring in Sweden" (Hicks 1965, p.77 and p.77 n.1).

Hence, one revolution was concerned with dynamic methods and in this field the Stockholm School played a major role, while the other one was the Keynesian revolution in a narrow sense, i.e. the principle of effective demand. In this perspective Keynes' contribution in the General Theory and the contribution of the Stockholm School are complementary rather than antagonistic.

Bibliography

A. Published works.

Benassy, J-P. (1975). "Neo-Keynesian Disequilibrium Theory in a Monetary economy". Review of Economic Studies, Vol. 42, (October 1975).

Brems, H. (1978). "What was new in Ohlin's 1933-34 macroeconomics?". History of Political Economy, Vol. 10, (Fall 1978).

Bryce, R.B. (1938). Review of Lundberg (1937). Canadian Journal of Economics and Political Science, Vol. 4, (February 1938).

Cassel, Gustav (1923 A-B). The Theory of Social Economy. Vol. I-II. London: T.Fisher Unwin, 1923.

----- (1929). Fundamental Thoughts in Economics. First edition in 1925. London: Ernest Benn, 1929.

----- (1934). Teoretisk Socialekonomi. Revised Swedish edition of Cassel (1923A-B). Stockholm: Kooperativa Förbundets Bokförlag, 1934.

Caplan, B. (1941). "Some Swedish Stepping Stones in Economic Theory: A Comment". Canadian Journal of Economics and Political Science, Vol. 7, 1951.

Clark, J.B. (1899). The Distribution of Wealth. London: Macmillan, 1899.

Debreu, G. (1959). Theory of Value. New Haven: Yale University Press, 1959.

Ellis, H. (1940). Review of Myrdal (1939). Journal of Political Economy, Vol. 48, (June 1940).

Frisch, Ragnar (1929). "Statikk og Dynamikk i den Økonomiske Teori". Nationaløkonomisk Tidskrift, Vol. 67, (1929).

Garegnani, P. (1976). "On a Change in the Notion of Equilibrium in Recent Work on Value: A comment on Samuelson". In Brown, M. (et al.). Essays in Modern Capital Theory. Amsterdam: North Holland, 1976.

Grünbaum, I. (1945). "Inkongruente Førventninger og Begrebet Monetaer Ligevaegt". Nationaløkonomisk Tidskrift, Vol. 83, 1945.

Hahn, F.H. (1952). "Expectations and Equilibrium". Economic Journal, Vol. 62, (December 1952).

----- (1973). On the Notion of Equilibrium in Economics. Cambridge: Cambridge University Press, 1973.

Hammarskjöld, Dag (1932). "Utkast till en algebraisk metod för dynamisk prisanalys". Ekonomisk Tidskrift, 1932.

----- (1933A). Konjunturspridningen. En teoretisk och historisk undersökning. Stockholm: P.A.Norstedt, 1933.

Hansen, Bent (1951). A Study in the Theory of Inflation. London: George Allen & Unwin, 1951.

Hart, A.G. (1942). "Risk, Uncertainty and the Unprofitability of Compounding Probabilities". First printed in Studies in Mathematical Economics and Econometrics, 1942. As reprinted in Readings in the Theory of Income Distribution, edited by H.S.Ellis. Philadelphia: The Blakiston Company, 1946.

----- (1951). Anticipations, Uncertainty, and Dynamic Planning. First edition in 1940. Preface to the 1951 edition. Reprinted, New York: Kelley, 1965.

Hawtrey, R.G. (1928). Currency and Credit. First edition 1919. Third edition. London: Longmans and Green, 1928.

Hayek, F.A. (1928). "Das intertemporale Gleichgewichtssystem der Preise und die Bewegungen des Geldwertes". Weltwirtschaftliches Archiv, Vol. 32, 1928.

----- (1933). Monetary Theory and the Trade Cycle. First edition 1933. Reprinted, Clifton: Kelley, 1975.

----- (1935). Prices and Production. First edition published in 1931. Second edition. London: George Routledge & Sons, 1935.

----- (1937). "Economics and Knowledge". Economica, Vol. 4, 1937. As reprinted in Hayek: Individualism and Economic Order. London: Routledge & Kegan Paul, 1949.

----- (1941). The Pure Theory of Capital. London: Routledge & Kegan Paul, 1941.

Hicks, J.R. (1934). Review of Myrdal (1933A). Economica, Vol. 1, (November 1934).

----- (1946). Value and Capital. First edition 1939. Second edition. Oxford: Clarendon Press, 1946.

----- (1956). "Methods of Dynamic Analysis". In 25 Economic Essays in Honour of Erik Lindahl. Stockholm: Svenska Tryckeriaktiebolaget, 1956.

----- (1963). The Theory of Wages. First edition 1932. Second edition. London: Macmillan, 1963.

----- (1965). Capital and Growth. Oxford: Clarendon Press, 1965.

----- (1973). "Recollections and Documents". Economica, Vol. 60, (February 1973). As reprinted in Hicks: Economic Perspectives. Oxford: Clarendon Press, 1977.

Bibliography   259

Johansson, Alf (1934). Loneutvecklingen och arbetslösheten. Stockholm: P.A.Norstedt, 1934.

Kahn, R.F. (1931). "The Relation of Home Investment to Unemployment". Economic Journal, Vol.41, (June 1931). As reprinted in Kahn: Selected Esssays on Employment and Growth. Cambridge: Cambridge University Press, 1972.

----- (1938). Review of Lundberg (1937). Economic Journal, Vol. 48, (June 1938).

Keynes, John Maynard (1921). A Treatise on Probability. First edition 1921. As reprinted in Vol. VIII in The Collected Works of John Maynard Keynes. London: Macmillan, 1973.

----- (1930A-B). A Treatise on Money. Vol. I-II. First edition 1930. As reprinted in Vols. V-VI in The Collected Works, London: Macmillan, 1971.

----- (1933). "A Monetary Theory of Production". A contribution to Festschrift für Arthur Spiethoff, 1933. As reprinted in Keynes (1973A).

----- (1934). "Poverty in Plenty: Is the Economic System Self-Adjusting?". Published in The Listener, November 1934. As reprinted in Keynes (1973A).

----- (1936). The General Theory of Employment, Interest, and Money. First edition 1936. As reprinted in Collected Writings, Vol. VII. London: Macmillan, 1973.

----- (1973A-B). The General Theory and After. Part I-II. Collected Writings, Vols. XIII-XIV. London: Macmillan, 1973.

----- (1979). The General Theory and After. A Supplement. Collected Writings, Vol. XXIX. London:Macmillan, 1979.

Knight, F. (1921). Risk, Uncertainty and Profit. Reprinted New York: Kelley, 1964.

Koopmans, T.(1957). Three Essays on the State of
Economic Science. New York: Mc Graw -Hill, 1957.

Landgren, Karl-Gustav (1957). Economics in Modern
Sweden. Washington: Library of Congress, 1957.

----- (1960). Den 'nya ekonomien' i Sverige.
Uppsala: Almquist & Wicksell, 1960.

Lange, O. (1938). Review of Lundberg (1937).
Economica, Vol. 5, (May 1938).

Lindahl, Erik (1924). Penningpolitikens mål och
medel. Malmö: Förlagsaktiebolaget, 1924.

----- (1929A). Om förhållandet mellan penningmängd
och prisnivå. Uppsala: Almquist & Wicksell,
1929.

----- (1929B). "Prisbildningsproblemet från
kapitalteoretisk synpunkt". Ekonomisk
Tidskrift, 1929.

----- (1929C). Review of Myrdal (1927). Economic
Journal, Vol. 39, 1929.

----- (1930). Penningpolitikens medel. Malmö:
Förlagsaktiebolaget, 1930.

----- (1932). "Offentliga arbeten i
depressionstider". Ekonomisk Tidskrift, 1932.

----- (1934). "A Note on the Dynamic Pricing
Problem". Stencil dated Gothenburg 23 October
1934. As reprinted in Steiger (1971). (Also
reprinted in Keynes (1979).)

----- (1939). Studies in the Theory of Money and
Capital. London: George Allen & Unwin, 1939.

----- (1939A). "Preface". Preface to
Lindahl (1939).

----- (1939B). "The Dynamic Approach to Economic
Theory". Part one in Lindahl (1939).

Bibliography   261

----- (1939C). "The Rate of Interest and the Price Level". Translation of Lindahl (1930). Part two of Lindahl (1939).

----- (1939D). "The Place of Capital in the Theory of Price". Translation of Lindahl (1929B). Part three of Lindahl (1939).

----- (1939E). "The Problem of Balancing the Budget". Ekonomisk Tidskrift, 1935. Appendix to Lindahl (1939).

----- (1941). "Professor Ohlin om dynamisk teori". Ekonomisk Tidskrift, 1941.

----- (1942). "Metodfrågor inom den dynamiska teorien". Ekonomisk Tidskrift, 1942.

----- (1953A). "Om Keynes ekonomiska system". Ekonomisk Tidskrift, 1953.

----- (1953B). "Not angående multiplikatorteorien". Appendix to Lindahl (1953A), but not published in Lindahl (1954).

----- (1954). "On Keynes' Economic System". Translation of Lindahl (1953A). Economic Record, Vol. 30, (May 1954 and November 1954).

----- (1957). "Full Employment without Inflation". Three Banks Review, March 1957.

Lundberg, Erik (1930). "Om begreppet ekonomisk jämvikt". Ekonomisk Tidskrift, 1930.

----- (1937). Studies in the Theory of Economic Expansion. First edition 1937. Reprinted New York: Kelley & Millman, 1955.

----- (1938A). Konjunkturläget hösten 1937. Stockholm, 1938.

----- (1938B). Konjunkturläget våren 1938. Stockholm, 1938.

----- (1948A). "Keynes system och de ekonometriska
sanningarna". Review of Klein: The Keynesian
Revolution. Ekonomisk Tidskrift, 1948.

----- (1948B). "Inflationsanalys och ekonomisk
teori". Ekonomisk Tidskrift, 1948.

----- (1960). "Om att begripa Keynes och att första
andra". Ekonomisk Tidskrift, 1960.

Malinvaud, E. (1972). Lectures on Microeconomic
Theory. Amsterdam: North Holland, 1972.

Marshall, Alfred (1920). Principle of Economics.
Ninth (variorium) edition London: Macmillan,
1961.

Metzler, L.A. (1941). "The Nature and Stability of
Inventory Cycles". Revue of Economic and
Statistics, Vol. 23, 1941.

Milgate, Murray (1979). "On the Origin of the Notion
of 'Intertemporal Equilibrium'". Economica,
Vol.46, (February 1979).

Myrdal, Gunnar (1927). Prisbildningsproblemet och
föränderligheten. Uppsala and Stockholm
^lmquist & Wicksell, 1927.

----- (1931). "Om penningteoretisk jämvikt. En
studie over den 'normala räntan' i Wicksells
penninglära". Ekonomisk Tidskrift, 1931.

----- (1933A). "Der Gleichgewichtsbegriff als
Instrument in der geldtheoretischen Analyse".
In Hayek (ed.). Beiträge zur Geldtheorie.
Vienna: Julius Springer, 1933.

----- (1933C). Konjunktur och offentlig hushållning.
Stockholm: Nordisk Rotogravyr, 1933.

----- (1939). Monetary Equilibrium. First English
edition 1939. Reprinted New York: Kelley, 1965.

----- (1958). "Postscript". In Myrdal: <u>Value in Social Theory</u>. London: Routledge & Kegan Paul, 1958.

Ohlin, Bertil (1924). <u>Handelns teori</u>. Stockholm: Nordiska Bokhandeln, 1924.

----- (1927). "Den danska kronan efter 1914". <u>Nationaløkonomisk Tidskrift</u>, Vol. 65, 1927.

----- (1931). "Den internationella penningpolitiken och dess inverkan på konjunkturutvecklingen". <u>Ekonomisk Tidskrift</u>, 1931.

----- (1932A). "Ungelöste Probleme der gegenwärtigen Krisis". <u>Weltwirtschaftliches Archiv</u>, Vol. 36, 1932.

----- (1932B). "Now or Never. Action to Combat the World Depression". <u>Svenska Handelsbankens Index</u>, May 1932.

----- (1932C). "Prisstegringens problem". <u>Det Ekonomiska Läget</u>, August 1932.

----- (1933). Ohlin's report to "Recent Periodicals and New Books". <u>Economic Journal</u>, Vol. 43, (December 1933).

----- (1933A) "A Note on Price Theory with Special Reference to Interdependence and Time". In <u>Economic Essays in Honour of Gustav Cassel</u>. London: George Allen & Unwin, 1933.

----- (1933B). Draft to Ohlin (1933C). As translated in <u>History of Political Economy</u>, Vol. 10, (Fall 1978).

----- (1933C). "On the Formulation of Monetary Theory". A translation of Ohlin (1933D) in <u>History of Political Economy</u>, Vol. 10, (Fall 1978).

----- (1933D). "Till frågan om penningteoriens uppläggning". <u>Ekonomisk Tidskrift</u>, 1933.

----- (1934). Penningpolitik, offentliga arbeten, subventioner och tullar som medel mot arbetslÜsheten: Bidrag till expansionens teori. Stockholm: Norstedt, 1934.

----- (1937A-B). "Some Notes on the Stockholm Theory of Savings and Investments. I-II." Economic Journal. Vol. 47, (March 1937 and June 1937).

----- (1941A). "Professor Lindahl om dynamisk teori". Ekonomisk Tidskrift, 1941.

----- (1941B). "Metodfrågor inom den dynamiska teorien". Ekonomisk Tidskrift, 1941.

----- (1949). The Problem of Employment Stabilization. New York: Columbia University Press, 1949.

----- (1960). "Erik Lindahl - några minnesord." Ekonomisk Tidskrift, 1960.

----- (1977). "Some Comments on Keynesianism and the Swedish Theory of Expansion Before 1935". In Patinkin-Leith (eds.): Keynes, Cambridge and 'The General Theory'. London: Macmillan, 1977.

Palander, Tord (1941). "On the Concepts and Methods of the 'Stockholm School'. Some Methodological Reflections on Myrdal's Monetary Equilibrium." Ekonomisk Tidskrift, 1941. As translated in International Economic Papers, No. 3, 1953.

Patinkin, D. (1965). Money, Interest and Prices. First edition 1956. Second edition. New York: Harper and Row, 1965.

----- (1976). Keynes' Monetary Thought. First edition 1976. Second printing. Durham: Duke University Press, 1978.

----- (1978). "Some Observations on Ohlin's 1933-Article." History of Political Economy, Vol. 10, (Fall 1978).

Robbins, L. (1930). "On a Certain Ambiguity in the Conception of Stationary Equilibrium". Economic Journal, Vol. 40, (June 1930).

----- (1935). An Essay on the Nature and Significance of Economic Science. First edition 1932. Second edition. London: Macmillan, 1935.

Robertson, Dennis (1926). Banking Policy and the Price Level. London: P.S.King, 1926.

Robinson, Joan (1939). Review of Myrdal (1939). Economic Journal, Vol. 50, (September 1939). As reprinted in Collected Economic Papers, Vol. I. Oxford: Basil Blackwell, 1951.

----- (1969). The Accumulation of Capital. First edition 1956. Third edition. London: Macmillan, 1969.

----- (1973). "Essays 1935". New introduction to Essays in the Theory of Employment. First edition 1936. As reprinted in Collected Economic Papers, Vol. IV. Oxford: Basil Blackwell, 1973.

Rosenstein-Rodan, P.N. (1934). "The Role of Time in Economic Theory". Economica, Vol. 1, (February 1934).

Schumpeter, J.A. (1954). History of Economic Analysis. New York: Oxford university Press, 1954.

Shackle, G.L.S. (1967). The Years of High Theory. Cambridge: Cambridge University Press, 1967.

Steiger, Otto (1971). Studien zur Entstehung der Neuen Wirtschaftslehre in Schweden. Eine Anti-Kritik. Berlin: Duncker & Humblot, 1971.

----- (1976). "Bertil Ohlin and the Origins of the Keynesian Revolution". History of Political Economy, Vol. 8, (Fall 1976).

----- (1978). "Prelude to the Theory of a Monetary Economy: Origins and Significance of Ohlin's 1933 Approach". History of Political Economy, Vol. 10, (Fall 1978).

Svennilson, Ingvar (1938). Ekonomisk Planering. Uppsala: Almquist & Wicksell, 1938.

Weintraub, E.R. (1979). Microfoundations. Cambridge: Cambridge University Press, 1979.

Wicksell, Knut (1898). "The Influence of the Rate of Interest on Commodity Prices". Ekonomisk Tidskrift, 1898. As translated in Wicksell: Selected Papers on Economic Theory. London: George Allen & Unwin, 1958.

----- (1908). "Varför inskränkes fabriksdriften". Ekonomisk Tidskrift, 1908.

----- (1909). "Penningranta och varupris". Ekonomisk Tidskrift, 1909.

----- (1919). "Professor Cassel's System of Economics". Ekonomisk Tidskrift, 1919. As translated in Wicksell (1934).

----- (1925). "The Monetary Problems of the Scandinavian Countries". Ekonomisk Tidskrift, 1925. As translated in Wicksell (1936).

----- (1934-1935). Lectures on Political Economy. I-II. Translated from the third Swedish edition 1928-1929. London: George Routledge And Sons, 1934-1935.

----- (1936). Interest and Prices. Translation of Wicksell (1968). London: Macmillan, 1936.

----- (1954). Value, Capital and Rent. German edition 1893. London: George Allen & Unwin, 1954.

----- (1966A-B). Föreläsningar i nationalekonomi. I-II. First edition 1901-1906. Fifth edition. Lund: Gleerups, 1966.

Bibliography   267

----- (1968). Geldzins und Glüterpreise. First
edition 1898. Reprinted Aalen: Scientia Verlag,
1968.

Winch, D. (1966). "The Keynesian Revolution in
Sweden". Journal of Political Economy, Vol.74,
(April 1966).

Yohe, W.P. (1959B). "An Analysis of Professor
Lindahl's Sequence Model". L'Industria, 1959.

----- (1978). "Ohlin's 1933 Reformation of Monetary
Theory". History of Political Economy, Vol. 10,
(Fall 1978).

B. Unpublished works.

Cassel, Gustav (1927). Minutes from a meeting held
11 April 1927 in the Faculty of Law and
Political Science at the University of
Stockholm.

Eatwell, John (1977). "The Rate of Profit and the
Concept of Equilibrium in Neoclassical General
Equilibrium Theory". Unpublished paper.
Cambridge, December 1977.

Frisch, Ragnar (1935). "Et generelt monetaert
begrep- og symbolsystem". Stencil of lectures
held in Oslo in 1935.

Hammarskjöld, Dag (1933B). Memorandum to a
manuscript to Ohlin (1934), circulated among the
members of the Unemployment Committee. Dated 17
August 1933.

Lindahl, Erik (1927). Manuscript to the oral
examination of Myrdal's dissertation.

----- (1935). "Introduction to the Theory of Price
Movements in a closed Community". Being chapter
1 (the only surviving) of Monetary Policy and
its Theoretical Basis. Unpublished manuscript
from the beginning of 1935.

Myrdal, Gunnar (1925). Report sent to the Royal
Academy of Science (Stockholm). Unpublished
manuscript to Myrdal (1927).

----- (1933B). A manuscript to the oral examination
of Hammarskjöld's dissertation.

Ohlin, Bertil (1937C). Further Observations on
Keynes' Terminology and Theory in General.
Planned as part III of Ohlin (1937A-B).
Unpublished manuscript. (Partly published in
Keynes (1973B).)

Yohe, W.P. (1959A). The Wicksellian Tradition in
Swedish Macroeconomic Theory. Unpublished
Ph.d.-dissertation. Ann Arbor (Mich.). 1959.

C. Correspondence.

Erik Lindahl's correspondence. Under trusteeship of
Mrs. Getrud Lindahl. Uppsala.

Gunnar Myrdal's correspondence. Deposited in
Arbetarrörelsen's Arkiv. Stockholm.

Lundberg, E. (1979), Private communication to the
author. February 14, 1979.

Appendix

Keynes' General Theory

We will now analyse the meaning of Keynes' principle of effective demand; the result of this analysis is always used as a reference in the comparison between the Stockholm School and the Keynesian revolution. There is also a tentative sketch of how the notions of ex ante and ex post could be applied to the principle of effective demand, i.e. a fusion of the Swedish method with Keynes' theory.

Keynes' system is first formulated as a set of simultaneous equations which clearly brings home the equilibrium character of his theory, since this is its distinctive mark in relation to the Swedish methods. Thus, Keynes' determination of the equilibrium level of output and employment is considered to be his main contribution, and the same ideas are not to be found within the Stockholm School. However, Keynes also stresses the role of uncertainty and anticipations in the determination of the rate of interest as well as in the behaviour of the entrepreneurs and the investors. It is therefore in accordance with the spirit of Keynes' analysis to attempt to extend his system in such a way that it explicitly includes plans and the revisions of plans, and it will then have some of the main features of the Swedish ex ante/ex post analysis.

1 - The principle of effective demand.
We will give a formulation of Keynes' system which shows how he determines his quaesitum:

"Our present object is to discover what determines at any time the national income of a given economic system and (which is almost the same thing) the amount of its employment" (Keynes 1936, p.247).

The quantity of money ($\bar{M}$) is determined by the action of the central bank:

271

(1) $\bar{M}=M_1+M_2$

The speculative demand for money (M_2), i.e. liquidity preference:

(2) $M_2=L_2(i)$

The transaction demand for money (M_1), where the velocity of circulation (V) is supposed to stay constant in the short run:

(3) $M_1=L_1(Y)=Y/V$

The demand for investment goods, i.e. the marginal efficiency of capital:

(4) $I=f(i)$

The demand for consumption goods, where the marginal propensity to consume is greater than zero but less than one:

(5) $C=g(Y)$ $0<dC/dY<1$

(5') $S=Y-C$

The equilibrium condition that total production is equal to total demand, or that savings is equal to investment ex ante:

(6) $Y=C+I$

(6') $S=I$

The employment function which is just an inverse of the aggregate supply function:

(7) $N=h(Y)$

In this system it is also assumed that the money wages are constant so all value terms could be expressed in wage units. Furthermore, the capital equipement is given as well as the quantity of available labour (N*).

272

The principal of effective demand is now made up of three components: that aggregate supply has to accomodate to aggregate demand and the latter sets thus a limit for the former, that changes in income are the equilibrating mechanism between savings and investment and not the rate of interest or other prices like in orthodox theory, that the level of income and employment represents an equilibrium position and which will generally involve a certain amount of unemployment, i.e. N<N*.

To propose that Keynes' theory is a general theory and which therefore completely substitutes the orthodox theory, it is also necessary to show that Keynes' system holds for a long run equilibrium with unemployment, which would refute the claim that Keynes' theory is just one short run specification of the orthodox theory. But before we tackle this problem we have to make two digressions: to analyse Keynes' equilibrium approach, and to show the relation between the unit period and Keynes' notion of long run equilibrium.

2 - Digression I: Keynes' equilibrium method.

The equilibrium method is very obvious in Keynes' analysis of the relation between the aggregate supply function, Z=Q(N), and the aggregate demand function, D=f(N). The former function shows a relation between the aggregate supply price (Z) or "the expectation of proceeds which will just make it worth the while of the entrepreneurs to give that employment [i.e. N]" (ibid., p.24). The latter function shows "the proceeds [D] which entrepreneurs expect to receive from the employment of N men" (ibid., p.25). If the entrepreneurs maximize profit, then they will increase (decrease) employment as long as D>Z (D<Z). There is an equilibrium point where the two curves cut each other which determines the volume of employment. However, Keynes does not analyse this adjustment process whereby the equilibrium is reached, and he is satisfied to directly determine the equilibrium point, i.e. he goes straight to an analysis of the equilibrium condition by setting Q(N) equal to Z(N). In his rough notes from the 1937 lectures Keynes gives the rationale for this equilibrium approach:

273

"Now Hawtrey, as it seems to me, mistakes
this higgling process by which the
equilibrium position is discovered for the
much more fundamental forces which
determine what the equilibrium position is
... . The main point is to distinguish the
forces determining the position of
equilibrium from the technique of trial and
error by means of which the entrepreneur
discovers where the position is" (Keynes
1973B, p.182).

Hence, Keynes considered his theory to be basically
the same even if it is assumed "that short-period
expectations are always fulfilled" (ibid,, p.181),
and he is therefore "more classical than the Swedes,
for I am still discussing the conditions of short
period equilibrium" (ibid., p.183).

This equilibrium approach is almost always used
by Keynes in the General Theory, which is the reason
why we above have formulated his system as a set of
simultaneous equations, since such a formulation
presumes that the short period expectations are
fulfilled.

3 - Digression II: The unit period and the notion of
a long run equilibrium.
Keynes defines his unit period or 'day' in the
following way:

"the shortest interval after which the firm
is free to revise its decision as to how
much employment to offer. It is, so to
speak, the minimum effective unit of
economic time" (Keynes 1936, p.47 n.1).

We will here also assume that the day is equal to the
length of the production period, which means that the
entrepreneurs have given production plans.
The entrepreneurs will now be guided by their
short term expectations:

"[which] is concerned with the price which a
manufacturer can expect to get for his
'finished' output [which can be consumer
goods or capital goods] at the time when he
commits himself to starting the process
which will produce it; output being
'finished' (from the point of view of the
manufacturer) when it is ready to be used or
to be sold to a second party" (ibid., p.46).

An entrepreneur's plan for the coming daily output is
then exclusively based on his short term expectations
and this plan implies a particular demand for
employment and other inputs. These expectations and
plans are based on the existing capital equipment,
the stock of intermediate products and half-finished
materials in the hands of the entrepreneur at the
time when the plans are drawn up. The day will
therefore have the same characteristics as Marshall's
short period. Hence, if the plans are consistent the
output and employment are determined for the day, and
the system of equations in the first section is
supposed to depict such a situation. However, there
is a slight problem due to the fact that liquidity
preference refers to a stock equilibrium which may be
assumed to rule at almost every point of time, and
the interval within which it is possible to revise
decisions is therefore much shorter than a day.
Nevertheless, we assume that the plans of the
entrepreneurs are drawn up on the basis of the given
stock equilibrium which rules at the point of time

275

when the plans are formed.[1] The changes in the stock equilibrium during the period can therefore not influence the volume of output and employment for the current day. But strictly speaking, if our system describes an equilibrium, then the only possible endogenous change between two periods is the change in the capital equipment and the stock equilibrium should not change during the period.

Keynes also speaks of the long term expectations:

> "[which] are concerned with what the entrepreneur can hope to earn in the shape of future returns if he purchases (or, perhaps, manufactures) 'finished' output as an addition to his capital equipment" (ibid., p.47).

These expectations determine the purchasing plans of capital goods which are executed during the coming day. We now call this buyer, and owner of the equipment, an investor, and it is assumed that the entrepreneur, or manufacturer, rents his capital equipment for its physical lifetime from the investor.[2]

----

1 This is assumed by Keynes in a draft of chapter 2 from the last 1933 draft table of contents:

> "we must suppose that the spot and forward price structure has already brought into equilibrium the relative advantages, as estimated by the holder, of holding money and other existing forms of wealth. Thus if the advantage in terms of money of using money to start up a productive process is increased, this will stimulate entrepreneurs to offer more employment" (Keynes 1979, p.83).

2 Cp. Fragment of the chapter on Capital from the second draft table of contents from 1933, Keynes 1979, p.75; A draft of chapter 3 from the last 1933 draft table of contents, ibid., p.89.

At each point of time there exists a <u>state of</u>
<u>expectations</u>, which comprises short term and long
term expectations, which determines production and
purchasing plans for the period ahead. In an
equilibrium, as described above, the two types of
expectations are congruent in the sense that
production plans for capital goods coincide with the
purchasing plans for these goods. But there is of
course no guarantee that the long term expectations
which determined the purchasing plans will be
fulfilled, since they refer to expected events in
subsequent periods. However, Keynes also proposes
that <u>a state of expectation determines a particular</u>
<u>level of long period employment</u>:

> "If we suppose a state of expectation to
> continue for a sufficient length of time for
> the effect on employment to have worked
> itself out so completely that there is,
> broadly speaking, no piece of employment
> going on which would not have taken place if
> the new state of expectation had always
> existed, the steady level of employment thus
> attained may be called the long-period
> employment corresponding to that state of
> expectation. It follows that, although
> expectation may change so frequently that
> the actual level of employment has never had
> time to reach the long-period employment
> corresponding to the existing state of
> expectation, nevertheless every state of
> expectation has its definite corresponding
> level of long-period employment" (Keynes
> 1936, p.48).

In such a situation the equilibrium for the day does
not only represent a congruence between short term
and long term expectations, but it is also based on
the fact that every piece of existing capital
equipment for the current day is the result of
previous long term expectations <u>which actually have</u>
<u>been fulfilled</u>. We would here follow Joan Robinson
and denote such a situation as a <u>state of</u>
<u>tranquillity</u>:

We may speak of an economy in a state of
tranquillity when it develops in a smooth
regular   manner   without   internal
contradictions or external shocks, so that
expectations based upon past experience are
very confidently held, and are in fact
constantly fulfilled and therefore renewed
as time goes by. In a state of perfect
tranquillity the prices ruling to-day, in
every market, are those which were expected
to rule to-day when any relevant decisions
were taken in the past; the quantities of
goods being sold, costs, profits and all
relevant characteristics of the situation
are turning out according to expectations;
and the expectations being held to-day about
the future are those that were expected in
the past to be held to-day" (Robinson 1969,
p.59).

However, we now reach the problem whether
liquidity preference could really exist in such a
tranquil situation, since liquidity preference
thrives on the fact that wealth holders have
different expectations about the future and they do
not hold these expectations with perfect confidence;
that is the basis for the continuous existence of
bulls and bears. But the process by which a state of
tranquillity is reached may incite the bears to leave
their camp and join the bulls, because this process
implies that expectations are gradually fulfilled,
which may lessen the fears of capital losses. It is
therefore necessary to assume that the liquidity
preference is kept alive by a fear of forthcoming
unexpected changes. We therefore hold that Keynes'
concept of a long period employment, or a long run
equilibrium, is a notional construction with the
supposition that the state of expectations which
rules for the subsequent day will also rule in the
future. It plays the same role as Marshall's idea of
a long run equilibrium in the sense that it shows the
position towards which the economy will be moving
over the coming periods. However, in the nature of
the case, this equilibrium position can probably
never be reached because of exogenous disturbances.

278

This interpretation seems to tally with Keynes' assertion that his theory is a theory of shifting equilibrium:

> "the theory of a system in which changing views about the future are capable of influencing the present situation" (Keynes 1936, p.293).

His theory is therefore not concerned with a stationary state:

> "In a static society ["where there is no changing future to influence the present" (Keynes 1936, p.145)] or in a society in which for any other reason no one feels any uncertainty about the future rates of interest, the Liquidity Function L_2 ... will always be zero in equilibrium" (ibid., pp.208-209).

The preference for a theory of shifting equilibrium stems from the simple fact that a stationary state has no foundation in the 'real' world:

> "I should, I think, be prepared to argue that, in a world ruled by uncertainty with an uncertain future linked to an actual present, a final position of equilibrium, such as one deals with in static economics, does not properly exist" (Keynes in a letter to H.D.Henderson, 28 May 1936, Keynes 1979, p.222).

Hence, Keynes' theory, formulated as a system of simultaneous equations existing at a particular point of time and derived from the given state of expectations, will always determine the equilibrium level of output and employment for the coming day. But it is also plossible to envisage a system which would describe the imaginary future situation which would exist if the current state of expectations would rule for all future periods.

4 - Unemployment equilibrium in the long run.

We now analyse whether there exists any self-adjusting forces which in the long run will pull an economy, which over several periods have been characterized by an underemployment equilibrium as determined by our set of simultaneous equations, back to full employment. If such forces exist that would be the same as saying that the state of long period employment, related to each state of expectation, is a full employment equilibrium. In this context, it is interesting to notice that Keynes already in the early thirties divided the economists into the following two groups:

> "On the one side are those who believe that the existing economic system is, in the long run, a self-adjusting system, though with creaks and groans and jerks, and interrupted by time lags, outside inference and mistakes. ... On the other side of the gulf are those who reject the idea that the existing economic system is, in any significant sense, self-adjusting" (Keynes 1934, pp.486-487).

In the orthodox theory the self-adjusting forces are made up of an flexible interest rate which would equilibrate investment and savings at the full employment level, and flexible prices and money wages.

The way we have defined Keynes' notion of long run equilibrium it is implied that liquidity preference will not be obliterated in the long run. Hence, it will all the time function as a barrier for the expansion of the demand for investments. Furthermore, there are no inherent reasons why the liquidity preference curve should shift over time in such a way that it would lead to a rate of interest which is compatible with full employment. But changes in prices and wages will in Keynes' system lead to movements along the liquidity preference curve. Keynes therefore sees the following role for the self-adjusting forces within his system:

"It is ... on the effect of a falling wage-
and price-level on the demand for money
that those who believe in the self-adjusting
quality of the economic system must rest the
weight of their argument" (Keynes 1936,
p.266).

The important point is that the fall in prices and
wages will increase the value of M_2 in terms of a
particular price index or in terms of the wage-
unit.[3] But he more or less rule out this possibility
because flexible prices and/or wages will in Keynes
theory imply a very unstable system:

"we must have some factor, the value of
which in terms of money is, if not fixed, at
least sticky, to give us any stability of
values in a monetary system" (ibid., p.304).

It is difficult to explicitly encapsulate this effect
in a system of equations which does not contain any
relations over time. However, if Keynes' theory was
formulated as a system of difference equations, then
the system must have the property of being very
unstable for larger changes in prices or money wages.
We have to add for 'larger' changes, since Keynes has
not completely ruled out the positive effects of
falling prices and money wages, namely, if the full
employment equilibrium could be reached by "a
moderate reduction" (ibid., p.267).
    We therefore conclude that Keynes' equilibrium
approach with fixed money wages is in fact an
assumption which makes the analysis realistic and not
just an arbitrary numeraire, since flexible prices
and money wages would imply a system which rushes
between three possible 'resting-places': full
employment, a position determined by the liquidity
trap, a position where the money wages can not fall
any longer (cp. ibid., p.191; p.304). Keynes on the
other hand envisaged a different economic system:

----
3 The same effect could of course be reached by an
exogenous increase in $\bar{M}$ from the central bank or an
endogenous increase in V.

"it is an outstanding characteristic of the economic system in which we live that, whilst it is subject to severe fluctuations in respect of output and employment, it is not violently unstable. Indeed it seems capable of remaining in a chronic condition of sub-normal activity for a considerable period without any marked tendency either towards recovery or towards complete collapse. Moreover, the evidence indicates that full, or even approximately full employment is of rare and short-lived occurence. Fluctuations may start briskly but seem to wear themselves out before they have proceeded to great extremes, and an intermediate situation which is neither desperate nor satisfactory is our normal lot" (ibid., pp.249-250).

5 - Keynes' system in Swedish clothes.

We will now formulate Keynes' system in ex ante/ex post terms. This is a tentative attempt to show the meaning of Keynes' equilibrium approach in Swedish terms; if the system is not in equilibrium, then we can see the first step in an adjustment process.

It is assumed that the system is disturbed by the central bank issuing new money which in the first instance will have the following effect:

"a relaxation of the conditions of credit by the banking system, so as to induce someone to sell the banks a debt or a bond in exchange for the new cash" (ibid., p.200; cp. p.205).

We assume that there is an instant stock equilibrium on the market for money and debts, and that the banks reserve, according to their income expectations, a certain portion of the new money for the transaction purposes of their customers (M_1').[4]

(1) $\bar{M}=M_1'+M_2'$

(2) $M_2'=L_2(i_1)$

(3) $M_1'=L_1(Y')=Y'/V$

The investment plans are made up on the basis of this rate of interest:

(4) $I=f(i_1)$

The manufacturers' production plans (which are realized) are based on what they expect to supply and sell (Z'), i.e. no planned changes in stocks. The value of this production is equal to its costs of production (E) [5], which, like in Lindahl's case (cp. sect. IX:4:2), is the same as the contractual income, inclusive of normal profit, for the current period:

(5) $E=Z'$

The consumption plans are based on the contracted income for the coming period (E):

(6) $C=g(E)$

(6') $S'\equiv E-C$

It is assumed that the consumption and investment plans are realized, and realized purchases (Z'') are equal to realized income, i.e. $Y''\equiv Z''\equiv C+I$.

---

4 Z',Y' etc. denote ex ante values while Z'' etc. denote ex post values. Variables with no sign are realized values determined at the transition point to the current period. i_1 is the rate of interest determined at the point of transition to the current period while i_2 is determined at the end of the period.
5 This is the same as if the entrepreneurs choose a point on Keynes' aggregate supply function, $Z=Q(N)$ (cp. Keynes 1936, p.25).

In equilibrium for the goods market total supply must be equal to the planned and realized purchases:

(7) $Z'=I+C=Z"$ [6]

Hence, this equilibrium presumes that the producers has rightly anticipated the aggregate demand. In fact, Keynes here invokes the instantaneous multiplier which assumes that the multiplier can fully work itself out during the current period.[7] It was this way of arguing which was so difficult for the Swedes to swallow (cp. sect. XI:1:3).

We now have to look at the market for money and debts:

(8) $M_1"=Y"/V$

(9) $M_2"=\bar{M}-M_1"$

(10) $i_2=L_2(M_2")$

Hence, to preserve the equilibrium on this market the banks must have made the right anticipations of the income for the current period and thereby they have reserved enough money to circulate the current income without upsetting the value of M_2. If that is not the case, then the outgoing rate of interest will not be the same as the ingoing one and the period can not be considered to have been in equilibrium. This example shows that there is a certain causality within Keynes' system:

$$\bar{M} => M_2' => i_1 => I$$
$$=> Z",Y" => M_1" => M_2" => i_2$$
$$Z' => E => C$$

---

6 We can see that $I=S'$ leads to equilibrium, i.e. $Z'=Z"$. Since $I'\equiv I"\equiv S"\equiv Y"-C$ and $S'\equiv E-C$, $I'=S'$ implies that $E\equiv Y"\equiv Z"$ i.e. $Z'=Z"$. In equilibrium we have that $E=Z'=Z"\equiv Y"$, i.e. cost of production is equal to realized income.
7 Joan Robinson remarks that this type of analysis "ought properly to be conducted in terms of comparative statics" (Robinson 1973, p.175).

Furthermore, there is no doubt that the system has the following feedback:

> "I have many pages on the theme that increasing investment involves increasing output and that this kicks back on the rate of interest by draining away more money into active circulation" (Keynes' letter to D.H.Robertson, 13 December 1936, Keynes 1973B, p.91).

Thus, the equilibrium is dependent on the fact that two agents, the banks and the producers, have the same expectations for the income during the forthcoming period plus the fact that enough investment and consumption are forthcoming to take the supply off the market.

We will now look at an example where the goods market is not in equilibrium, which comes closest to the Swedish analysis. It is assumed that there are no stocks of finished goods which implies that the production (Z') will be supplied and sold whatever the price. If $Z'>Z"\equiv I+C$ then the producers will make a loss equal to $Z'-Z"$ and the vice versa if $Z'<Z"$ holds. Hence, ex post losses/profits for the producers will balance the difference between planned investment and planned saving.[8] They are windfall categories, like in the Swedish analysis, which will not affect the behaviour for the current unit period. The Swedish show therefore the first step in an adjustment process. It is true that supply has to accomodate to demand and changes in income equalizes savings and investment ex post (in the Swedish model the rate of interest is mostly exogenously determined), but there is no determination of an equilibrium level of income. Hence, all three criteria of the principle of effective demand are not fulfilled (cp. sect. 1).

It also possible to assume that prices are fixed and there are plenty of stocks. In this case a difference between Z' and $Z"$ will lead to adjustment in stocks. The stock changes will now balance the

----

8 If $E-Z"=G$ (G is profit) and $I'\equiv I"\equiv S"\equiv Y'-C$ and $S'\equiv E-C$ then $I'-S'=Y"-E=Z"-Z'=G$ i.e. $S"=S'+G$.

difference between savings and investment ex ante[9],
as in the Swedish case, the producers will try to
fill or deplete the stocks in the next period.

---

9 $I'' \equiv I' - (Z'' - Z') \equiv S''$ since a reduction in stock is
counted as a disinvestment ex post. In this case the
realized income (Y'') is equal to the cost of
production (E), since a decrease in stocks is not
counted as income but as a disinvestment. Hence,
$S''=S'$ since $S' \equiv E-C$, $S'' \equiv Y''-C$ and $E=Y''$, thus $I'-S'=Z''-Z'$.

286